Praise for *PowerHunch!*

"No one but Marcia Emery could have written this book. It gives us the opportunity to be with this gifted intuitive, teacher, and researcher. We hear the stories she collected from hundreds of people—some famous—and begin to realize that the intuition they have is the intuition we have. At the same time, she gives us a structure and principles that we can use every day. Slowly but surely, with *PowerHunch!*, we can bring a flow of intuitive decision-making into our lives. Then we begin to see greater beauty, even in difficult times. We turn fears into breakthroughs. We develop a higher vision for our lives, know how to take risks, become timely, and bring balance and peace to our lives. There are many books on intuition but virtually all of them fail to deal with intuition's central paradox: it is both potentially powerful and seemingly ephemeral. In this book Dr. Emery serves as a master guide—drawing on her vast experience, powerful courses, extensive interviews, and consulting work—to offer a practical guide that can make our lives more exciting, meaningful, magical, rich, and, simply, more fun."

—*Michael Ray, Ph.D . professor of creativity and innovation, Stanford Business School*

"*PowerHunch!* is not only an excellent reminder that we are always receiving internal and external guidance, but its practical exercises and wonderful stories can help everyone immediately tune up his or her intuition!"

—*Carol Adrienne, Ph.D., author of* Find Your Purpose, Change Your Life

"Marcia Emery is one of the world's foremost teachers of intuition. Here she helps us to discover answers from within ourselves to the problems of everyday life. This book is full of both warmth and wisdom. It contains a treasure of intuitive gems."

—*Jeffrey Mishlove, Ph.D , president of Intuition Network and author of* The PK Man

"*PowerHunch!* is a delightful book. I recommend it to everyone who has a curiosity about developing their own intuitive skills—and that should be everyone."

—*Caroline Myss, Ph.D., author of* Anatomy of the Spirit

"*PowerHunch!* brings practical wisdom to everyday life. It's a treasury of potent techniques and sensible tips for tapping the mind's hidden resources."

—*Philip Goldberg, author of* The Intuitive Edge

"Marcia Emery knows intuition. She knows it from the businessperson's viewpoint, the healer's viewpoint, the dreamer and artist's viewpoint. In *PowerHunch!* Dr. Emery distills her vast experience with intuitive development into a handbook you can easily understand and really use. Her wonderful generosity of spirit, story-telling ability, and sense of humor make this book a great addition to the important new field of extended perception."

—*Penney Peirce, intuitive trainer and consultant, and author of* The Intuitive Way *and* Dreams for Dummies

"*PowerHunch!* is an exhilarating invitation for us all to truly trust ourselves! Marcia Emery engagingly illuminates those inner voices and feelings we all have every day and shows us how to recognize and even develop those senses. When you actually follow Dr. Emery's suggestions for trusting your intuition, the world around you changes and you feel more alive! This is a terrific and truly liberating book and a veritable treasure trove of fun and fascination."

—*Stephen Simon, producer of* What Dreams May Come

"Dr. Emery does it again! *PowerHunch!* is rich with stories that we can all relate to. The techniques and exercises she presents are useful tools to help us tap in to the vast wisdom we each hold inside. Her understanding of intuition and the clarity in which she presents it is both practicable and applicable to every facet of our lives."

—*Carol Ritberger, Ph.D., medical intuitive and author of* What Color Is Your Personality?

"Intuition is wisdom from your soul. It's an ever-present guide to help you live your life with joy and passion. *PowerHunch!* provides you with both practical exercises and down-to-earth philosophy to put you in touch with this valuable resource. Insight and common sense shine through on every page."

—*Lynn A. Robinson, author of* Divine Intuition

"Once again, intuition expert, Marcia Emery, has provided a well researched and easy to read book that gives us the tools, inspiration, and trust to follow our hunches every day in every way. Read this book and power your intuition into action!"

—James Wanless, Ph.D., *author of* Strategic Intuition for the 21st Century *and* Way of the Great Oracle

"A clear explanation of how intuition works with examples and exercises that can help beginning, intermediate, and advanced students of intuition."

—Laurie Nadel, *author of* Dancing with the Wind

"Everyone has intuitive experiences. Most don't know what to make of them. Marcia Emery, in her latest book, *PowerHunch!*, takes the extraordinary and makes it ordinary by proving hundreds of examples of 'normal' people who have had powerful hunches and benefited by listening to them. Read this book and you'll have an easier time integrating your own hunches."

—Janelle Barlow, Ph.D., *co-author of* A Complaint Is a Gift

"It is time we got past cute intuition 'trickniques' and start living an intuitive life, one that elicits our true, meant-to-be self that is in harmony with the whole. *PowerHunch!* comes at the right time, intuitively, to give us what we need to enter the flow of a fulfilling intuitive life."

—Henry Reed, Ph.D., *senior fellow at Edgar Cayce Institute for Intuitive Studies and author of* Your Intuitive Heart

POWERHUNCH!

Living an Intuitive Life

POWERHUNCH!

Living an Intuitive Life

Marcia Emery, Ph.D.

BEYOND
WORDS
Publishing
I N C

Beyond Words Publishing, Inc.
20827 N.W. Cornell Road, Suite 500
Hillsboro, Oregon 97124-9808
503-531-8700
1-800-284-9673

Editors: Naomi Lucks and Laura Carlsmith
Managing editor: Julie Steigerwaldt
Copyeditor: Kathy Kattenburg Astor
Proofreader: Leia Carlton
Cover design: Lynn Brofsky
Cover art: Martin Jarrie
Interior design: Dorral Lukas
Composition: William H. Brunson Typography Services

Printed in the United States of America
Distributed to the book trade by Publishers Group West

Library of Congress Cataloging-in-Publication Data
Emery, Marcia.
     PowerHunch! : living an intuitive life / Marcia Emery.
          p.   cm.
     Includes bibliographical references.
     ISBN 1-58270-065-6 (pbk.)
     1. Intuition.   I. Title.

     BF315.5 .E47   2001
     153.4′4—dc21

                                                            2001037462

The corporate mission of Beyond Words Publishing, Inc.:
     Inspire to Integrity

Dedication

This book is dedicated to

My beloved husband, Jim Emery

My Intuitive Fisherman

Contents

Appendix

Acknowledgments

The Rose in my heart opens up as I give a fragrant petal of gratitude to everyone who contributed to the creation of this book.

First and foremost is the God-like energy that pours into my soul when I write.

Kudos to Cindy Black and Richard Cohn and the staff at Beyond Words—Laura Carlsmith, Julie Steigerwaldt, Joy Collman, Sylvia Hayse—for using their vision to see a book that has the potential to deeply touch humanity during this transformative time. In the true spirit of synchronicity, the title of this publishing company is the best description of intuition—beyond words.

Sheryl Fullerton, my extraordinary agent, used her periscopic vision to help me turn this book around and direct it to the perfect publisher. Naomi Lucks, my talented editor, has such an exciting way with words. She wields her fine-tuning fork and transforms the page.

Lynn "Buck" Charlson initially funded my research on intuition and decision making ten years ago. The substance of this book has undergone many incarnations since that time. I am so incredibly grateful for his spiritual and material support, which have allowed me to be a guiding force in bringing intuition out into the world.

Carol and Bruce Ritberger are intuitive trailblazers. I treasure their friendship and appreciate how they encourage me to stand tall and tell my intuitive tales. My "family" in Carol Ritberger's Medical Intuition Training has validated my work and given me untold support and nods of encouragement, helping me reach the finish line of this book.

All my students on the undergraduate and graduate level have been my teachers. They go back to Aquinas College in Grand Rapids, Michigan, through my public and private workshops up to the current classes I teach for the Holmes Institute, Kaiser Institute, JFK University, and private workshops in Berkeley, California.

Teachers came forth to inspire me to write this book. They included the 225 people I interviewed and all the members of the Intuition Network I knew over the years. Everyone provided me with whole-brain thinking so I could translate the pictures, symbols, and images rambling in my mind into intuitive terms.

My chiropractor, Patrick Tribble, helps vitalize my physical body so the radiant light can continue to pour into my being.

A special Rose to my late mother, Naomi Rose, a magnificent enamelist whose words are still etched in my heart. Thank you for letting me know that I was "the most beautiful thing you ever created." What a legacy to carry around in my heart forever. Speaking of mothers, I acknowledge the loving support of my mother-in-law, Mildred Emery.

And to my beloved husband, Jim: You are the light of my life. I am so blessed to have you as my best friend. You cloak me in love and support with everything you do and say.

Foreword

Of course you are intuitive! Why would you think otherwise? The question is: What are you doing to develop your intuition?

The great thing about this book is that it takes you from where you are to however far you want to take your intuitive talent. There is no substitute for a gifted teacher. Marcia Emery is that teacher. She is a superb coach and an experienced intuitive guide. I have observed her in action. She knows what works. The real issue is: Are you willing to work?

As good as this book is, you will not become more intuitive by simply reading it. You have to practice, practice, practice. This book is chock-full of great tools and exercises to help you do just that. Use them. I guarantee your powers of intuition will vastly increase. In fact, you may become so intuitive, you will astound both yourself and your friends.

If you keep a record of your progress in your PowerHunch Journal, it is worth it! You'll get constant feedback from yourself and reap maximum gain from this book. Your inspiration may follow your perspiration rather then precede it. But the good news is that this work is not drudgery. It is fun!

You will be amazed as you read this book to learn how many folks rely upon intuition to assist them in the challenges of daily living. People from common folks to the rich and famous have discovered the value of their "inner splendor." Intuition is both a spiritual gift and a practical tool for use in our material world. It will assist you in so many ways. You'll learn how to use your intuition to reconstruct the past, reorganize the present, or re-vision your future. Now that is a big payoff for a little effort on your part.

As Dr. Emery points out, intuition stimulates your creativity, generates new visions of possibility, gives you a sense of timing, prepares you to take necessary risks, enhances your relationships, enables you to find a new balance in life, and reveals hidden symbols in your dreams. It also tunes you in to your environment and opens doors of opportunity. With a developed intuition you will be in the "flow" and will experience frequent synchronicity as the universe helps you achieve your intentions.

Intuition is a powerful ally. It is a constant source of wonderment to me that we do not emphasize it more in our religious institutions, schools, and workplaces. Intuition, a right brain function that balances our culture's left brain preoccupation, is at least as valuable as logic in problem solving. It takes us beyond outward facts into a deeper level of consciousness.

Whether you are a man or a woman, young or older, this book is for you. Intuition is not gender- or age-based. It is a brain function open to development by anyone interested in investing the necessary time and effort.

You have picked up this book for a reason. You are ready to move ahead in your life and the universe is answering your call for assistance. It is not by chance these words reach you. Nothing happens by chance in our connected world. You are simply experiencing the power of synchronicity—a cosmic law of cause and effect. You have put out a call for this book (cause) and it has come right into your hands (effect). You have set in motion a desire to release your higher powers of consciousness.

An excellent way to develop your intuition is to play the role of the missing piece. Our life's events are something like a giant jigsaw puzzle: always trying to fit together to create a larger pattern. Often, two pieces could come together if a middle piece could be found to join them. By using your intuition, you can play the role of the missing middle piece.

The universe loves connectivity and will work with you to become a master connector. If you are in the right place, at the right time, with the right folks, you can play a key role in creating a higher state of order (putting the pieces together).

To become an intuitive connector, you must always be tuned in to the possibilities that are waiting to happen. This requires a distinctive mental focus on the background activities, not on what is presently occupying your attention. By becoming sensitive to context; i.e., by honing your intuition, you sense pieces that are moving toward one another. By resonating with these pieces and bringing them together, a connection is formed through you. However, you don't have to stay in the equation. Once there is a strong enough magnetic attraction between the two pieces you are holding together, they will form a new middle piece to join them. You can then step out of the picture and the new union will hold.

Your skill as an intuitive connector is to be able to create these new bonds and then move on to other arenas of action. This is where your ego is tested. If you want to stay center stage and continue to be "needed" by the two parties you have joined, you defeat your role as an intuitive connector and encumber the relationship you have formed. The universe can only use you effectively if you avoid this kind of ego contamination. Your sole motivation and full reward is to see yourself as a "temporary intervening variable" that permits higher levels of connectivity. Dr. Emery's excellent chapter on timing—being at the right place at the right time—will help you fill the role of the "missing piece."

Intuition is your pipeline to inner space. It extends your perception to inner worlds. You will experience quite a perceptual shock when you finally realize how limited your perception has been.

Physicists have demonstrated the existence of eleven dimensions. Most of us live in only three. Intuition will introduce you first to the fourth dimension and then lead you into the higher dimensions.

You can easily fall under the spell of inner space. It offers new worlds of experience with fewer limitations than our third dimension. This is one of the dangers of intuition. It can take you out of this world into higher dimensions. Yet, one of the most valuable functions of intuition is to help you work more effectively in this dimension. You must avoid becoming distracted whenever you encounter phenomena in higher dimensions.

The intention of Spirit is to incarnate in you fully, thereby bringing a little heaven to earth. Volunteer yourself to become a living channel of Spirit. If you are faithful to the work of Spirit in this world, Spirit will occasionally reward you with a visit to a higher dimension. But of course, you don't want to float away. A good preventive for this in Zen is the admonition: Chop wood, carry water. In other words, stay grounded. This is another place where *PowerHunch!* shines. It keeps you grounded in real life and focuses your efforts on practical issues. Oh, it's fun to soar, but there is a lot of work that needs to be done right here all around you.

We could talk a great deal more, but I am keeping you from the best part. Let's finish this foreword and let Dr. Emery do her magic with you. Welcome to the intuitive life!

—Leland Kaiser, Ph.D.
Associate Professor
Executive Program in Health Administration
University of Colorado, Denver

Introduction
A Lifetime of PowerHunches

Cindy was flying from a business meeting in Calgary to her home in St. Louis, with a connecting flight in Minneapolis. She started to worry when her flight out of Calgary was delayed for over an hour. To make matters more irritating, the departure gate in Minneapolis was the farthest possible distance from the arrival gate. Her mind raced with "what-if" thoughts—she knew there were no other flights to St. Louis that evening. What if she missed the flight and had to spend the night in a hotel? What if there were no hotel rooms and she had to sleep in the airport? As she ran to the gate at top speed, her bladder uncomfortably full, the image of a "thumbs-up" sign suddenly flashed through her mind. *Her intuitive mind was sending her a clear message that she would make her flight.* Immediately, she slowed down. She took a moment to stop in the restroom, and then walked directly to the gate. As she arrived, a woman was kissing a very tall man good-bye at the gate. When she boarded the plane she realized this man was the LA Lakers basketball star, Shaquille O'Neal. Not only did she make the flight, but her seat was across the aisle from Shaq. As a bonus, she was thrilled to obtain his autograph for the youth group she worked with. In the end, her flight home was not at all what her logical mind would have had her believe!

Every day, life hands you a dilemma and asks you to make a decision:

- "My friend asked me to start up an e-business with him. He's a brilliant businessman with great ideas, and I'd love to learn more about the Internet, but I've got a full-time job and a family—I'm spread pretty thin right now. I'm really not sure how to respond."
- "My girlfriend and I have been talking about marriage, but every time the subject comes up my stomach hurts. The

thought of us being together legally—forever—I don't know. I don't know if it's just this person, or if it's the whole idea of getting married. I just can't keep putting off a decision."

- "I'm going through a divorce right now, and we're putting our house up for sale. I know I will have to move soon, but I'm freaked out by the decision. Where am I going to live? Where should I look? What should I do?"
- "I had a cold a couple of weeks ago, and it just won't go away. The congestion in my throat and sinus area seems to be going on and on. My doctor wants me to take antibiotics, but I don't *like* to take antibiotics—they mess up my digestive system. I'm not sure what to do."

Whether it's relationships, career, balance and healing, or simple everyday decision making, intuition gives everyone an edge. When we feel stuck and uncertain, it's often because we're only seeing a part of the whole. A flash of intuition illuminates and clarifies everything. We see the big picture and an array of new options we never thought of before.

What's intuition? It's a clear understanding that comes not from our logical mind—the part that knows how to do the math—but from a deeper part of our being. It's the secret of heeding premonitions, acting on bolts from the blue, and paying attention to your quiet inner voice, which is what successful people always do, whether they are conscious of it or not.

An intuition is not a whim, a good guess, or even blind luck. Intuition is a real force in every human psyche—the inner spark that ignites vision, creativity, inspiration. The inventor, designer, poet, and futurist Buckminster Fuller called intuition "cosmic fishing." But, he warned, "Once you feel a nibble, you've got to hook the fish." Too many people, he said, "get a hunch, light up a cigarette, and forget about it." In this book, you will learn to tap into this inner sense to discover when and where the fish are going to bite, and how to enhance your intuitive skills to reel 'em in!

Intuition can be a powerful ally in a world obsessed with pragmatic solutions. Unfortunately, most of us are trained to ignore our intuitive mind and depend solely on logical thinking. Intuition is often discredited because it is associated with sloppy, seat-of-the-pants type analysis or even that "woman's thing." When we honor intuition as an equal partner with logic, however, we can make decisions and solve problems effectively and well. I am a whole-brain advocate: I honor logic and intuition as necessary companions. Logic helps us organize and assess the forest of information in which we live. Intuition ignites the visions and insights that inspire and awaken the highest in us. Both are required to turn our visions into reality, to make our dreams come true.

Intuition is not just for a few gifted people—it's a powerful tool we all have, and one we can learn to tap into and use every day. This great asset resides within you now. If it has been dormant over the years, this is your chance to awaken it. As you learn how to identify, develop, and utilize your intuitive judgment, you will be able to integrate that input with logic for more effective whole-brain thinking.

Today, intuition seems to be everywhere and is recognized as an important decision-making tool for the twenty-first century. Leaders and the majority of businesspeople are using intuition more and more in the decision-making process to achieve success. And outside the corporate boardroom, down through the ranks, from the management team to the workers, out to the social arena and the home, that gut feeling or PowerHunch, also called intuition, is there to inspire us and show us where to look next.

Everyone has intuitive flashes. Intuition is your inner advisor and counselor, an oracle-to-go that you can access anywhere, anytime, day or night: in the office, on a commuter train, at home doing the dishes, in the shower, walking, relaxing, even sleeping. Your intuition can help you go beyond the bare data to reach surprising conclusions, tune in to a friend's needs, choose the right partner, come up with an innovative solution, help your children

xxi

through difficult times … in fact, there is no area of life intuition does not touch. Accept the challenge of learning how to tap into this powerful tool and use it every day. As parapsychologist Jeffrey Mishlove points out, you can use intuition to examine some of your most fundamental values—to find out what is good, beautiful, true, and just. You can learn how to access and implement your deepest wisdom in order to achieve your greatest happiness.

Storytelling

All the stories and examples in this book are real (in some cases, I have changed names to respect privacy). During the past twenty-two years, I have taught people from all walks of life how to cultivate their intuition. I hear so many stories about how the principles of intuition have been incorporated into their lives. I love watching people's faces as they make these intuitive discoveries, and their experiences teach me new ways to apply intuition.

Hearing other people tell their stories is a magnificent way to learn. Stories can trigger memories of similar situations you may have experienced but not labeled as intuitive. I found this to be true of virtually all the 225 people I interviewed for this book.

Here's a story from one of my students. The other day, Harriet's thirteen-year-old son seemed especially distracted—even for a teenager. She had a hunch he had something to say but hadn't yet found the right time, place, or person. She decided to take him out for some errands so they could enjoy private time in the car, and, she hoped, get to the heart of the matter. Soon, they were involved in a deep discussion and meaningful exchange. Afterward, they both felt better. Harriet credits her intuition for prompting her to invite her son to come along for the ride. I credit Harriet for *paying attention* to her intuition. Does this story trigger any memories for you? How often do loved ones, friends, and co-workers want to communicate a secret or feeling and don't know how to take that dramatic first step? If you are aware enough to hear the intuitive voice cry out, *"Pay attention!"* You will reap immeasurable rewards when you see a grateful smile on the face of your friend or child.

Here's another story. Just after boarding a plane bound for Hawaii, Sharon realized she didn't have her purse. She felt very calm, because her mind showed where she left it in the waiting area. Sharon explained the situation to the flight attendant, and retrieved her purse from the ticket counter at the gate. Someone had already turned it in, with all its contents intact! I don't know about you, but in my house losing or misplacing things is a regular occurrence. Now, when my husband frantically looks for his wallet, glasses, or important papers, I get quiet, and tune in within to find out if the item is really lost or just misplaced. I always thank my intuitive mind for the relief it brings.

One of my students, Chuck, was a middle manager with no previous experience or particular belief in intuition. The following story, however, showed him that intuition can have definite practical applications:

> *I was doing my morning stretching exercises as part of a program called Corporate Aerobics. While exercising, I suddenly had a sense that something was wrong and hurried to the area where we had placed a new product on display. As I looked once again at the product in the showcase, I discovered a problem that no one had caught in all the testing we had done. By finding this problem, I prevented the company from future liability. When the supplier was called in to fix this defect, he spent five days looking at the problem with their engineers and ours, and finally arrived at a very costly fix. The next day I spent a few minutes looking at the problem myself and came up with a much less expensive solution that all the engineers had overlooked. Being led to the problem initially and discovering a reasonable solution as well has led me to believe in my intuition more than I ever did before.*

Stories like these ensure that my classes never have a dull moment. Sometimes, however, the story emerges in the moment. On one occasion, in the middle of class, a student abruptly put on her coat, picked up her belongings, and ran out the door with tears streaming down her cheeks. I looked to my own intuition: Did the class content provoke her discomfort, or was it something else? I felt the latter was true, and my hunch was validated at our next class. The student had had a sudden prompting from her intuitive mind to call home immediately. Her husband, who had been making repairs on the roof, had just fallen off and the paramedics had been called. Fortunately, her husband was not badly hurt. She was very pleased that she had heeded the sound of her intuitive voice, which directed her to call and go where she was desperately needed.

I have learned from my students, and from the interviews I conducted for this book, that most people have used intuition daily but don't attach a label to the process. Each of them sensed that a guiding force helped them sail through unfamiliar seas. Not everyone sat down and consciously said, "Now I am going to call upon my intuition to make this decision," but they tapped into this reservoir of information nevertheless. During interviews, I asked people to tell me about the riskiest decision they ever made. I didn't hear anyone say out loud that "my intuition told me" to build a new facility, adopt a radical marketing campaign, get married, quit their job, have a baby, or move to a new town. I did hear them mention having a "hunch" or a "gut feeling," or making a "judgment call" before taking such a risk. Whatever words were used, they listened to the intuitive voice in order to remain open to new possibilities.

The Invitation

I invite you now to embark on this personal training course to strengthen your source of inner wisdom so that you can call on it regularly and reliably. You will learn how to consistently and accurately apply your hunches to any issue or problematic area. These exercises will help you develop your intuitive muscle and show you how to put these lessons into practice in the workplace and with your friends and family.

Call it a gut feeling, a sudden knowing, a judgment call. In this book, we call it a PowerHunch to underscore the strength of this quiet yet powerful force within you. *PowerHunch!* will give you the basic tools and principles you need to make intuition a part of your everyday life, whether the problem has to do with work, family, personal relationships, or life decisions. You'll soon discover how intuition can help you create a vision and make it happen, take appropriate risks, be in the right place at the right time, tune in to others' unspoken needs, and find balance and relief from stress. In part 1, you will learn the basic principles of intuition. In part 2, you will apply these principles to living an intuitive life. In addition to reading, practice is a necessity. This reminds me of the joke: How do you get to Carnegie Hall? And the answer of course is practice, practice, practice. There are two types of practice exercises in each chapter to help you develop and strengthen your intuitive muscle. The PowerHunch Tool exercises will help you take immediate steps to develop this muscle. The PowerHunch Workshops, the second type of exercise, give the opportunity to practice what you have just learned over a longer period of time.

Throughout this book I encourage you to record your insights in a special journal you can use to keep track of your progress. You can use a notebook divided into sections, or a loose-leaf binder with dividers. I hope you will identify with the student who told me, "When I consider the progress I made in understanding intuition just by being aware of it, it becomes evident that through frequent use and further understanding, I will rely on it more."

The prerequisite to getting in touch with your intuition is to become relaxed and draw inward, letting go of your logical, thinking mind and inviting yourself to open to more subtle messages. Throughout this book, I will introduce simple breathing and relaxation techniques to help you in this process. Any time you need to pull one out, you can find them listed in the Breathing and Relaxation Exercises at the end of this book.

Enjoy *PowerHunch!* as you learn how ordinary people have achieved extraordinary success using a winning combination of intuition and logic. Through these stories and the intuition exercises in each chapter, you will learn the methods and underlying principles to help you live an intuitive life. *PowerHunch!* reveals the "secrets" of intuition, and shows you, step by step, how to cultivate and harness this innate human gift in your business and your personal life, and ride it into the winners' circle. With knowledge, practice, and attention, you will learn how to access this powerful tool. You will be living an intuitive life by creating a vision, following a dream, guiding a successful business, having rewarding partnerships, understanding family members, and moving with ease and confidence through the turbulent and exciting world of opportunity that is all around you.

Have a wonderful journey!

PART ONE
PowerHunch Principles

1

The First Secret
Tap Into Your PowerHunch Source

Most people are living in the periphery of consciousness.
Intuition invites us right into the center.

— Willis W. Harman

Your intuition is speaking to you all the time. In fact, you can tap into it whenever and wherever you want. You probably already have—without knowing it. Have you ever:

- followed an urge to take a different route, and discovered later that you avoided a horrendous traffic jam?
- listened to your friend tell you about her engagement, silently heard an inner voice say, "It won't last"—and watched her break it off a few months later?
- quit your job without knowing what your next step would be, only to have a better opportunity land in your lap within a few days?
- suddenly come up with just the right words to say to help your child open up to you about a difficult situation at school?
- had a flash that adding a new and unusual ingredient would turn your tired spaghetti sauce recipe into something special?

The hunch, gut feeling, judgment call, sudden insight, or flash out of the blue are all intuition. Your intuitive "Aha!" can compel you to take a risk, come up with a creative solution, meet a new friend, choose the right school for your child, put ingredients together in a new way, resolve a longstanding problem ... you name it.

Intuition is not a talent reserved for very special folks: It's a gift we use every day, whether we know it or not. The secret is that you don't have to wait for lightning to strike in order to put your intuition to work: *You can learn to listen and understand what the deepest wisdom of your soul is telling you.* It's easier than you may think!

Do You Get the Picture?

Close your eyes and imagine that you have an *inner compass* that is always pointing you in the right direction. See it in as much detail as you can, and know that it is inside you, where you can always find it when you need it. This is a marvelous metaphor to represent your intuitive mind. I love to collect intuition metaphors. If you don't resonate with the inner compass, find a metaphor that speaks to you. Don't worry if you can't come up with one right away—you'll find many more in this book.

As you begin this chapter, take a moment to become aware of the metaphors, or symbols and images, that you already use to describe intuition. Have you ever talked about having a kind of "radar" or an "inner alarm"? Does a "light" go on? Does a "piece of the puzzle" fit? Has "lightning struck"? These metaphors or guiding images are truly worth a thousand words because they graphically show how *your* intuition communicates to *you.*

Here's one of my favorites: the intuitive antenna. Imagine you have an intuitive antenna inside your body that picks up the pictures, symbols, images, ideas, and feelings from your intuitive mind and beams them onto the screen of your conscious awareness. This antenna is constantly receiving and transmitting messages from within and without. With your intuitive antenna, you can tune into four different channels. You can listen to your:

- body send out sensations on the *physical* channel
- mind send a flash of insight on the *mental* channel

4

- heart transmit feelings on the *emotional* channel
- soul connect with universal truth on the *spiritual* channel

The Physical Channel

Have you ever had a tight stomach before an important meeting, a pain in the neck after a confrontation, grinding teeth when you're chewing over a dilemma, or a frog in your throat before making a presentation? That's your body trying to tell you something! Physical cues like these are screaming, "Pay attention to me!" Listening and becoming aware of the messages your body sends is pivotal when you begin to cultivate your intuition.

Sometimes it's your entire body that gets the message. Marie was having a job interview, and she thought it was going quite well. But as soon as the interviewer mentioned hiring her for full-time employment, her body just wanted to get up and run away. She had to hold herself down to keep from jumping out of her chair. Fortunately, she paid attention to this warning and asked for time to think over the offer. Her discomfort stayed with her for the entire day, so she turned down the offer—even though she really needed the work. Weeks later, a friend who did take that job told her she was very unhappy with this incredibly disorganized company. Marie's body knew this way ahead of her logical mind.

Writer and producer Arielle Ford, author of *Hot Chocolate for the Mystical Lover*, told me about a client who wanted her to do a big project involving huge sums of money. After the meeting, Arielle had a sick feeling. She somehow knew that working with this man would be a nightmare. She canceled the deal, and others later validated her intuitive assessment—he really was a pain to work with.

Many people literally get intuitive input from their gut or stomach. Writer Ray Bradbury said we can stay well if we pay more attention to our stomachs. The late J. Peter Grace, chairman of W. R. Grace & Company, said simply that intuition "is what your

5

stomach tells you." For Bradbury, Grace, and many other people, the "gut feeling"—which emanates from the stomach or solar plexus—acts as an intuitive barometer. The late Brandon Tartikoff, whose genius at television programming is legendary, was called the "man with the golden gut" because of his unerring ability to pick successful shows. Since executives in the entertainment field are immersed in a fast-moving and ever-changing industry, it is not surprising that people who rise to the top are highly intuitive. That is the only way they can survive.

Daniel Goleman's work on emotional intelligence indicates that emotional skills like self-awareness, empathy, motivation, and paying attention to gut feelings will contribute more to your well-being and success than your intellect or technical expertise. An integral part of emotional intelligence is knowing what you're feeling—which includes noticing your gut feelings or intuition about important life decisions. After a decade of research, Goleman has isolated a large class of neurotransmitters, or brain chemicals called peptides, which were first discovered in the gut. He says, "They're identical mates to brain-cell receptors, and that means that what's working in large parts of the brain is also active in the gut, and the central nervous system is wiring the two together. So it's not really a surprise that gut feeling should be a way you get messages."

POWERHUNCH TOOL

Body Awareness

Begin now to become aware of your body's messages. Notice, for example, when your stomach feels tight or heavy, your lower back hurts, your knee feels locked in place and can't move, or your gums ache. Ask yourself what's going on at that moment or in your life. Are you facing an unsettling decision at work, in relationships, in your personal life?

Begin to connect these bodily sensations to messages from your mind, heart, or soul. This is called making the mind-body connection. Sometimes they send messages in the form of puns, as dreams often do. If my neck abruptly begins to ache, for example, I ask myself, "Who's the pain in my neck annoying me right now?"

Start noting these instances in the first section of your PowerHunch Journal (title this section "How I Tap into My PowerHunches," or any name that reflects your growing awareness of your intuition) to keep track of the correlation between these body bulletins and what's happening in your life. As you begin to become aware, you'll probably notice that you respond more quickly and appropriately.

Sensory Signals

Once you've begun to pay attention to the messages your body sends, you can begin to appreciate how your five senses reach out to receive intuitive input from sounds, sights, smells, feelings, and tastes. This isn't much of a stretch for most people. In fact, the great majority of men and women I have met through intuitive development training sessions and classes initially made contact with their intuitive voice through their extended senses.

See if you identify with one or more of these examples:

- "A little voice told me to do it." Your intuition may work best through your ears: your *auditory* sense. Your intuition extends your hearing so you can hear what is *really* being said, beyond mere words.
- "I see what you mean." Your intuition may work best through your eyes: your *visual* sense. Your intuition helps you "read between the lines" or use "X-ray vision" to see beyond the apparent into the real.
- "I can put my finger on it." Your intuition may work best through your sense of touch: your *tactile* sense. Your intuition helps you get a "feel" for what's really going on.

7

- "It just doesn't smell right." Your intuition may work best through your sense of smell: your *olfactory* sense. Your intuition lets you "sniff out" a situation.
- "I've got a real taste for it." Your intuition may work best through your taste buds: your *gustatory* sense. Your intuition intensifies your ability to "get a taste" for any condition.

Animals already live on this level. But people can do it, too! According to animal communicator Sam Louie, extending your senses can help you drive defensively, surround yourself with trustworthy people, find a safe street to walk down, and make a good choice on your career path.

My own discovery of how the senses are connected to the intuitive mind came through Jim Stark, a student in my class "Whole-Brain Thinking for Managers." At the time, Jim was the circulation sales and marketing manager for Michigan's *Muskegon Chronicle*. As a class project, he was interviewing businesspeople to find out how they used intuition in their decision-making activities, and he noticed that they all processed his questions differently. The *listeners* would tilt their head to one side as if they could hear an answer "out there." The *visuals* would squint and then look up as they saw their answer to the asked question. The *feelers* picked up a pen, as if the answer felt good to the touch. The *sniffers* unconsciously changed their breathing, as if to search for the answer that smelled right. Several tried to get a *taste* for it, by rolling the answer around in their mouth with their tongues before replying.

People engaged in experiential exercises seem to amplify one or another of the senses in order to retrieve intuitive information. Each person reaches inside to process the information through his or her dominant sense, and out comes the "right" response. I had a stunning discovery of my own strong auditory nature, which I had always taken for granted. I thought that everyone sat down and "heard" dictation while writing. Now I honor this dominant sense when I am stuck for a word or a sentence, quietly waiting until the words pour forth from my intuitive mind.

Let's walk through each of these extended senses so you begin to identify which sense is dominant for you.

Hearing: Lend Me Your Ear

If you're old enough, you may remember ventriloquist Edgar Bergen and his dummy Charlie McCarthy. Charlie was always outrageous, and Bergen often said, quite seriously, "Sometimes Charlie knows things that I just don't know." Was Bergen listening to his intuitive voice speaking through Charlie?

My friend Janice told me about an unusual occurrence. She was awakened one night from a deep sleep by the ringing phone, and had a brief phone conversation with a troubled friend. The next morning, when she mentioned the midnight caller at the breakfast table, her family gave her a blank stare. No one else had heard the ringing phone! When Janice phoned her friend later that morning, she told her that she had had a crisis and considered calling her early in the morning—*but she never made the call.* Janice's auditory sense pulled in a sound from the universe to alert her that someone was calling out to her.

Many of the people I interviewed reported having an internal conversation with their "intuitive voice." Author Leo Buscaglia was guided by his intuition throughout the day. In fact, he told me that everything he did came out of listening to what he needed. Hearing the message is one thing, but paying attention is what counts. He emphasized that you have to *hear* and heed when your inner voice tells you "That's enough routine" or "That's enough work." When we press on regardless, it may be because we simply don't hear the word "Stop."

Author Cay Randall May hears gentle, fluttering ideas going through her mind. She calls them her "butterfly thoughts" because they flit in and out. Have you ever noticed these? They can be anything on a scale from banal to profound. Sometimes they can be lifesaving. Karen had just come back from a long visit with her daughter, and she was tired. She tried to ignore nagging thoughts that she should take her car to the mechanic.

She knew there was no emergency, and really there was nothing wrong with the car. After two days, however, she started listening to her butterfly thoughts and took her car to the repair shop. The mechanic lifted the hood and immediately said, "I smell gas." Then, after looking at the engine for a moment, he said, "Who's been working on your car?" "No one," she replied. But the metal shavings he found showed that someone had filed down the throttle valve, allowing gas to escape into the car. Listening to her intuitive voice probably saved her life and the lives of others.

Hearing the intuitive voice often leads to uncharacteristic but important actions. During the fall of 1941, British Prime Minister Winston Churchill made regular visits to the antiaircraft batteries surrounding London. One evening, he turned to leave one of the sites. As usual, his driver opened the near-side car door for him. Uncharacteristically, Churchill walked around the car, opened the door on the far side, and sat down. As his car sped off into the dark, a bomb explosion lifted the car onto two wheels—on the side Churchill normally sat on. As the car righted itself, Churchill joked, "It must have been my beef on that side that pulled it down." Later, he told his wife that something said, "*Stop*" before he reached the car door held open for him. That prompted him to open the door on the other side and sit down.

Seeing: Let Me Paint You a Picture

Sooner or later, a visual person will talk about the "pictures in my head." Whenever nursing CEO Sharon Buursma talks to someone, she always looks up and to the right to "see" if the details are true—she sees the different parts coming together and watches the scenario unfold. Many of her nursing colleagues appreciate this visual approach because they, too, tend to see a picture about what's happening with their patients.

Randy Arnold, the national sales manager for Barefoot Champagne, is a strong visual person who gets ideas "out of the blue." A lot of his work in marketing involves "just staying awake and noticing what is happening." For example, while driving through Ashland, Oregon, he noticed a banner for the Oregon Shakespeare Festival. Instantly, he *knew* he could do a promotion with them, and actually "saw" a fund-raising event. He pulled off the road, called the marketing director, and together they set up a whole program.

James Wanless helps his business clients define what they really want. He begins by eliciting their passions, desires, and needs, then he asks them to vividly picture their greatest desire and describe it. Next, in a lesson learned from Tibetan Buddhist practices, he asks them to "see" what they want in their mind's eye, and then frame this desire in a golden light. You might want to try this, too. Periodically focusing on your vision is a powerful way to manifest your heart's desire.

Touching: Get in Touch

This kinesthetic sense manifests in all sorts of ways: You may get a chill, have a "hair-raising" experience, get goose bumps, feel sudden warmth or light-headedness, or get "bad vibes" about someone. Some people unconsciously rub their stomachs as they contemplate a difficult decision. If a particular risk intuitively feels right for me, my stomach is the first to know—it feels comfortable and at peace. When I feel good about a person, my entire solar plexus is flooded with a pleasant feeling.

Here are some "chilling" examples. Margaret Sellers Walker is a professor in the School of Public and Nonprofit Administration at Grand Valley State University, in Grand Rapids, Michigan. When she gets a kind of chilly feeling, she asks herself, "Why do I feel uncomfortable with this? How should I proceed?" She says, "If I don't have to make a decision right this minute, I will hold off and sleep on it. It is also perfectly all right to go ahead and move on a decision based on what I know right now, even though I am experiencing a slight discomfort with it. I may reserve the right to do it differently later or look into it further. Action depends on what I know and the level of discomfort."

One afternoon, Brenda Knight, marketing director at Conari Press, was watching an interview on *Oprah!* when she was struck by an idea for a book. She says, "It was like WOW— this is an incredible idea and I think I have my first best-selling book idea. I got chills and the title came fully formed into my mind: *Attitudes of Gratitude*. I thought, *That's it.*" Conari's executive editor, Mary Jane Ryan, wrote *Attitudes of Gratitude* in four months, and the book sold 200,000 copies in less than a year.

Don Hewitt, the producer of *60 Minutes*, says he and his staff "all live by our fingertips." According to Don, "There are certain things you just know because you know them. If you play the piano for twenty-five years, you know where the notes are. Your fingers just take you there."

Don and his staff do not believe in meetings or memos. He says, "I figure if you hold meetings, your whole broadcast looks like a meeting. If you write memos, your broadcast looks like a memo. Everything is a hunch around here—the producers walk in here, the door is open and they say, 'Hey why don't we do it. I don't know... it sounds pretty good.' All of us live by the gut feeling. If you have been around in the business as long as I have, you just know in your gut what is right and what is wrong. You don't need a rule book, you don't need meetings to sit down and puzzle out facts and figures and slide rules." Don's word choices reflect his keen awareness of the senses. Talking about how they choose stories for *60 Minutes*, he says, "You sort of *smell* them out. You say that *sounds* like it could be great. And what *smells* right and *sounds* right is usually right."

My friend Marc's pet cockatiel, Casper, lets out a piercing whistle whenever he's feeling lonely. Marc couldn't devote every moment of his time to the bird, and the incessant noise was beginning to make him frantic. Marc got very quiet, and opened himself to his intuition. All at once, he felt he was touching a wooden object that was covered in buttons. This was intriguing, since Casper loves to remove buttons from clothing. This insight led Marc to create a new toy for Casper—he attached a number of buttons to a piece of wood, and successfully kept the bird occupied during his solitary time.

Smelling: Let's Sniff It Out

Getting a smell for a situation or having a taste for it may not come up in conversation as often as getting a picture or hearing a voice. Yet these sensory signals still trigger many intuitive insights—you may have said at least once that something "smells fishy."

Charles McCallum emphasizes that lawyers talk about the "smell" of a transaction or making sure something passes the "smell test." Regardless of what is set forth logically on paper, it has to "smell right" or "pass the smell test." In the final analysis, an intuitive sniffer like Charles is giving the logical mind the pass or fail signal.

My friend Jay and his wife were in the middle of a weeklong visit with his family in Oregon, some 500 miles away from their home in Northern California. Suddenly, Jay—and no one else— smelled smoke. There was no trace of any smoke in the house or grounds. Jay felt an overwhelming need to leave right away, and insisted they return home immediately. When they got to their house, they found their next-door neighbors sitting on top of the roof watering down smoldering shingles—flames had engulfed part of their house. Jay was pleased his sniffer had alerted him to this potentially disastrous event.

Tasting: Passing the Taste Test

It helps to give your intuitive muscles a workout. Seasonal sporting events are great for this. One year, during the NCAA basketball tournament, I gave my students the informal assignment of intuiting whether the University of Michigan would win any of their next five games. The challenge to keep wishful thinking suppressed was ever present, since everyone was rooting for the home team. We were all amazed at one student's accuracy: Al picked every game correctly! How did he do it?

Al, an engineer working for General Motors, had a simple technique: He put it to the taste test. Each night before the game began, Al silenced his logical mind (as he had been taught in class) and brought forth his intuitive mind. As he mentioned the name of each team, he became highly aware of how his taste buds responded. A sour taste always alerted him to the loser. A good taste signaled the winning team.

You might think Al's mouth could be the secret ingredient for winning the lottery or making a bundle at the racetrack. Scratch that thought immediately! Using intuition to attain monetary gain simply doesn't work. Keep the intent pure. In Al's case, his sole motivation was to develop his intuition so he could retrieve the appropriate word of encouragement or discipline to use with any of his staff.

For the past nine years, whenever Carol's adult stepchildren came for their summer visit, she would fight with them the entire time. The night before they were to arrive, she had a sour taste in her mouth that just wouldn't go away. She realized she was feeling sour about the visit, and knew she had to talk to her husband about her concerns. Doing this led them to agree on a few ground rules that would minimize potential problems. After this talk, the sour taste left her mouth. To everyone's delight, the visit went smoothly.

Opening All Your Senses

As you become aware of your senses, you will realize that you are usually being guided by more than one sensory modality. Can you imagine what happens when *all* of the senses are activated simultaneously? Then the intuitive door is flung wide open so you can consistently and accurately access the intuitive mind.

Here's how Melody extends her senses to receive intuitive input about other people. When her young children's friends come over, she likes to monitor their play to make sure a friendly atmosphere prevails. She greets each child with a gentle *touch*, and pays attention to how she feels after doing that. She finds that her fingers allow her to sense each child's mood, alerting her to the possibility of problems. Then she gets quiet and inwardly *sees* the children at play. Her inner sight shows her if the cooperative mood among the children will be sustained or if an argument will ensue. She *hears* her inner voice warn her about a potential disturbance by saying, "This could be trouble." She can *smell* if there is a disturbance in the air and get a *taste* of any problems. Activating her inner olfactory sense to smell smoke signals a fiery situation or dissension coming up. With a bitter *taste*, an acrimonious dispute is in the making, in contrast to a sweet taste foreshadowing harmonious play activities. Armed with this valuable information, she is able to improvise. If she senses that the kids have a lot of pent-up energy that could erupt in fights, she directs them into active games. If they seem low-energy, she helps them find quiet games. It's not brain surgery, says Melody, and it allows her to relax in the knowledge that the children are interacting in a way that is positive for them.

15

POWERHUNCH TOOL

Make the Sensory Connection

After attending a day-long intuitive development workshop, Charles called to tell me about the new connection he had made between the senses and intuition. The day after the workshop, Charles had given a potential client an envelope containing a business proposal for consideration. He noticed that the client was rubbing his hand up and down the envelope, while exclaiming, "I want to see what this *feels* like. Let me call you in a couple days." His discovery that the senses were operating gave Charles a suggestion for how to communicate effectively with this potential client—by speaking the client's sensory language. He told me that the next time he contacted this client, he planned to ask, "Does this project *feel* good to you? Is there something else you want to *get in touch* with? Can you *get a handle* on this project?"

Take a moment now to check your sensory antenna. What does it mean to you when you "hear a voice" or "have a picture" pop into your head? What are you really hearing or seeing when this occurs? What sense(s) do you use?

Become vigilant about noticing the language you use. This will reveal how you are receiving intuitive information from your senses. Do you say, "Can we come to grips with this?" (tactile); "You're not listening" (auditory); "Can you see what I mean?" (visual); "This leaves a bad taste in my mouth" (gustatory); or "This stinks!" (olfactory).

Record these connections in the first section of your PowerHunch Journal.

The Mental Channel

Victoria Weston was having a logical conversation with a friend when a thought flashed through her mind: Don would be calling momentarily to cancel lunch. Within seconds, the phone rang. As soon as she heard Don's voice, she said, "You are calling to cancel lunch." And he was. As a gifted intuitive, Victoria Weston calls herself "clairvoyant," which comes from the French word for "clear seeing." Yet this intuitive impression did not come from sight or any other sense. It came from Victoria's mental channel, to which she was highly attuned.

Whenever you have a sudden illumination, an "Aha" or "Eureka!" experience, or a flash of understanding, you are tuned into the mental realm of the inner mind. How do you know you are in the mental realm? Futurist Lee Kaiser told me that he gets a little mental "acceleration" and feels an energy that announces an impending insight. He can feel the change in the energy field around him as the thought-form comes in. He can tell these insights are different from everyday thoughts because the information comes in fully developed and with a sense of completeness. In contrast, when he is generating ideas from his logical mind, the thought process is usually step-wise and progressive, with a little bit added at a time.

Albert Einstein was a strong mental intuitive. He said that "man's conquest over his own ignorance must rest on intuition. It is imagination that makes man able to talk to the stars." By extending his mind, Einstein conversed with the universe. This ability was clearly evident in published accounts of Einstein's discovery of his theory of relativity. He had a vivid daydream of riding on a beam of light, which he followed in his mind's eye back to its point of origin. He then spent years formulating the questions that would lead to his theory of relativity. He wrote, "The intellect has little to do on the road to discovery. There comes a leap in consciousness, call it intuition or what you will, the solution comes to you and you don't know how or why."

Can you identify with this last sentence? When a resolution to a seemingly troubling situation blows in and "you don't know how or why," it means that your intuitive antenna is tuned to the mental channel. Alan Vaughan was an intuitive who functioned in this realm. A situation simply gave him an intuitive hunch, which quickly became an idea about the future. A restaurant conglomerate that was considering acquiring a rib restaurant franchise asked Alan to predict what their best-selling item might be. For no logical reason, his intuitive mind strongly registered that chicken was outselling everything else. So the prospective owners heeded Alan's advice, abandoned the idea of the rib franchise, and bought a chicken chain called El Pollo Loco, which went on to become very successful.

Willis W. Harman was the former president of the Institute of Noetic Sciences, a research foundation devoted to interdisciplinary study of the mind and its diverse ways of knowing. For Harman, intuition had to do with the operation of the hidden mind, which presents you with a bit of wisdom or a solution to a problem. You recognize that it is not something you put together with your rational mind, yet it seems valid. You learn to trust it.

POWERHUNCH TOOL

The Mental Channel

Ask your subconscious to go to work and give you the answers you seek. Find a quiet place where you can be undisturbed for at least fifteen minutes. Take three deep breaths in and out, and begin to quiet your mind and body. Imagine you are walking down a flight of stairs that has ten steps. With each step, you become more and more relaxed. If you like, you can find a special name for your subconscious so you can communicate in a very personal way. I call mine Subby. I say, "Dear Subby, There's something that concerns me and I need help. Can you give me an answer or show me how I can take the first step toward a resolution? My concern is . . ."

Remain quiet and receptive to the pictures, images, symbols, ideas, or feelings your subconscious tosses back to you. When you're done, thank your subconscious and then take your leave. Record these messages in your PowerHunch Journal.

At some point, we all get intuitive messages from the mental channel. The challenge is to become more aware of them. To see how powerful they can be, keep track of these instances in your PowerHunch Journal. Note how the clear knowing feels, how it presented itself. What is the quality? How do you feel about the certainty or completeness of the insight?

The Emotional Channel

Have you ever met a person who didn't meet any of your criteria for a perfect friend or partner, yet you felt compelled to explore the relationship? This is exactly what happened to Azriela Jaffe, the author of *Create Your Own Luck*. When she met her future husband, he seemed to be everything she *didn't* want: He was a kosher, vegetarian, orthodox Jew with two teenage kids. She wanted to marry someone who had never been married, and she wasn't interested in raising adolescents, accepting Jewish orthodoxy, or following a vegetarian diet. Yet, while her logical mind was saying "No way!" her heart was shouting, "This is the one!" Listening to her heart's intuition led her right to the perfect marriage.

Your heart sends you intuitive information when you are attuned to the emotional channel. You may feel a sudden attraction or aversion to someone, or an unprovoked mood change. For example, you invite someone you barely know to join you on a work project because a positive glow radiates from your heart. Or you reluctantly go for a job interview where the salary is less than you are currently earning and the location is undesirable. Yet your heart sends you an intuitive message to accept this growth opportunity.

For many ancient cultures, the heart symbolized the center of integration for emotion, will, thought, and feeling. You can always count on your heart for profound wisdom and integrity. You can trust the insights that come from it.

19

Pure intuition comes right from the love centered in your heart. This is a pure feeling without any judgment. Yet the insights here are not attached to any emotion; they have an objective, detached, and impartial quality. Paradoxically, perhaps, you can be sure your intuition is genuine when it comes to you as an impersonal hit.

Theresa Tollini directs and produces her own documentary films on women's and children's issues. Her hunches are centered right in the heart area. When her heart is feeling tugged or pulled, she feels deeply and is motivated to see a project through. For example, Theresa had a chance encounter with a female police officer who had just quit the force. The officer worked in the crimes against children unit and was continually involved in incest cases. She felt emotional pain for the kids whose cries for help were not believed. Theresa had a powerful heart-centered hunch that someone needed to talk about this topic, and this strong intuitive feeling led her to direct and produce the highly acclaimed PBS-TV special on incest called *Breaking Silence*, which has been shown all over the world and translated into ten languages.

Lenny Wilkins, former basketball coach of the Atlanta Hawks and current coach of the Toronto Raptors, views intuition as a feeling. Lenny says, "Certainly, intuition is used in coaching. You have a feeling how the player is going to play off the bench that night. You make a move, put him in, and he performs. Sometimes, even in business, you have a hunch abut something or decide to do something because it just feels right." To help encourage intuition in his players, Lenny urges them to trust their own instincts combined with their experiences, especially if it feels good.

Watch Out for Emotional Intruders

If the heart knows so much, why do we sometimes choose the wrong partner in the name of love or accept a job that turns out to be disastrous? It happens when emotional intruders— the voices of blame, criticism, and judgment—block the heart's intuitive flow. These culprits are subjective ego-based emotions driven by wishful thinking, fear, projection, and stress. In contrast to the pure feeling emanating from the heart, these emotions are judgmental and attached to the ego. They subtract from intuitive clarity.

Wishful Thinking

Wishful thinking operates when we make a decision based on a fantasy of what we want to happen. For example, Jack was tired of the single life. He was captivated by Maria, a woman he worked with. They went out a few times and felt some mutual attraction. Jack had been lonely for a long time, and he tried to convince himself that he was in love. He felt that his heart was telling him to ask Maria to marry him, and he did. Maria, who knew she was not in love but just having fun, was horrified. Jack misread his wishful thinking as real intuition.

Fear

Fear can enter into decision making simply because human beings are resistant to change and afraid of the unknown. When Michael bought a day care center, his friend Shelley immediately asked for the director position. This seemed on the surface to be perfect—Michael was afraid he wouldn't be able to fill this position before he went on a long-planned vacation, and he knew that Shelley was qualified. Still, he had an uncomfortable feeling. In his heart, he felt his friend was wrong for the job, but he wanted to get everything settled before he left. He convinced himself that she had all the right qualifications, gave her the job, and left on vacation. When he came back, however, it was clear that Shelley was in over her head—he realized that he should not have let his need to take a vacation and his fear that he wouldn't find the right person override his original intuition. It was a costly deal for Michael to get out of the agreement.

Projection

21

Projection occurs when you project your needs and wants onto someone else. For example, Steve saw his colleague Dennis as a close friend and associate, and told everyone about their harmonious relationship. When Steve was having trouble in his love life, he just "knew" that Dennis would be the perfect person to go to for advice. But when he did, Dennis was embarrassed to be taken into this intimate conversation. In reality, Dennis didn't see Steve as a close friend at all. Steve actually needed a father figure to give him comfort and advice, and he projected his need for that close, trusting friendship onto Dennis.

Delia was positive that her daughter, Chloe, would go to medical school after college. She had always pictured Chloe as a doctor and often bragged to her friends about how far her smart and charming daughter would go in this field—perhaps she would even be a surgeon! So when Chloe announced that she was going to get a master's degree in fine arts, Delia was devastated and confused. Delia's projection of her own unfulfilled desires had clouded her vision: When she thought about it later, she realized that Chloe had always been drawn to painting and drawing, interests Delia insisted she would "outgrow."

A projection is a like a movie you watch in a dark room: Once you turn on the light and see what is really going on, you can address the situation more realistically.

Stress

Stress can also interfere with intuitive decision making. If you have been working longer and harder than usual to make a decision, your mind might be reeling from "analysis paralysis"—you continue to bounce back and forth between alternatives. The challenge is to go beyond the facts and logic to the genuine intuitive input so you can make the right decision. If you feel restless and wonder, "How will I know the right decision to make?" trust your intuitive voice to speak loud and clear.

Economics professor Roger Frantz realizes that his focus on analytical thinking makes him "try" to come to the logical conclusion that he wants. There's a heaviness to this energy, and he feels like his mind is in an enclosed space. Roger contrasts this limiting activity to the moments when he uses his intuition: There's no heaviness, no weight, and absolutely no trying. For Roger, this state is analogous to being in the ocean, catching the next wave and effortlessly riding it to the shore.

Pat Sullivan writes a monthly column on spirituality for the Sunday *San Francisco Chronicle*. When we were talking about intuitive culprits, she was reminded of that section in *The Christmas Carol* where Scrooge says to the ghost, "You could be a bit of undigested meat." She said that any of these nonintuitive intruders could be the result of "indigestion"—that is, leftover business with family or wishful thinking.

It is important to be able to distinguish what is useful and has integrity from leftover business that really isn't relevant. Here are some hints:

- Always ask yourself if an insight resonates with your deepest values.
- When your insight is loud, scary, critical, and full of "shoulds," you are in your logical mind.
- Let the intuition come in easily and effortlessly, with no attachment to the outcome.
- A valid insight is usually accompanied by an overall feeling of well-being, a sense of inner calm, balance, or even a sensation of light in your chest area.
- If a particular alternative feels incorrect, you might have an uncomfortable feeling in your stomach or another part of your body.
- If you clearly know the insight is wrong *in the deepest part of your being*, it probably is.

POWERHUNCH TOOL

The Emotional Channel

We reach out to partner with other people in many situations, not just in love or friendship. When Jeffrey Mishlove invited me to partner with him in a postconference workshop for the Institute of Noetic Science, we had never met. We had only a brief exchange over the phone. Yet we knew in our hearts that our partnership would provide a rich workshop to the participants.

The next time you have a partnership opportunity, put it to the feeling test. Ask yourself:

- Do you feel warm and comfortable when you mention this person's name?
- Can you picture your joint endeavor?
- Do you get a thumbs up or down? A smiling or frowning face?
- Let an image bubble up to represent your relationship. How does this validate your joining in partnership?

Then listen to the answers your heart gives you.

In your PowerHunch Journal, note your feelings at the time. Later, write about what really happened after the activity with your partner.

The Spiritual Channel

Martin Rutte, co-author of *Chicken Soup for the Soul at Work*, likens intuition at the spiritual level to an "in-breaking" that metaphorically cracks your skull open and jumps in. This, he says, is God speaking, saying "Now, this is what you must do." In contrast, a gut feeling is a subdued, muted message. Author Leo Buscaglia also felt that this higher power or inner voice was the voice of God. He emphasized that God speaks only in whispers, and we don't hear because "Number one, we don't believe it, number two, we don't listen, and number three, we then plow ahead making all kinds of mistakes that go counter to our needs and personalities." The inner voice is loud and clear, but the personal static we create makes hearing impossible. Even if we do hear, we don't trust our own voices and are more apt to listen to the voices of others than to what our own intuition tells us. He said, "When we are reticent to accept the voices, we miss whatever messages are coming from the God in us."

Actress Anna Maria Horsford also feels that God whispers in her ear. Whenever she has taken actions that have surprised her family and friends, she has felt that everything would be all right because she listens to God's voice directing her. Anna Maria affirms that, since it is a whisper, you have to keep quiet to hear. You don't hear it, for example, when you are loud or trying to prove something.

Candace tunes in to the spiritual channel whenever she needs strength. At her high school reunion, she was invited to give the opening prayer. She got centered, took a deep breath (which she felt as the breath of God), and then let the words flow. She doesn't remember what she said, but afterward her teachers, former headmistress, and friends sought her out. Everyone thanked her for taking them to a place where they needed to be. She knows it did not come from her but through her. By being attuned to the spiritual channel, the perfect words flowed through her. Where did these words come from?

If the word "God" makes you uncomfortable, use whatever word or words feel right to describe this spiritual channel: higher mind, higher self, higher consciousness, essence. Leah has always shied away from traditional religion, but she has remained open to other worlds. She experiences her spiritual channel as an opening just above the top of her head. She pictures an empty chalice. When she asks for spiritual wisdom, she sees a waterfall of white light pouring into it, and feels the warmth and power of that light course through her body.

As you become more comfortable with the spiritual channel, you will tune in to the realm of infinite possibilities rather than view your circumstances based on your prior experiences. You will also become aware of a greater design than you could experience from your limited ego-based mind.

POWERHUNCH WORKSHOP

25

Listening and Becoming Aware

The first step in cultivating your intuitive abilities is to become aware. Ready? Let's get started.

1. *Write It Down*

The biggest lesson you can learn is to *pay attention!* Begin by recording in your PowerHunch Journal intuitive impressions you might ordinarily discount or not even notice. For example, your stomach might hurt before you have to make a major decision; you might have an unexplained aversion to a neighbor; you might feel a "buzz" at the sudden thought of moving. Even if you think these feelings have nothing to do with anything, write them down.

The entries you make in your intuition journal will open you up to potential PowerHunches by making it clear that you *already* use intuition, even if you didn't know it. This is your opportunity to *track* and validate the intuitive voice. As you review your journal entries, you will be amazed at how many times you disregarded important warnings that would have been very useful. As you pay attention and become more aware, you will develop a greater sensitivity to your intuitive abilities.

2. *Yes or No?*

Have you ever tried to solve a problem by making a list of pros and cons? No matter how many you list on each side, you *still* can't solve the problem! A better—and much faster—way to cut to the heart of the matter is to activtate your yes/no button. You already have the right answer inside—all you have to do is listen.

Sometimes, it's the little questions that really get us: Should I stay at work a little longer? Should I take the freeway or the street route? Should I cook dinner at home or go out? Should I wear my blue jeans or my khakis? How do we answer these questions intuitively? By shutting out the outer noise and hearing the intuitive mind respond with a "yes" or "no." The type of answer you get at first will depend on what is your strongest sensory modality. Practice with small questions like those above. When you feel ready, you can extend your intuitive antenna to each of the four channels. Here's a format you might find useful when you are trying to answer a nagging question. Let's say you are considering a career change. Put the question to your intuitive mind: "Should I take this new path?"

The Physical Channel: First, check in with your senses. Try to activate at least one of them. With practice, they will all give you input.

- Do you *hear* a "YES"?
- Do you like the *feel* of the new job title?
- Do you have a good *taste* in your mouth?
- Can you *see* yourself flourishing in this new capacity?
- Can you *smell* success?

Now put the question to the body test. Do you feel contentment or agitation?

The Mental Channel: What's the first thing that pops into your mind? The answer may surprise you! Even if it seems off-base, don't discount it.

The Emotional Channel: Check in with your heart. What positive feelings are flowing through you? Do you feel an expansiveness coming from your heart? Or even a warm vibration emanating from the chest area?

The Spiritual Channel: Close your eyes and feel yourself expanding beyond your body and connecting with the universe. Allow a connection with all that is and will be, and feel an energy pouring into every cell of your being. What have you discovered about the higher nature of this question?

2

The Second Secret
Listen to Environmental Cues

*Synchronicities transcend time and space, revealing the unified field,
the Mind of God in which we live and move and have our being.
Coincidences, on the other hand, lack the dimension of inner
meaning that defines synchronicity.*

—Joan Borysenko, *Pocket Full of Miracles*

Book publicist and author Arielle Ford was being tugged in two
directions. She felt that it was time to move on to a new city
and a new living situation, but at the same time she felt pulled
to stay with her work, family, and friends in Los Angeles. She
just couldn't seem to make the decision to move on. Finally, she
asked for help: "OK, universe, give me a sign that it is time to
move." Two hours later, a powerful earthquake rocked L.A.
Point taken!

Our environment sends us messages all the time—although
most are not as direct as the ground shaking under our feet.
Stephen Simon, producer of the film *What Dreams May Come*,
found himself in a sticky situation and feeling more and more
uncertain and hesitant. Obsessing over the problem as he drove
to work one morning, he suddenly caught sight of a billboard that
read, "You have more power than you think." *I guess I do*, he
thought, and knew that it was time to take action.

Meaningful Connections

Meaningless coincidence? Absolutely not! When our intuitive
mind suddenly links two seemingly unrelated events, *synchronicity*

is operating. Then it becomes a meaningful connection. When you learn to pay attention and honor such messages, the world becomes a rich tapestry of connections.

Psychiatrist Carl Jung first established the concept of synchronicity in the early twentieth century. It was further defined by Jungian psychiatrist Harry Wilmer as "the simultaneous occurrence of two meaningfully but not causally connected events in which an inner psychic subjective state or event parallels an outer event in the objective world. Not only is the cause unknown, but the cause is not even thinkable." This clarification connects an inner need to the outer event.

Pat Seiler, a family practice physician in Ohio, was looking forward to a job interview in another state, and was quite prepared to accept an offer. But as soon as her plane landed, a thunderstorm began, and it continued throughout her visit. Her experiences during the course of the interview were equally stormy. She began to reconsider. A few weeks later, Pat traveled to Grand Rapids, Michigan, to interview for a similar position. This time, sunshine welcomed her right into the heart of the city. The weather left a strong impression that intuitively guided Pat to her final decision. She knew in her heart that Grand Rapids was to be her new home, and that an environmental cue was literally giving her a golden key to the city.

John was upset when his teenage son, Greg, repeatedly disregarded his midnight curfew. Grounding him seemed pointless, since it had failed to work the last three times. John didn't know where to turn. Looking for something to take his mind off his dilemma, he picked up the newspaper lying on the chair and was riveted by a story about an actress who had been sentenced to community service for a minor infraction of the law. Then and there, John decided Greg should serve ten hours a week to each community—his family, his friends, and his neighborhood. The article in the paper was an environmental cue that triggered a creative solution to a seemingly insoluble problem.

Learn to Recognize Environmental Cues

How can you become more sensitized to the richness embedded in environmental cues? In this chapter, we'll explore three basic techniques you can always use:

- Open your mind to environmental cues.
- Dig for the deeper meaning.
- Actively ask the environment for input.

Open Your Mind to Environmental Cues

The environment is speaking to us all the time. What a wonderful gift! Let your mind go free and be open to this kind of input:

Damien had been in a bad mood for days, but couldn't say why. While drinking coffee one morning, his gaze fell on a pile of CDs on his coffee table and he understood: "I've been going in circles for a while, just like those CDs!"

Jessica was concerned. Her cat, Cleo, did not eat or drink for four days. Curled up in a tight ball in the closet, she would not come out. Jessica did not want to lose her beloved pet, who was only three years old. She asked her higher mind, "Show me a sign of Cleo's prognosis." When Jessica looked up, her eye was drawn to a new leaf that was opening. Aha! What a wonderful cue from the environment. Cleo, like the leaf, will be opening and unfolding soon.

Out of the blue, Jalen became interested in photographing flowers. He was particularly drawn to the beauty of the roses, and he found himself noticing them wherever he went. A few days later, he met a woman to whom he was very attracted. When he found out her name was Rose, he was not surprised!

Once you begin to look at the things around you in this way, environmental cues can provide direction and guidance on a wide range of concerns—even one as trivial as looking for a restaurant. Bob and Fred were new in town, driving around and trying to decide where to have dinner. After too much discussion, they finally decided to go to an Italian restaurant two miles from

31

their hotel. At that moment, a car suddenly pulled out of a metered space right in front of a different restaurant. Bob said, "Fred, this is it. Let's eat right here." Several times during their delicious meal, they mentioned how glad they were that they had paid attention to an empty parking spot that said "This is it!" This is not an earth-shattering example of intuitive decision making, but it presented them with a great meal. Without any effort, when they looked to the environment, the answer rolled in.

POWERHUNCH TOOL

Open Your Mind to Environmental Cues

Title the second section of your PowerHunch Journal "Environmental Cues." Record the help you get from the world at large. Write down the cue and the message you got from it. As you document these experiences, you will become more and more aware of the richness available to you everywhere you go. Eventually, your intuitive mind will come to your assistance more readily and reliably.

Here's an example from my journal:

"December 29: Noticed a flyer on my desk about an art show in the neighborhood. Somehow, I didn't notice this flyer before but now it jumped out at me. I decided to take a new route walking over there. On the way, I ran into Cousin Ken. He doesn't even live nearby but had to return something he purchased weeks ago. What a delightful surprise. The environmental cue prompted me to go to the art show and then my intuitive mind led me into this new route, where I met Ken."

Dig for Deeper Meaning

Sometimes just noticing an environmental cue is not enough; you have to dig deeper to get to the real meaning. Gail did not want to attend her PTA meeting—she knew she would be asked to chair yet another committee!—but out of a sense of duty decided to go anyway. When she tried to start her car, however, she found that it was out of gas. This environmental cue made a clear-cut decision for her and reflected her real needs: She was feeling overworked and stressed, and was ignoring the inner voice that shouted, "Don't go!"

Like Gail, if you listen you will soon find that your environment provides answers not only to your conscious needs, but to needs that are simmering just below your awareness. Marlene's boss asked her to work overtime for the third night in a row—another job that just had to get out. Even though she was dead tired, she agreed, and started in. But her work came to an abrupt halt when her computer screen froze up. The in-house support tech said he wouldn't be able to get it fixed until the next day, and she might as well go home. This was a strong message from the environment that Marlene needed rest and repair because she, like the computer, was burned out.

It's important to heed environmental cues, even (perhaps especially) if they run counter to your logical mind's agenda. Ira lived in Indiana, and his brother Norman was coming for a visit from the West Coast. Ira had been meaning to cut down the huge, dying tree in front of his house, and figured this would be a perfect time—in college, Ira and Norman had summer jobs felling trees for the Department of Forestry. After Norman arrived, Ira tried to get the electric saw started but it wouldn't work. He tried and tried, but to no avail. Finally, he picked up an old saw that was a bit rusted, and it started right away. The brothers began to cut down the tree. Ooops! They hadn't worked together on a tree-cutting job in twenty years, and they weren't as coordinated as they once were. The tree hit a power line, causing an electric outage to the entire neighborhood. If only Ira had listened to the message from the defunct first saw, a clue not to do the cutting at that time.

Many times, things that happen to us in daily life—especially things that happen over and over—reflect what's going on in our inner lives. Learning to understand the symbolic messages in daily events can help solve simple and knotty problems alike. Hanna was trying to reach her daughter, Jen—they hadn't spoken in a couple of weeks, and Hanna was upset that Jen hadn't called her. But every time Hanna dialed the phone, she got a busy signal. And each time she hung up, Hanna got more and more frustrated with Jen. *What's wrong with that girl? Doesn't she ever get off the phone? She's so insensitive!* And on and on, until Hanna realized maybe she was overreacting. Since she couldn't reach Jen, she decided to check in with herself instead. How did this situation symbolically reflect her inner life? She saw that she was trying to make an emotional connection with her daughter, but, like the phone connection, it just wasn't working. She was angry; her thoughts were going around and around to no purpose. Then she looked at her body. She became aware that her fists were clenched and her muscles were in knots. When she checked in with her intuition, she got the answer: You're trying too hard to make a connection with Jen. This is the wrong time—Jen is connecting with someone else right now. Stop now, and try later. Feeling relieved, Hanna went on with her day. A few hours later, Jen called her—just to chat.

34

POWERHUNCH TOOL

Dig for Deeper Meaning

Put the synchronicities you record in your PowerHunch Journal under the microscope and look for deeper meaning. In your journal note the incident, what it signifies, and any action or attitudinal change you need to make.

For example: Jack noticed that the battery in his watch had stopped working. A few minutes later, his wife stomped into the house complaining that her car battery was dead. This caught his attention, and he recorded these synchronicities in his journal. The act of taking a moment out of his life to write them down actually gave him the answer: Like the batteries, both he and his wife needed recharging! He spent a few more moments in his journal, jotting down ways they could both get a break.

Actively Ask the Environment for Input

Have you ever heard people say, "If you need something, just ask"? It works with PowerHunches, too!

Ray, a self-employed woodworker, had just finished a two-month restaurant remodel. He had no idea where his next job would be coming from, but he knew he needed one, and he had a plan. Ray decided to use his intuitive mind to broadcast an explicit two-fold message to the universe: He needed to work on a big job to make a lot of money fast, and he also wanted to hire someone to pick up the slack at the small cabinet-making business he ran out of his garage. The next day, out of the blue, he got a call from a contractor friend who wanted him to work on a big project. That call answered his first need. An hour later, he got a call from his ex-wife's son, who was looking for temporary work until something permanent showed up.

The connection between inner need and outer events is strikingly clear: Ray didn't make any calls to find work or a helper. Instead, he focused on exactly what he wanted, sent that energy out into the environment, and waited confidently for a response. This is how the intuitive mind rapidly and pointedly addresses our unmet needs.

Seeking answers does not have to be an arduous task: The intuitive mind easily makes connections. Just ask—then wait for the answer. One day, Sarah was worrying about her income and wondering if her finances would ever get off the ground. In some desperation, she asked her intuitive mind, "What does the future hold for me?" and waited for a sign. Then, looking up, she saw a sign—a real sign—on a café that said "Rich's." She laughed out

35

loud. What more could she have asked for than—with a slight spelling change!—"riches"?

Here's a highly significant connection that came in response to a question I actively posed. West Michigan was my home for twelve years, and I was eager to move. My husband wasn't as strongly motivated to relocate, since he had lived in our Grand Rapids neighborhood all his life. I attended a conference in San Diego, California, and that sunny city only strengthened my conviction that it was time to leave the Midwest—but where should we go? In San Diego, I decided to pose the question to my intuitive mind: "Where should we live?" I became totally focused on finding the answer.

The next day before lunch, I scanned the 1,200 bodies sitting down at tables and asked the universe to guide me to the seat that held a key to my moving dilemma. As soon as I sat down, a woman exclaimed, "I am so happy to see you! You were sitting across the table from me at lunch yesterday, but you were so busy talking to everyone I couldn't get a word in." When she mentioned she lived in the San Francisco Bay Area, I spontaneously said, "I'd love to house-sit or animal sit there for three weeks to get a feel for the area." Her eyes lit up and she said, "Are you serious? I'm leading a Qigong tour to China, and need someone to live in my house for three weeks and take care of my cats." I called my husband in Michigan, and he agreed to accompany me on this house sitting assignment. We came out to Berkeley, fell in love with the area, and after five days bought a house. What synchronicity!

Whenever I tell this story, people are alarmed to hear that we bought a house that cost five times more than our house in Michigan, and moved to a new state where we had no promise of employment. This defied all logic. And yet inwardly we were both singing "California Here I Come!" Whenever we checked in with our intuition, we felt calm and peaceful. We have now lived in California for five years—happily ever after.

POWERHUNCH TOOL

Ask the Environment for Help

Here are three ways to actively ask the environment to help you. Try each of them, and note in your PowerHunch Journal which method feels most comfortable. Use them as many times as you like.

1. *Reach Out from Where You Are*

Become quiet, close your eyes, and breathe deeply in and out. Pose your question. Make this query focused and uncomplicated. For example: Who will take care of my dog this weekend? Is this a good time to buy a new car?

After you pose the question, reach out for an object in your surroundings. You can reach actively (for example, by sticking your hand in your pocket and seeing what you pull out); or with your eyes (relax your gaze and let it fall on whatever it is drawn to); or with your ears (what's the first sound you hear?). How is this input answering your question?

2. *Go Outside.*

Go for a walk in your neighborhood, or take a drive. When the time is right, and you feel centered, pose your question. Then look around you for a sign. It might be as loud as a thunderclap or as quiet as a stop sign

3. *Read All About It*

Pose your question, then find a book or magazine. Open randomly to any page and read the first sentence your eyes fall on. How does it speak to your question?

People Are Part of Your Environment

You may receive the message you need from a person in your environment. It may not necessarily be a person you would seek out for help or advice. It may even be a stranger. Liam, for example, said the conversation between two strangers that he overheard while waiting in line for movie tickets galvanized him to quit his job the next day and start his own business.

Gia was looking for a new person to cut her hair and wanted a recommendation—she didn't want a bad haircut from an unknown person. One day, while shopping, she ran into her friend Bobbie, who lived way across town and rarely came to that neighborhood. "What are you doing here?" Gia asked. "I just came from my hair appointment," answered Bobbie. "She's so good I travel twenty miles every six weeks just to see her."

Tim Clauss teaches business and marketing in New Mexico. He was working with the students in his class on identifying their true purpose and the limiting beliefs that held them back from achieving their goals. One of his students, Francesca, complained, "This sounds great, but these fun miraculous things never happen to me." Together, Francesca and Tim focused on identifying her true purpose and limiting beliefs. She finally isolated two distinct parts to her identity: One was a traditional mother and businesswoman. The other part of her wanted to be a dog sled trainer in Alaska, a wild woman who wanted to have fun. Tim suggested Francesca open to these two parts of herself, and see what happened.

The following week, Francesca told Tim that the day after the last class, while she waiting for a doctor's appointment, she started up a conversation with the woman sitting next to her. "What do you do?" asked Francesca. "I'm a dog sled trainer from Minnesota," the woman replied. By letting go of her limiting beliefs, she allowed the environment to connect her with the very person who mirrored her inner desires. She saw that maybe her secret identity might have some basis in reality after all, and she determined to look into what it might take to realize this dream.

When Howard asked, "How can I find more joy in my life?" he got the answer not from people, but from *pictures* of people. One evening, in San Francisco for business, he sat for a sidewalk portrait artist. The painting portrayed him as a cross between Al Pacino and Sylvester Stallone. Afterward, he wandered aimlessly and ended up at a café advertising "Brooklyn-style pizza." On the wall were pictures of Pacino, Stallone, Arnold Schwartzeneggar, and other "tough guy" actors. Suddenly, he realized that these pictures of macho men were the answer to his question about finding joy. For him, the message was to develop the more "masculine" qualities that would balance his sensitive and emotional nature.

You never know who will lead you to that perfect pearl of wisdom. As I was writing this chapter, I was searching for another metaphor to graphically describe the environmental cue. To find it, I went for a walk—just as I suggested you do in the previous exercise. I had already asked my intuitive mind for a lead, and there he was—Tom Cintron, the clerk in the post office. After I received my stamps, Tom asked how my writing was coming along. I told him about the chapter on environmental cues. His face lit up as he said, "Oh, that's like when I make a wrong turn in my life and end up in the right place!"

I loved that image: We think we're going the wrong way, because it's not the direction we had in mind, but we end up in a better place than we ever imagined; or we keep hitting dead ends until finally we realize we were going the wrong way, and we reach our destination successfully. If you ever experienced the precipitous ending of a job or relationship, you know what Tom means. It reminded me of my client, June, who moved out of state and found work right away. Then four months later, she was let go without explanation. This "wrong turn" was followed by losing *another* job. But someone she met at her last place of employment led her to an incredible position she would have missed if she hadn't been laid off from the first job. Knowing about synchronicity, she knew inwardly that the layoffs would ultimately lead to her good fortune.

39

Most people have experienced the indescribable pain of making a "wrong turn" in the relationship lane. But is it a wrong turn? I know that whenever I stepped out of a romantic relationship that was clearly wrong for me, it created the space to meet a more suitable partner. Have you ever made wrong turns and ended up in the right place?

Environmental Cues Are Everywhere!

Some years ago, after she graduated from college, Anita LaRaia went to Europe and soon found herself in London—without money or a place to stay, and too proud to ask her parents for help. As an American living abroad, she knew she would need a work permit just to work as a waitress. One night, Anita was walking the dark streets of London feeling depressed and at loose ends, when she came upon a huge, red neon sign that read: TAKE COURAGE. She took this as a sign, and decided to stay in London and get a work permit. The next day, she answered an ad for a full-time job in a wine store. She soon developed a keen interest in wine, and later found success in the United States as a wine consultant. Only later did Anita find out that the huge, red neon sign that told her to TAKE COURAGE was a beer advertisement that meant "Drink Courage Beer"! She thought it was speaking directly to her despair, and was literally telling her to "take courage." And, for her, it was.

An environmental cue can be used as an inner compass to direct a person to the right spot. Helen had been searching for over a year to buy a house that would serve as a tax break and provide a larger living space for her growing family. She employed realtors, asked friends, and looked at every house listed in the paper, but just couldn't find what she was looking for. Driving around one day, she suddenly ran into roadwork that forced her to take a detour down a street she had never been on. And there it was—a white house sitting back from the street between two apartment buildings. Even before she went inside, she felt, *This is it!* After brief negotiations, she bought the house.

Sometimes we need an environmental cue about how to approach a painful situation. Filmmaker Teresa Tollini knew she was coming to a tense and sensitive moment when she brought a mother and her three daughters in front of the camera. They were bitter and hurt and had not talked for years. How would this go? Would the meeting be futile and incur more hostility? Teresa asked for an intuitive sign to give her guidance, in hope that the filming would not end in disaster. Just before the shoot, she wandered into another room and looked up at the ceiling. She saw thousands of stars flickering in the heavens and was transported to a distant place. The stars existed only in her imagination, of course, but they signaled to her that a breakthrough was imminent. Instead of the family becoming even more estranged, as Teresa feared, an incredible healing took place. The sisters and their mother, who had felt like enemies and hadn't been in the same room for years, came together, hugging and crying.

The comfort provided by an environmental cue can be unfathomable to the logical mind. Sharon had recently lost her husband to Hodgkins lymphoma at the young age of forty-five. After the funeral, she went to sleep feeling desolate, alone, and frightened about her future. Suddenly, she heard a phone ring in the bedroom. The only phone there was an antique phone that was not yet connected: It was the last purchase she and her husband had made together. Sharon was perplexed, but she took the ringing as a message: "I have arrived in this next dimension and all is well." She felt comforted that an object in her environment gave a clear signal that helped her though the grieving time.

41

There's a Song in the Air

Have you ever heard one line from a song replay over and over in your mind? That snippet of lyric can be an environmental messenger. At other times, a song on the radio may speak to you. It was Sunday, and Pattie was taking a long drive through the countryside. She was relaxed and singing along with the radio. As she sang the words "has not invited into parts of his heart," she knew this was a message about her partner, Charles. She was very frustrated about the challenges in their relationship, and didn't know how to resolve them. Charles was on vacation, and Pattie decided to call him that night and share these words with him. He told her that he would reflect on what these words meant. This conversation opened the door to another, in which Charles did some heartfelt sharing that energetically recharged their union.

Ken found that a song was a potent environmental cue when he began questioning whether to enter a bicycle race after some years away from the sport. Suddenly, the song "Ride Like the Wind" by Christopher Cross came into his mind. He had not heard this song in years and was struck by the clarity. He decided that he wanted to try to win a race again, and entered the next day.

I learned the song lesson in a most poignant way when I missed the opportunity to say a conscious good-bye to my mother, Naomi Rose, before she died. I just didn't make the connection when the words from one of my favorite Tom Paxton songs, "The Last Thing On My Mind," went through my mind over and over for days. The phrase that kept echoing was, "Are you going away with no word of farewell?" This refrain wouldn't leave my mind. I still didn't make the intuitive connection when we were suddenly called away from our Michigan home to visit my folks in Doylestown, Pennsylvania, because my mom was hospitalized. During that visit my mother, who was rarely ill, had a massive heart attack and died suddenly. She truly went away "with no word of farewell." My intuitive mind had been frantically trying to prepare me for this event by sending me the line from the song, but I just wasn't ready to receive it. If a phrase plays in your mind over and over, go within and ask, "What are you trying to tell me?" Then take the opportunity to say good-bye, hello, peace, or take whatever action the situation calls for.

POWER**HUNCH** WORKSHOP

Environmental Cues Are Everywhere

Environmental cues truly are everywhere. If you still need convincing, this workshop will change your mind! Do these exercises every day for one week and see what happens.

1. Choose a quiet time to communicate with your intuitive mind. Many people prefer the early hours of the morning, before they become involved in daily distractions. Pick three issues that you haven't been able to wrap your mind around. Let one focus on career, another on family, and the last on your social life, including your relationships. Frame each concern as a question that you will pose to your intuitive mind.

2. Now imagine that the universe is doing a computer search to select the very person, object, chance phrase, song, or other environmental cue you need to address each question. Hold this belief as you go through the week, and be alert for answers to your questions. You have used the third technique you practiced in this chapter (ask for environmental input) to begin this exercise.

3. As you go through the week, use the other two techniques you learned in this chapter—being open to environmental cues and looking for the deeper meaning. Note in your journal all the cues you notice, and search for deeper meaning if necessary. Don't force yourself to find them, just be open to the possibility that they will find you. Remember, the universe is doing a special search just for you, so be patient!

43

3

The Third Secret
Make the PowerShift

The intuitive mind will tell the thinking mind where to look next.

— Dr. Jonas Salk

We've all gotten stuck in issues large and small, from trying to figure out what to cook for dinner to trying to decide what to name a new baby; from wondering where we hid the remote to trying to decide whether we should take our current relationship to the next level. Brainstorming meetings come to a screeching halt, creativity fails, indecision takes up permanent residence. From this moment forward, at moments of panic or perplexity, please remember this simple maxim: Shift needs to happen!

Making the PowerShift

Albert Einstein said, "No problem is solved by the same consciousness that created it." Does that mean that if you created a problem, you can't possibly solve it? Fortunately, no! It means that you must move out of your usual way of thinking and into your intuitive mind. The PowerShift is a subtle but effective technique for doing this quickly, effectively, and reliably. This basic PowerHunch tool silences the chatter of habitual thought patterns, stills agitation, and creates a channel in which new ideas and solutions can flow.[1]

The PowerShift consists of eight simple steps to move you from where you are to where you want to be:

1. issue
2. centering
3. receptivity
4. imagery
5. deciphering the image
6. incubate
7. go deeper
8. implementation

Let's look at these steps in detail.

Step 1: Issue

First things first: Define or determine the exact nature of your issue or concern, and formulate it as a concise question. Be careful not to ask two questions in one. For example, it would be incorrect to ask, "Should I change jobs and move to another city?" These are two separate inquiries: "Should I change jobs?" and "Should I move to another city?" The type of answer you receive may be determined by the way in which you frame your questions. For example, the question "Should I move?" will elicit a simple "yes" or "no," while the more open-ended question "Where should I move?" will give you a more graphic response. When you have your question, write it down.

Example: In preparation for moving, Sherry is packing, carrying boxes, and putting a lot of stress on her body. Suddenly, her left foot begins to swell—on the top of the foot, below the toes. After a few days, the swelling is still there and her foot is becoming increasingly more painful and uncomfortable. She applies ice and elevates the foot, but nothing works.

46

Issue: Sherry formulates her question like this: "What should I do to fix my foot?" She writes it down on a piece of paper to fix it firmly in her mind.

Step 2. Centering

Once you've got your question, it's time to draw your energy back into yourself and get centered. Use any or all of the following techniques to release the mental tension.

- **Use an affirmation.** Create a positive statement that you can say repeatedly. For example: "I already know the right answer."
- **Use a focusing word or phrase.** You might consider using words like courage, joy, relax, one, serenity, peace, be still.
- **Use a visual focus.** You can focus on any object or picture in your environment, particularly one that is geometric in shape. You can also look at a soothing picture of a natural setting, such as the seashore, mountains, or a pastoral scene, or focus on an object, such as the leaf of a plant, a clock, the wood pattern in your desk, or a flower.
- **Use an auditory focus.** Listen to a slow, restful piece of recorded instrumental music, or to sounds of nature.

Example: Sherry walks into her family room and gazes out at the ocean. As she looks out at the water, she begins to relax. Then she lights a candle, gazes at it, and lets her thoughts pass through her mind without grasping on to them.

Step 3. Receptivity

Now that you're centered, you'll release your physical tension and become receptive. Sit quietly with your eyes closed. (Use the following PowerHunch Tool to learn ways to become quiet.) Use a breathing and/or a relaxation technique to release your tension. This will make it easier to become receptive to the messages of your intuitive mind.

47

Example: Sherry takes three energizing breaths. She starts by exhaling all the air from her lungs. Then, she takes six short inhales in quick succession through her nose. 1 breath (sniff) 2 — (sniff) 3 — (sniff) 4 — (sniff) 5 — (sniff). She holds, and then takes one more breath (sniff), and holds for two counts before exhaling completely. She then relaxes using the "Progressive Relaxation Technique." She feels the tension flow out through the soles of her feet as she visualizes rays of energy releasing from each body part, beginning with the feet and ending with the head. (See the Breathing and Relaxation Exercises at the end of this book for the complete exercise)

POWER**HUNCH** TOOL

Learning to Be Quiet

In silence, ideas proliferate, sparks ignite, and flashes come from out of the blue. This is when you clearly hear your intuitive voice. Finding the time to be quiet, however, is another story. In our dizzy, busy world, it can be difficult. Being quiet is even more challenging when you are sitting in your home or office surrounded by Post-It notes and other reminders of things to do, and family members or colleagues are asking for your attention. Even when you go out for a quiet walk, sirens wail and horns honk. Is it possible to find clarity in the midst of confusion, quiet in the midst of sound? Yes! The trick is to practice disconnecting from daily routine.

Quiet time can take any form: prayer, meditation, being out in nature, walking, inspirational reading, or engaging in an artistic or sporting activity. Use whatever name you prefer for these periods of stillness: introspection, meditation, reflection, contemplation, quiet time, in the silence, prayer.

Here are some ideas to get you started. Choose the practice you like best, and begin with five minutes of quiet once a day. Aim for thirty minutes every day, and allow yourself as long as you need to quiet the mental hubbub so you can hear the gentle voice of intuition when it speaks!

Morning and evening reflection. Go to a room where you can be alone. Take a moment each morning to welcome the day, and a moment in the evening to reflect on the day that has passed. You might do this after you brush your teeth in the morning, and as you are getting ready for bed at night. Welcome any intuitive thoughts that come at this time.

Let intrusive thoughts go. Our minds are never noisier than when we aim for solitude. When random thoughts try to catch your attention, try not to become attached to them. Just watch them pass through your mind. Sometimes I take a moment to silently let these important thoughts know that I will come back to them later. At other times, when negative thoughts intrude, I say *NUTS!* I learned this acronym from Ruth Fishel, author of *Time For Joy*. It stands for *Negative Uninvited Thoughts Stop!*

Contemplate. Sit in a meditation area, garden, or even in your office with the door closed, and empty your mind of all thoughts and concerns. Simply cease all activity, close your eyes, and turn within. Breathe deeply and evenly, and imagine yourself retreating to your favorite quiet place. Focus on your breathing as you say "breath in, breath out." This will quiet your chattering mind.

Take a water retreat. Water is a wonderful intuitive conductor. Albert Einstein valued his periods of relaxation to balance the strenuous mental demands of his work. He loved to play and relax on his sailboat, or drift aimlessly in his canoe. You don't need to have a boat, a lake, or an ocean to take advantage of water's soothing properties. You can relax in a hot tub, and take "intuitive showers"! In reality or even your imagination, you can sit by a lake or still body of water. Even having a bowl of still water nearby will also slow your energy down.

Be active. For many people, quiet time involves activity. Long, solitary walks are the best tonic for many people. Solitude and quiet time can prevail whether you are taking a walk, going out for a run or bike ride, or even working out in the gym. This immersion in an enjoyable activity, particularly an athletic movement, ignites the intuitive flow. One of my students finds that she has some of her most intuitive moments when she is alone in the car driving to the grocery store!

Take a Breather. Take time each day—more than once a day, if possible—to focus on your breathing. For at least five minutes, sit in a comfortable chair, soften your gaze or close your eyes, and breathe deeply. Practice any of the four breathing techniques and six relaxation exercises at the end of this book.

Step 4. Imagery

Now you will bring forth imagery: When you ask your question, your intuitive mind will communicate by sending you the answer—but it may not be in the form you expect. You may get an image, picture, symbol, voice, feeling, taste, or smell. Don't be put off by the word imagery. This doesn't mean you have to "see" an image inwardly. In chapter 1, you discovered which sensory mode is dominant for you. Through any of these senses, you can "sense" the image. For example, pick up a pen or paper clip. Close your eyes. How do you "see" this object? If not with the inward seeing, you get a clear sense of what it looks like even with your eyes closed.

You may get your answer right away, in a yes or no, a red or green light, or a sudden flash of understanding. More likely, you'll receive an image you don't quite understand. Whatever you get— even if it seems nonsensical—don't discount it. Take it with you to the next step, interpretation.

Example: When Sherry asks, "What should I do to fix my foot?" the image of a large fish pops into her mind. Her first inclination is to ignore it because it seems to have nothing to do with her foot. Instead, she stays with it and it grows more vivid—in fact, it's a big, beautiful fish.

POWERHUNCH TOOL

Finding an Intuitive Trigger

You can easily learn to trigger your intuition. With a little practice, you can learn to center yourself and become receptive to intuitive input in just a few minutes, or less. Everyone has a personal technique, and you'll discover yours.

I've trained myself to do a quick "meltdown" to reach my intuitive mind when I need an instant answer—an instant PowerShift. I exhale deeply, heaving an audible sigh. Then I raise and lower my shoulders to release tension, tighten and release my abdomen, tighten my hands into fists, and release any anger I may have. Then I gaze at a pattern on the wall or ceiling. As soon as I pose my question, an image pops up or an intuition flows in.

A friend of mine uses another simple technique. She repeats silently, "Let all that is for my highest good come forth, all else return from whence it came." She breathes deeply and slowly and lets go of tension. Then she asks her question and waits for the answer.

A student of mine told me that he closes his eyes and visualizes himself sitting underneath a waterfall. He relaxes as the water flows over him, and imagines it is also the flow of intuition coming to his aid. You will find your own technique.

Choose one or two phrases, images, or physical techniques, or a combination. Experiment with them. Ask your questions, receive answers, and simply be receptive to the flow of intuitive ideas into your mind. Then, in the third section of your journal, called PowerShift Notes, write the answers to the questions you have posed to your

51

intuitive mind. Notice how different they are from the answers you generally get from your logical mind.

Once you've found the practice you resonate with, take time each day to practice getting to this space. Note in your journal how long it takes. The time should get shorter and shorter!

Step 5. Deciphering the Image

Now you can work on interpreting your intuitive answer, in much the same way you would interpret dream imagery. Use any method you know to decipher the underlying meaning. Sometimes, the associations may be clear. If, like Sherry, your answer just doesn't make sense, try using the amplification method: Start with a central image, and continue to associate until you get to the core meaning. It is important to let this stream of association flow through without censoring any ideas. You can do this in your mind, you can speak the associations out loud, or you can make a diagram, like Sherry did (see below).

Come up with as many associations as you can. I love watching people while they are engaged in this process. Their eyes always light up with an "Aha!" look when they make the intuitive connection.

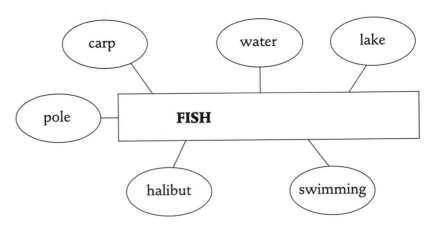

Example: Sherry's first associations to the fish are shown in the following diagram.

She felt she was getting closer, but she wasn't there yet.

POWERHUNCH TOOL

Learning to Decipher the Imagery

This is really fun, and you will delight at the images your intuitive mind sent to you. Sometimes, you have to stretch a bit! In one of my classes, Sue shared her dilemma: Should she and her husband have a fourth child, or build an extension on their house? After the students became centered, receptive, and retrieved their images, Sue raised her hand immediately and said, "All I got was a picture of the sun coming up over the horizon." Immediately, I saw the intuitive wisdom embedded like a pun in the imagery: "You have a son coming up 'over the horizon'—in time." She couldn't accept that conclusion. It was too easy! But ten months later she sent me a card announcing the birth of her son, Alex Stephen.

Start using the centering and receptivity techniques to become still and retrieve an image central to any issue or concern. Have fun playing around with the "punny" interpretations you may get. You will not only have fun, which is a stress reliever, but most importantly get a new view to a vexing situation.

Step 6. Incubate
Like Sue, you may not immediately understand the message. This does not mean the symbol was nonsense. Take a break, do something else, sleep on it. Let the image incubate in your intuitive mind. Chances are, the "Aha!" will emerge spontaneously while you're engaged in a mundane activity like driving to work or doing the dishes.

Just forget about it for the moment, and go on with your life. Even if you're not consciously thinking about it, your intuitive mind will work on the problem for you. The answer will usually come up when you're least expecting it.

Example: Sherry decided to incubate the insight and let the right connection emerge spontaneously. While grocery shopping, she thought fish might be good for dinner—considering the circumstances. As she stared at the whole salmon on ice, she got her "Aha!" Gills! Several years ago, she had seen a podiatrist named Dr. Gill. The fish symbol was telling her to make an appointment with Dr. Gill.

Unfortunately, Sherry couldn't get in to see Dr. Gill for several days. In the meantime, her foot was still painful. Her logical mind sprang into action. What if it was broken? What if something was really wrong? She decided then and there to go to the emergency room and have it x-rayed. After a three-hour wait in emergency, and more time taken for reading the x-rays, the ER doctor told her that there were no broken bones and suggested she see a podiatrist. Sherry realized that when she ignored her intuition and acted out of fear, she created a lot of extra work! Within minutes, and without added cost, her intuitive mind had given her the same information.

Step 7. Go Deeper

You may or may not want to go deeper with your answer. If your question is something simple: "Where did I put the remote control to the TV?" further interpretation of the answer "under the sofa pillows" is not necessary! However, you may want to let your intuitive mind play with the word association method to get to the bottom of a more complex issue. To do this, let one word trigger another until you have the intuitive insight.

Example: Sherry has a few days to wait until she can see Dr. Gill, and decides to do a word association to the word "foot." She thinks, "Foot › walk › direction" The word "direction" catches her attention immediately. "Aha!" She had not been following the directions Dr. Gill gave her over a year ago: to get a shoe insert that would keep pressure off her toes. Maybe that was the cause of her current problem. Had she followed his advice a year ago, she probably would not be having this problem today.

Step 8. Implementation
The final step is to use your intuitive input to create a solution to your problem and implement it. To find the remote, look under the sofa cushions. If the answer to your travel questions was "airplane," buy your plane tickets.

Example: Sherry's appointment with Dr. Gill was quite satisfactory. As she suspected, the shoe inserts were exactly what she needed. She ordered them as soon as she got home, and they made an immediate difference. Within a day, the swelling began to go down. Soon, her foot pain was gone.

Variations on the PowerShift Theme

As you will soon discover, the best part of the PowerShift practice is that you can customize it. Here are some examples to help you get started. (See the Breathing and Relaxation section at the end of this book for help with the exercises described under Receptivity in each example.)

Example 1: Maria's Career Change

Maria has a consulting business that offers corporate seminars and wellness services. Her largest client contract is taking up far too much of her time. Not only that, the fee she asked them for has turned out to be far less than she needs. She feels like she's reached a dead end, and would like to (a) work fewer hours, (b) make more money, and (c) use the extra time to pursue her graduate studies.

1. **Issue:** Maria writes down her central issue: "What direction should my business take to help me accomplish my goals?"

2. **Centering:** She listens to soft jazz and focuses on the pattern in her living room carpet.

3. **Receptivity:** Then she takes several deep, slow breaths and tenses and releases each muscle in her body one at a time, starting with her toes and moving all the way up to her scalp.

4. **Imagery:** She asks the question silently, in her mind. Into her mind pops the image of a bonsai tree.

5. **Deciphering the Image:** When Maria starts associating on the bonsai tree, many words pour forth: trim, short, planned, clean, neat, well cared for, nurtured, loved, tough, old, shaped, structured, rooted, and beauty. Three of the words resonate: planned, tough, and rooted. Aha! She has to be *tough* and *rooted* during the transition with a clearly *planned* business direction. Maria decided to add to this image with another, and went back to step three to see if she could retrieve another image. This time she saw a street in New Orleans, and got the following associations: old, play, joy, heritage, sidewalk, closed down, hat, secrets, treasures, witch doctor, voodoo, and magic. The words that resonate are secrets, treasure, and magic. These words suggest that she wants to continue her work in wellness, which she feels is *magical* and certainly has several *secret treasures.*

6. **Incubate:** Still, she doesn't feel she received a clear answer to her question, and decides to incubate the answer. Later that day, the image of the instructor in *The Karate Kid* pops into her mind and won't go away.

7. **Go Deeper:** Maria focuses on his face, and gets the word "coach." Hmmm. She used to have a personal coaching practice in lifestyle changes, and really enjoyed the one-on-one approach. She realizes that she should move away from corporate work and into personal coaching. In a few months, this business could make twice the amount she is currently receiving.

8. **Implementation:** To build this practice, Maria begins to network. She joins the National Association of Women Business

Owners, and participates in their monthly roundtable groups. Right now, the women are helping her come up with a marketing plan and select a business name.

Variation on the PowerShift Technique: Maria keeps recovering imagery until the answer to her question is clarified.

Example 2: A Relationship Dilemma

Carl feels his relationship with Beth is not as exciting as when they first met. They share many mutual interests and also have their own hobbies. At times he wonders, "Why were we brought together? Will this relationship last?"

1. **Issue:** Carl asks, "Should I end my relationship with Beth?"
2. **Centering:** In the quiet of his home office, he plays soft music to stimulate insight and wisdom. He looks at the pattern of wood on the desk as the thoughts going through his head start to fade.
3. **Receptivity:** He takes a few "Total Breaths" and allows himself to relax. Carl takes a deep inhale, lets his stomach expand, and then exhales. Silently, he poses the question as his body and mind become more relaxed.
4. **Imagery:** Darkness prevails until he notices a person's head, which is pointed toward him as if the person is bowing. He sees only the top of the head; the face and rest of the body are not visible. The hair is very black, but he especially notices a spot that is shiny with reflected light. As he observes that light spot, it grows larger and becomes more luminescent. Before Carl can even ask the question about this, he hears the word "enlightenment." He asks for a confirming image and immediately sees a bouquet of flowers and ribbons that could easily be used in a wedding. The fragrant roses in the bouquet emit a

57

powerful aroma. Tears rush into his eyes and he feels so happy, like a new groom.

5. **Deciphering the Image:** The luminescent head is showing Carl that his girlfriend brings him enlightenment. The fragrant bouquet passed the smell test and definitely resembled a marriage bouquet. This additional information assures him that he can make a serious commitment and not have any regrets.

6. **Incubate:** Not needed.

7. **Go Deeper:** Not needed.

8. **Implementation:** The commitment to Beth is now sealed in his heart and he is already imagining the scenario for "popping the question."

Variation on the PowerShift Technique: Carl's intuitive antenna is tuned into the physical channel.

Example 3: Kate Understands Her Cat

58

Kate has a serious problem with her cat, Wizard. After eight years of good behavior, Wizard started to avoid the litter box and began to pee on the carpet. The problem escalated and a carpet had to be replaced in one of the rooms, since Kate is selling the house. Although that room was blocked off, Wizard started to pee in the basement. As this behavior continued Kate became really angry. Her first thought was to take Wizard to the veterinarian and make sure this wasn't a health problem. Fortunately, the vet said that Wizard was in perfect health, and this was a behavioral issue.

1. **Issue:** Kate asks, "How can I get Wizard to use the litter box?"

2. **Centering:** Kate is pretty angry when her PowerShift process begins, so she puts on classical music, lights some candles, and repeats her affirmation: "My intuitive mind will lead me to the right answer."

3. **Receptivity:** She lies down on the carpet and feels her muscles softening and flattening out. She does several Hang-Sah breaths. She whispers aloud the word "hang" as she inhales and "sah" as she exhales. She does this ten times. Kate allows her body to relax further. With each breath she releases anger, judgment, and emotion and allows herself to just be open and receptive to any intuitive wisdom. Kate spends several minutes in this calm, quiet, and serene space.

4. **Imagery:** Two images emerge: a heart, and a table turned upside down. Kate gazes at the heart and feels an overwhelming sense of very deep love. This strong heart feeling connects her to the emotional channel.

5. **Deciphering the Image:** Kate feels that the image of the heart and the strong sense of love means that Wizard is in need of more love. She realizes that she hasn't spent a lot of time with her cat lately—she's been focused on selling the house. Aha! So this is how Wizard commands attention (which is often what peeing outside the box signifies). That part was fairly simple, but what about the image of the table turned upside down? Then it hit Kate: Turn the tables! Yes, turn it around. She had been so angry with Wizard that she didn't think about how the moving of furniture and the constant changes in the house might be affecting him. Instead of thinking about what Wizard was doing to her, Kate turned the tables and started to think about what she was doing to Wizard. He must be very stressed and traumatized by all the change. What he needed was more love, not punishment.

6. **Incubate:** Not needed.

7. **Go deeper:** Not needed.

8. **Implementation:** Kate begins by telling Wizard how much she loves him, and that she will spend quality time with him several times a day. She sets up a special space for Wizard that will not change, with his favorite blanket. Soon, she finds that when things are in turmoil, Wizard goes into his secure space.

Wizard now has lots of love to help him through this stressful time and has been faithfully using the litter box.

Variation on the PowerShift Technique: Kate received a heartfelt communication through the Emotional Channel.

Example 4: The Magic Carpet Rides to a Family Resolution

Candy has been having trouble getting along with her Aunt Esther. She was offended by a comment Esther made months ago and has avoided her ever since. This is difficult at times, since so many members of her family live nearby and get together frequently. She really wants to release the grudge but doesn't know how to take the first step.

1. **Issue:** Candy asks, "How can I change my negative feelings toward my Aunt Esther?"
2. **Centering:** She sits on the edge of her bed, looks at a beautiful multifaceted rainbow crystal, and says, "Peace, be still."
3. **Receptivity:** She does the Total Breath and uses a progressive relaxation technique to relax from her toes to her head, allowing each muscle group to relax completely and "melt into the bed." Once she has that very light, tingling feeling all over, Candy knows she is deeply relaxed.
4. **Imagery:** Candy sees a flat paperlike object floating in front of her. After a minute or two she realizes it is a magic carpet. She gets on and takes off for a ride. Suddenly, the carpet stops and she feels a sharp, pointy kind of pain in her chest. Then she feels a pointed pain in her lower abdomen, which makes her think of a poke in the gut. At the same time, she hears the sound of a bugle. Once again, the carpet takes off and she is walking on a beach with her aunt. The sun is shining brightly, she feels the sand beneath her feet, and she can't wait to jump in the waves.

60

5. **Deciphering the Image:** The pain in the chest reminds Candy that this issue is literally touching her heart in a very meaningful way. She associates to the word "guts" and immediately thinks of courage. She realizes she needs to have courage to forgive her aunt, and heeds this as a wake-up call (the bugle blowing) to take the first step. With this last stop, the carpet takes her to a place where there is a lot of sunshine. This brings the Bahamas to mind. Aha! This might be a good opportunity to invite her aunt to join her on a trip. That will be a wonderful setting to express her feelings about the past and then when amends are made, go into the future.

6. **Incubate:** Not needed.

7. **Go Deeper:** Not needed.

8. **Implementation:** From the imagery, Candy realizes the value of family ties and goes to get the Bahamas travel brochures to show her aunt.

Variation on the Powershift Technique: Candy's imagery took flight as she was propelled into motion.

Example 5: Looking for the Perfect Team to Win the Science Fair

Wendy teaches fifth grade. Every year, her students enter the science fair, but she's never had a winning year—not because her students aren't gifted, but because she can't seem to find a way to motivate them to work as a team on this project. This year, however, she is determined to give it her best.

1. **Issue:** Wendy asks, "What do I need to do to have my team of fifth-grade students win the science fair?"

2. **Centering:** Wendy looks down at the pattern on her carpet and says "serenity."

3. **Receptivity:** She takes ten Hang Sah breaths and listens to an autogenic relaxation tape, because it helps her set her mind

free right away. She silently tells each part of her body to relax, starting with her feet, and working her way up to her face and head. Then she feels totally relaxed.

4. **Imagery:** Wendy asks for a word or image to show up. At first the word "patience" comes, and she starts making associations: trust, be still, wait, and relax. Then she sees a wagon wheel and notices that all the facets are turning together. As she looks more closely at the image, she sees that the wheel is attached to a whole covered wagon with a team of horses galloping together. Teamwork! Then it pops into her mind that this is a chuck wagon: Wendy is a caterer! Perhaps she should give periodic rewards of pizza to the children for each completed segment of the project. She holds on to the wagon image, and it turns into a stagecoach with a driver. Sometimes he is cracking a whip, and at other times he is pulling in the reins. The people in the stagecoach are telling the driver what to do and where to go. They are not in alignment and harmony. They each want the driver to get to the designated destination by their route. The driver and horses come to a standstill. Then Wendy sees herself standing in front of the stagecoach, stopping it from going anywhere!

5. **Deciphering the Image:** This is like dreaming, where everybody in the dream is really a facet of yourself. Wendy is the stagecoach driver telling the children what to do, and at the same time she is pulling in the reins. Perhaps, Wendy thinks, she has been giving her students mixed messages that are impeding their progress.

6. **Incubate:** Not needed.

7. **Go Deeper:** Wendy carries on a dialogue with the image and asks what it wants from her. It says, "Get out of the way. You're blocking the way." As Wendy views herself from the perspective of the image, she sees herself waving her hands and arms frantically, preventing the "team" of horses from working together, from going forward. The road was even paved behind her, yet she was stopping the coach from going forward. Wendy

continues the dialogue and asks, "What would happen if I got out of the way?" She sees the coach burst forth with great speed. The driver is whooping and laughing and the horses are all pulling together. The passengers are sitting still in the coach and going along for the ride. Wendy realizes that the children can work as a team without her constantly directing them. She is giving conflicting messages and needs to nurture them more supportively—"cater" to their needs.

8. **Implementation:** In meditation, Wendy visualizes the students pulling together as the perfect team to win the science fair. From the stagecoach image, she is giving them the suggestion to pretend they are pioneers going forth to discover gold. The gold, of course, is the reward of a job well done. Wendy decides that every afternoon of the school week, she will give the science fair team an hour to work on their project without her intervention. Then, she will allot up to twenty minutes to give feedback.

63

Variation on the PowerShift Technique: A dialogue with the image provided the needed insight.

POWERHUNCH TOOL

A Moving and Talking Image

A well-known lucid dreaming technique asks the lucid dreamer to communicate with dream images, like Wendy did, in order to better understand the meaning of the dream. In a lucid dream, the dreamer becomes consciously aware of dreaming. You can engage your intuition in this same lucid way.

Return to any of the issues you started to work with in earlier PowerTool exercises, or focus on a new concern. Once you have an image, communicate with it. Write the results of this communication in your PowerHunch Journal.

Example 6: Making the "Punny" Connection

Hal is moving to Denver, and needs to find a mover. He's asked his friends and looked in the phone book, and he has a pretty long list. The problem is, they all look pretty good—there's no obvious choice.

1. **Issue:** Hal asks, "Which moving carrier should I choose?"
2. **Centering:** He affirms, "My intuitive mind will clearly know the right moving company."
3. **Receptivity:** Hal focuses on breathing in through the nose and out the mouth from the bottom of the lungs. He visualizes earth energies rising through his body on the breath in, and the negative energies moving out of his body on the breath out. Then he imagines the cosmic energy flowing downward through his body.
4. **Imagery:** He immediately gets the image of an ocean sunset as viewed from a seaside cliff. It is so beautiful and peaceful, with the wind gently breezing around him, and the calm waters reflecting the last rays of the sun, as he reflects on the serenity of the scene. In addition to this picturesque description, two other words came to him: conclusion and decision.
5. **Deciphering the Image:** Clearly, it's time to make a decision in favor of the candidate that resonates with the theme of water or oceans. The universe, being very "punny," is pointing him to Daryl *Flood* Movers.
6. **Incubate:** Not needed.
7. **Go Deeper:** Hal thinks this is pretty funny, but he's still not sure. He asks for another image to help him decide. He sits quietly for a few minutes, and the image of a feather floats into his mind. He uses word association to unravel the meaning of this puzzling imagery: feather → dove → Noah's Ark → flood. Once again, Daryl *Flood* Movers—a double whammy, to make sure he gets it!

8. **Implementation:** He calls Daryl Flood Movers, and they give him just what he wants: peace of mind and a speedy move.

Variation on the PowerShift Technique: Playing with the "pun on words" was pivotal.

Coming to Consensus

Sometimes, two or more heads are better than one. In the PowerShift consensus, you invite others to join you in your problem-solving endeavors. Each participant comes up with an image that represents a piece of the puzzle leading to a successful resolution. This technique works best with four to six people. For example, Ron wanted to resolve the continual bickering between his wife and his mother, who lived with them. Each harbored ill feelings toward the other, which created a tense atmosphere in their home, confused the children, and polarized other family members. Ron asked an aunt, uncle, and cousin to meet with him to resolve this dilemma. He used the PowerShift process to guide them into a space where they were open to the imagery presented by their intuitive minds, and posed the question, "How can my mother and wife reconcile their differences?" Each person came up with a different image: entangled roots, a passenger train, refrigerator, and waves crashing on the surf. What was the common theme?

65

The four images actually picture the dilemma. One way to make the connection is to put the images into one descriptive sentence: A big chill (refrigerator) is about to come crashing down (waves) on an entangled situation (roots) as two people decide to travel separately or together (train). Next, the group can delve further into each image to retrieve the intuitive clues showing what steps they can take toward a resolution. When Ron's group tried this, they came up with the following:

The "entangled roots" yielded associations like growth, bottom-up, nourish, moving, and the final Aha! of "long time to occur."

Associations to the "passenger train" are long tickets, fast, connecting doors, crowded, food car, and finally, "same destination."

The image "wave crashing on surf" suggested associations of cold, gentle sand, power, dangerous, and change can't be done easily.

When they used word association to the "refrigerator" image, they got refrigerator → cold → big chill → needed to keep from spoiling.

Now they had a more focused view of the problem and solution: It was a frosty situation that took a long time to occur and couldn't be undone easily—unless Ron's wife and his mother realize they are headed toward the same destination.

Ron's cousin really resonated to the "same destination" theme, and pulled up an image of "a graduation" and then "a wedding ceremony." This was the intuitive key that unlocked the door to a resolution. The group determined to find a way to communicate to Ron's mother and his wife that they were on the same journey—the journey of family—and that they might find mutual ground by attending memorable family events like graduations and weddings. They decided to begin by having a small family party centered around the project of sorting through all the old family pictures they had, and working together to put them in albums that told the story of their family.

Ron's mother and his wife were distant for forty minutes. Then, they found a photograph of themselves sitting on a bench during a family picnic. This triggered some hilarious memories that had occurred that afternoon. The tension completely dissolved as other experiences surfaced, clearly showing them how each made a unique and important contribution to their family.

POWERHUNCH TOOL

PowerShift Consensus

You can use the group consensus technique to solve problems in your family, among friends, and in work groups. The people in the group don't have to be experts—they just have to be open to using this method. Invite a group of friends or people from work to join you in this group intuitive problem-solving activity, and follow this general structure: Pose your question; get centered and relaxed; elicit images; intuitively interpret all the symbols using the amplification and word association techniques; and analyze the results. Then go into the next phase as you reframe the question to find out how you can take action to implement the solution.

POWERHUNCH WORKSHOP

Use the PowerShift for Problem Solving

In this workshop, you will practice using the PowerShift to get an intuitive perspective into three pressing issues in your life. Formulate three simple questions. Let one concern pertain to career, another to relationships, and a third to an everyday concern. Write them down in your PowerHunch Journal.

Now go through the process discussed in this chapter. For each question, write down exactly what you did for each step and note the outcome:

1. **Issue:** Identify your issue and write down your question.
2. **Center:** What did you do to become centered? Would you do anything differently next time?
3. **Receptivity:** Practice using both a breathing and a relaxation technique.

4. **Imagery:** What form was the imagery in? Visual, sound, words, understanding, or something else?
5. **Deciphering the Image:** How did you decipher the imagery? Make a diagram if necessary.
6. **Incubate:** Did you need to leave time for incubation? How long?
7. **Go Deeper:** Did any further interpretation surface? Were you surprised? Pleased?
8. **Implementation:** How did you implement the intuitive input? Write about how the intuitive resolution opened you to new options or a different perspective.

Be patient. If this is the first time you have ever done anything like this, it may take time to relax and become receptive. Your logical mind may want to hang on for dear life, giving you all sorts of reasons why you should not listen to your intuition. Hang in there and remember: Shift happens!

4

The Fourth Secret
Fire Up Your Creative Juices

People who say they are not intuitive call themselves creative. But if they are truly creative they come to the intuitive doorway. People who say they are creative but not spiritual also access spirit. And people who say they are not intuitive but just want to follow the spiritual path are also people who have strengthened their intuitive factor.

— Angeles Arrien, Ph.D.

With chisel in hand, Michelangelo sat in front of a huge block of marble. He gazed at the cold white stone, waiting for it to reveal the image of David that he knew lived inside, waiting to be set free. He believed in the truth of this intuitive vision, and used it to create one of the greatest sculptures of the Italian Renaissance. In this often-told story is the essence of the connection between intuition and creativity.

You may say, "But I'm not Michelangelo," meaning, "But I'm not as *creative* as Michelangelo—I'm no artist." If so, you are overlooking an important point, and the point of this chapter: Intuition and creativity are inextricably connected, and creativity is more than being able to paint or draw. It is creativity that allows us to think up new ideas, to find imaginative solutions to knotty problems, to put old ingredients together in a new way, to imagine a future and work toward it.

Intuition and creativity work hand in hand. Intuition is the impulse for the creative act. Intuition is the energy, or input, while creativity is the output. When we develop our intuition, the creative juices flow. And the more we allow our creativity to flow and flourish, the more access we have to our intuitive mind.

You can conceive of any invention as a creative act sparked by intuition. Clearly, logic cannot account for the invention of the hula-hoop, the pet rock, or the slimy, green, gooey stuff that kids love to play with. The safety pin, which many would argue is one of the greatest inventions of all time, was created by a man who was fiddling with a piece of wire while he was trying to figure out how to get out of debt. He suddenly looked down, and there was a safety pin!

What Is Creativity?

Better to ask, what does creativity mean to you? Take a moment right now to let your mind pour forth some words, phrases, or sentences about creativity, and jot them down in the fourth section of your PowerHunch Journal. Here are my words: new, different, better, improved, rearrange, reassemble.

To me, creativity means to make new. You can attach this word to anything: new products, new directions, new attitudes, new ideas, new approaches. It also means to make something not just new, but better.

If you already think of yourself as a creative person, then intuition is probably the first arrow in your quiver. But here's a secret: Anyone can shoot that creative arrow! As you explore your intuition, you are also setting free the creativity that already exists inside you. What, you? Yes! Many people think they are not creative because they can't sing, dance, paint, or act, but there's no reason to limit creativity to artistic pursuits.

You can incorporate creative problem solving into every aspect of your life, even the most mundane. Mark delights in putting ingredients together in new ways to create a meal. Jan's friends admire her unerring ability to create beautiful outfits from secondhand clothes. Alan has always been able to craft just the right gift for every occasion out of inexpensive materials. You may find your creative niche at work: Joan's creativity is expressed in the way she puts just the right combination of people together in task groups. Greg is a whiz at designing new software on the fly to implement new processes at his manufacturing firm. You may be creative at play: Tim's friends are always eager to discover what his next theme party will be. Rae's ability to rap on any subject has made her a winner at many poetry slams. You may even be creative in romance: All of his girlfriends say that Ken knows "just how to treat me to make me feel special." After thirty years of marriage, Shirley and Norm still find new ways to delight each other.

What prevents you from accessing your creativity at any time of the day or night? Often, the problem is simply that your fear creates a barrier, and your logical mind just won't get out of the way! In this chapter you'll find out how to:

- break through the fear barrier.
- make a judgment adjustment.
- endure creative confusion.
- shift your perspective.
- have fun!
- think outside the box.

71

Break Through the Fear Barrier

Chanting the fear mantra, "I'm blocked! I'm blocked!" creates a thick barrier that effectively silences the intuitive voice and blocks creativity. The challenge is to acknowledge that you are blocked and move past the fear. To do this, it helps to be able to understand what your own fear barrier looks like and how it works.

Bonnie was chosen to give a welcome speech to the new members of her social club. She is usually very funny and perceptive, and always knows the right thing to say in conversation. But when she tries to speak in front of large groups, she just dries up. This was an engagement she couldn't get out of, so Bonnie confronted this demon. She had no trouble picturing this fear: She saw herself actually nailed to the spot and immobile. A big bandage across her mouth prevented her from speaking. Now she watched this image change as a helper emerged to pull each nail out and take the bandage off. Bonnie wriggled around and felt free, flexible, and ready to give her speech.

Alice was writing a magazine article on dog training—at least, that's what she was supposed to be doing. Here's what was really happening: Each day, she sat down at her computer and froze. She couldn't think of a thing to say. Still, when her friends asked how the writing project was going, she always answered, "Great." She kept telling herself, tomorrow will be different; but as the days went on and nothing was written, she grew more and more fearful. She couldn't admit to herself or anyone else that she was afraid she wouldn't be able to complete the article by her deadline.

I advised her to begin dismantling her fear barrier by making a positive statement or affirmation to turn the negativity around. She decided to change "I can't write a word" into "I can write this article with ease." Next, she elicited an image of her fear: It was a shrunken hand that couldn't even grip a pencil. She replaced this image with a strong, healthy, full-size hand. Finally, she created a step-by-step success process to replace her failure scenario—beginning from where she was at the moment. Alice began with step 1, defeat: I crumple up papers in disgust and throw them in the trash. From there, however, she saw herself progressing to the point where the words actually flowed from her intuitive mind. Then she decided to establish two new boxes for her desk: an In box and an Out box. Now instead of throwing the pages away, which just made her feel worse, she allowed room for some work she liked and some she didn't like. Eventually, she saw that the pile of pages in her In box was much larger than the pile sitting in the Out box. For the final step, of course, she saw the completed article.

POWERHUNCH TOOL

Break Through the Fear Barrier

Are you ready to break through your fear barrier? OK, let's go!

Your fear may take any form: It may be a block of ice, a pack of barking dogs, a black cloud that covers your face. Why keep this useless imagery? With the help of your intuition, you can create new imagery to break up this barrier: Melt the ice, feed the dogs and silence them, let the sunshine in to make the clouds go away.

When you are relaxed and centered, say this affirmation: "I am unblocked and my creativity surfaces." Then ask for an image of your fear. You may be surprised by what it turns out to be! Once you've got the image firmly in mind, ask your intuitive mind to give you the key around which you will create a scenario to dissolve your fear. Finally, act this scenario out in your mind. Repeat this activity as many times as you need to, and anticipate your creative geyser gushing forth.

Make a Judgment Adjustment

Have you ever pushed a creative thought away by saying, "This is too weird," "No one would like that," or "I'm just not very creative"? When searching for original input, do you ever say, "This isn't good enough" or "Anyone could have thought of this idea"? Self-judgments like these are guaranteed to cancel creativity. Honor the precious insights that come from your intuitive mind; don't denigrate them.

If you've ever been in a brainstorming session, you know that participants are directed to say whatever comes into their mind without judging it. Most of us have been conditioned to think that what we have to say may appear silly or stupid to others, so we often silence our contribution. But that judgmental response limits our sharing and stifles creativity.

POWER**HUNCH** TOOL

Make a Judgment Adjustment

Pay attention to your judgmental thoughts. For one day, write down in your PowerHunch Journal every time you have one of these thoughts, what it related to, and if it stopped you from doing something or thinking or behaving in a creative way. This will increase your awareness of how many times a day you do this. You may be surprised!

The following day, continue to pay attention to these thoughts. But this time, immediately replace the thought with its opposite. For example, if you are thinking, "What a stupid idea!" replace that thought with a more positive one: "What an interesting idea!" and see where it leads. Write down in your PowerHunch Journal any creative links you made with a simple judgment adjustment.

Train yourself to listen to these judgmental thoughts and eradicate them as soon as they seep into awareness. Substitute a positive word or phrase to cancel the judgmental ones. For example, in place of the word "weird" you might say, "My unusual ideas will make a vital contribution to a brainstorming session."

74

Correct Your Conditioning

The judgment problem usually begins in childhood. Whenever Erica ventured her own opinion around the dinner table, her mother told her to be quiet—she had no idea what she was talking about. What did that do to her creative thinking ability? When she grew up and went to work, she was careful not to overstep her job boundaries—she did what she was told, and no more.

Tomas was always making creations out of cardboard tubes, scraps of fabric, and office supplies. His mother called them "trash" and threw them away. What did that do to his artistic vision? "I'm not an artist," he says now. "I can't create anything worthwhile."

Sadly, these kinds of stories are all too common. People who are not in touch with their own creativity do not recognize or encourage it in others. If these stories sound familiar to you, you are probably holding on to some old myths that are squelching your creativity.

A long time ago, I was told that I could never teach anyone how to develop their intuitive abilities. Instead of retreating or feeling defensive, I took up the challenge and formulated a course on both the undergraduate and graduate university level to teach people how to cultivate their intuition. If I had listened to the many naysayers, I never would have created my intuition course or written my books.

It's so easy to walk away from a creative idea if someone throws cold water on it. But why not try instead to stand your ground and decide for *yourself* whether your idea will work? One of my favorite musicals is *Annie Get Your Gun*. I especially love the singing duel between Annie Oakley and Frank Butler. When he repeatedly tells Annie, "No you can't!" she sings back loud and clear: "Yes I can, *yes I can*, YES I CAN!" So whenever anyone says to you, "No you can't," take a hint from Annie and shout back, "Yes I can!"

75

POWERHUNCH TOOL

Correct Your Conditioning

Reflect on your childhood and examine the myths or ideas that have held your creativity captive. Go into your intuitive mind and probe to see how you behaved according to expectations or in a way to achieve a certain goal. For example, were you told you had to have the facts to back up whatever you said?

What childhood myth would you like to correct? Often these are deeply buried but can surface as you let a story come to mind to trigger the childhood event. When Daniel tried this exercise, he remembered an incident that happened when he was eight years old.

He corrected something his teacher said, and she told him to stand in the corner because *he* was the one who was dumb. He had to stay there all day. Consequently, he believed his ideas were not worth expressing. When he tapped into this as an adult, he realized how cruel the teacher had been and that he no longer needed to believe this myth about himself. He decided to create a ceremony to rid himself of the idea that he was dumb. He made a dunce hat, put it on his head for a moment, and then threw it off and stomped on it. He found himself beginning to laugh aloud as he did this. When he had destroyed the dunce cap, he put on a new hat, one on which he had written, "I'm Tops." With this act, he felt strength physically seeping into him—if he could afford to be this silly and have so much fun doing it, maybe he could find the courage to stand behind other ideas. Correcting his old conditioning helped his creativity pour forth.

How about you? If your actions are based on expectations or goals that have limited you, you can now let go of that old conditioning. Create a ceremony where you wear an appropriate outfit and use any needed props to welcome back your creative mind.

Endure Creative Confusion

Oddly, one way to access your creativity is to persist through your confusion. When we feel blocked creatively—when the outpouring of pictures, symbols, ideas, images, or words is totally stopped—we panic. We think we'll *never* have an original thought again! The easiest thing to do is turn outward, looking for ideas in books or someone's well-intentioned words. More often than not, even if we do come up with a solution, we feel deep down that it wasn't *our* solution and we are creatively diminished.

The intuitive way is to simply *remain* in this confusing space and keep working with the assurance that the block will clear, that your creativity clicked out for a moment but it will click back in, and once again you will produce fluidly and effortlessly.

Replace panic and despair with the confidence that creativity will reemerge, and stay the course.

Have you ever heard the old cliché "It's always darkest before the dawn?" Struggle, confusion, even chaos precedes almost any creative outpouring. The following story is a powerful illustration of what can happen when we let things take their own time and don't force them.

A man was taking a walk through a park when he noticed a cocoon that was partially open. He saw movement within the cocoon, and soon became captivated by watching the new butterfly try to break through. After some time, he began to agonize over the pain of watching the butterfly struggle. Finally, he couldn't stand by and watch anymore, and decided to help the butterfly out. He carefully began unraveling the cocoon, and gently lifted the butterfly out onto the palm of his hand. The man was elated, and held his hand up toward the sky, waiting for the creature to fly away. But the butterfly died in his hand. Sadly, the man realized that he had taken away the process of struggling, which is what gives the strength to the wings and allows the butterfly to fly away.

77

As painful as it may be, many times it's the struggle that gives us the strength to fly creatively. It's OK if the strength you need to soar comes through a struggle. Bless those struggles, and use them to capture the strength for your movement forward.

POWERHUNCH TOOL

Welcoming Confusion

Are you struggling to put your ideas down in a letter, essay, or proposal? Are you searching for words to express what you really mean? Are you having trouble finding a solution to your financial problems? Don't panic! Know that you will find what you need—sooner or later. When you do, it will be accompanied by a euphoric feeling as you make the shift you need to have a creative breakthrough.

Welcome the confusion, knowing you can and will go from chaos to creativity. Are you in the middle of the ocean? Keep swimming until you sight land! Someone may even toss you a life raft! When you're in this state, pay attention to your breath. It's easy to breathe too deeply or not deeply enough, which can lead to even more feelings of panic. Once you get centered and relaxed, welcome your intuition and make a "patchwork quilt" of unrelated ideas.

Let any and all ideas flow into your mind, even if they are not connected to each other or to your creative conflict. Write them down in your PowerHunch Journal. Trust that an order will eventually appear. Perhaps one idea on the page will jump out or grab your attention. Remember cosmic fishing: You only need to net one good idea to get you started.

Shift Your Perspective

Pat Sullivan writes a column on business and spirituality for the *San Francisco Chronicle*. When she feels blocked creatively, she knows it's time to shake things up—literally. She shakes the snow globe sitting on her desk, and watches the sparkles go around and around as a visual reminder that things can change in an instant.

Sometimes the block seems so big that it covers our entire horizon and we forget that we have other options. But look at it this way: If you ran into a stone wall, would you stand there and bang your head against it, or would you simply turn and go in another direction? I hope it's the latter!

As Helen Keller wisely remarked, "When one door of happiness closes, another opens; but often we look so long at the closed door that we do not see the one which has been opened for us." The best way to find that new door is to look from a slightly different point of view—in other words, shift your perspective; do something different! Here are some suggestions that work.

If You're Sitting Down, Move

If you're working at a computer, it's easy to spend the better part of a day sitting and staring at it. Kevin is an advertising copywriter. He was up against a client deadline, and out of ideas. He'd been sitting at his desk staring at a blank monitor for what seemed like days. Finally, in frustration, he got up and went outside to take a walk around the block. Within five minutes, he was startled to find that the perfect idea had just floated into his mind! Where had it been hiding for a week?

Quite often, when we're not moving, our intuition and creativity are not moving either. I can't tell you the number of times I've sparked my own intuition simply by getting up from my desk and taking a walk or going outside and doing some gardening! Put on your chef hat and create a meal around whatever you find in the pantry. Put on your favorite CD and dance around the house until you feel free and unfettered and ready to return to your initial focus. When you build movement into your daily routine—walking your dog, swimming, pruning, working out, bicycling, yoga—you can get a creative flow going and keep it going. If you were looking for a reason to start exercising, this is it!

If You're Moving Too Much, Rest

Having four children under age twelve meant that Barbara spent the better part of each day in motion: getting them fed and dressed and off to school, driving to soccer practice, grocery shopping, and all the other chores that make up a typical day for moms everywhere. She recalls the days before she had a family, and remembered all the projects she used to enjoy: everything from writing songs and playing them on the guitar to creating personalized cards for her friends. Now when she considered creative projects, her mind was a complete blank. Clearly, she was so busy with her kids, running from one thing to the next,

79

that there was no room in her mind for intuition to spark a creative idea. I suggested that a time out might be in order—for her.

It took Barbara a few weeks to convince herself that she even had *time* to take a time out, but she finally decided to give it a try. Her solution was to get away to the one place she knew would be private: a hot bath with scented oil, low lighting, and candles. As she soaked in the tub, her tension began to drain away, her to-do list mind shut down, and her long-lost intuition ventured in to say hello in the form of helping her think of more creative ways she could take time off!

And Now for Somewhere Completely Different!

Just can't stand it anymore? Go somewhere completely different: the zoo, the park, a museum, into town. If you can't go to Hawaii, take a vacation right where you live. Do what tourists in your town do: Go sightseeing, take a boat trip, go shopping. Get out of the house or the office; smell the fresh air; take off your shoes; feel the grass under your feet; play in the snow; walk in the rain.

Have Fun!

My friend Carol Ritberger writes self-help books, and has learned a few interesting ways to help herself pass through creative blocks. When she reaches that closed door in her writing endeavors, she puts on a silly hat with bug antennae that she got in Disneyland. She moves her head back and forth; the antennae bounce around; and she feels the energy starting to move from her logical to her intuitive mind.

Sound silly? It is. And that's the point. Why agonize over a creative block when you could be having fun? Relax, and stop taking life so seriously. Be a kid: Get down on the ground and stare at the ants, throw a ball around, play with your pets, watch cartoons. Have fun, and let the creativity roll.

POWERHUNCH TOOL

Try It, You'll Like It!

Do something you've never done before. The more outrageous and contrary to your usual lifestyle or work habits, the better. If you already have some great ideas for breaking the mold, by all means do them. If not, this exercise will get you started. In your PowerHunch Journal, start writing a list of all the new things you can try. Don't censor these ideas, just write them down. Get as many as you can—the wilder the better. For example, it might occur to you to skip to your car each morning rather than walk, to take a different route to the grocery store, to eat spaghetti for breakfast, to buy some clothing that is totally "unlike" you, to read a biography instead of a mystery novel, to talk to a stranger, to rearrange the furniture, to take three days off.... For example, after Alexander and his family went to the zoo, they came home and shared what they liked about their favorite animal and even acted it out. Alexander tried to imitate a giraffe, and suddenly realized that he needed to stick his neck out and take more risks. What a hoot!

When you're done, read over your list. Pick the idea that sounds the most intriguing. Keep your list, add to it, and use it the next time you're blocked.

Think Outside the Box

"Thinking outside the box" is a popular phrase today. It means finding creative solutions that may be wildly different, but that really work. This kind of creative thinking is the kind that can revolutionize society. Everything from circumnavigating the globe to personal computers is the result of someone having taken the time to step outside the box of what is generally considered possible.

A big part of outside-the-box thinking is using intuition to see what's just around the corner (someone looked and saw the hula hoop rolling down the street), or to find a new path through the forest (Einstein found that path in the theory of relativity, Steve Wozniak and Steven Jobs found the personal computer). Let's look at three techniques for thinking outside the box: turning it around, turning it inside out, and brainstorming in a group.

Turning It Around

At the beginning of one stress management workshop, I wanted to do something different to shift the individuals in the group out of their habitual thinking processes. People were relating very stiffly. We were addressing each other as Mr. Jones, Ms. Sherman, and Dr. Emery. I wanted to free up their energy. I asked them to take off their name tags. Then I gave out new ones, and asked them to write down a frivolous pseudonym that represented who they are. After a few moments, they got the idea. Names appeared like Twinkle Toes, Fire Engine, Light Beam, Sunshine, and Caregiver. The formality abruptly ended, and people related freely to one another. This simple creative beginning energized them throughout the workshop and galvanized their input.

If you start your day quietly in meditation, try turning it around and have a loud gong wake you up. Sound is a great way to activate the creative process. According to Feng Shui expert David Raney, metal is the perfect element to move us out of an earthbound creative block. Just as a hoe breaks up the earth, a ringing bell opens us up and grabs our attention. I like to imagine a trumpet at the dawn of day, playing a wake up call just for my creative mind. My friend Elena keeps a small chime at home and rings it to remind herself to awaken her sleeping creativity.

Turning It Inside Out

Turning a situation inside out gives you a new perspective on something you may be tired of looking at. Time management expert Ann McGee Cooper suggests bypassing the logical mind by reading a book from back to front and seeing what passages jump out from the text. This gives you the sense of a book, and is especially valuable when you've lost interest in it. What this does is remind you of the value in shifting your perceptions.

You can even turn your own responses inside out. When you act unexpectedly, you are certain to get unexpected results! This is especially true in personal relationships. If you're in a committed long-term relationship, you've probably complained long and hard about your partner's snoring, sloppy habits, nitpicking, nagging, or other qualities that conflict with your own perfection! Big surprise: You always argue about the same things, and the argument always turns out the same. Here's a secret: If you change one part of a habit, the whole pattern changes. The next time you're upset because you found your partner's socks under the covers instead of in the hamper, change your usual response. If you say, "Why do you always do this to me?" and your partner always responds, "What about your forgetting to put gas in the car again?" try doing nothing, realizing nobody's perfect.

Brainstorming in a Group

Brainstorming is sometimes called an "ideation session" or a "think tank." Whatever it's called, it's a good way to foster creativity. Brainstorming shifts you away from the familiar and habitual to your intuitive mind, where new and provocative images are housed. It lets your ideas sneak past the censors of the logical mind.

Here's what happens. After one person gives the signal to begin, everyone else lets the associations flow, saying anything that comes to mind. One person writes down every idea—good, bad, and indifferent. In the middle of this flow, anyone can throw out a line that is seemingly unrelated to the project and ask for feedback. This can stimulate an entirely new line of thought. Afterward, you can look at any of these groupings for common themes. Eventually, some ideas can be perceived as belonging

83

together. You may come up with useless or irrelevant remarks and finally hear a useful contribution. When you are finished, ask, "What is new? What is unique?" During your session, have fun and don't hesitate to share the hilarious and offbeat picture coming into your mind.

Marketing consultant Judith Kahn frequently attends ideation sessions. She recalls the time the facilitator wrote the word "judging" on the board and put a line through it. He was pointedly telling them not to judge their own ideas or anyone else's ideas.

Here's an exercise from Craig Neal, co-founder of Heartland, which assists individuals and organizations in navigating change and transformation. Its Thought Leader gatherings begin with "the Opening Word," in which each person in the circle gives their name and affiliation and says in one to three words the first thing that comes to mind or heart when they think of a phrase like "life's passion," "life's meaning," "leadership," "challenge," and so on.

Ask yourself to respond in a word or two to the question, "How do I feel about (my job, my kids, my family)?" Or "How am I feeling right now?" Most people tend to go on and on in response to basic questions like that. This exercise gets you thinking intuitively—in a word or two that says it all.

POWERHUNCH TOOL

Solo Brainstorming

You don't need a group to brainstorm: You can engage in a solo ideation session to ignite your creative flow. Actually, in this exercise you may find that you have two participants—your logical mind and your intuitive mind!

You'll need your PowerHunch Journal and something to write with. Get comfortable and relaxed, and go as deeply into yourself as possible. See your hand around the pen or pencil as the vehicle for your ideas. Start writing by asking, "Here's what I want to do. Now what are the things that help me do this?" It might help to pose your question in the third person, so you can be even more objective.

Once you've posed your question, ask for input from your intuitive mind and wait for your pen or pencil to start moving. You may find your logical mind bringing you obvious information at first. Don't censor it; just write down what it has to say and keep going. Soon more intuitive ideas will flow out of your creative doorway. Even if they're outrageous, don't edit yourself—not yet. When you are finished, read what you have written. Have any unique ideas emerged that surprise your logical mind?

POWERHUNCH WORKSHOP

Make A Creative Breakthrough

The purpose of this workshop is to dissolve your barriers and jump-start your creativity in every part of your life. We'll break it down into work, social life, family, general, and work on each area for one week. Your goal is to bring a fresh vitality into any stale situation. As you work through the month, you'll probably find that some areas need more work than others. That's OK. Keep going; you can always come back for more later. Use any or all of the PowerHunch Tools you learned in this chapter. To remind you, you can break through the fear barrier, make a judgment adjustment, endure creative confusion, shift your perspective, have fun, and think outside the box. Do this exercise over the period of one month and see what happens. Don't forget to record what you have learned in your PowerHunch Journal.

Week I: Ask your intuitive mind how you can use any of your creative PowerHunch Tools to vitalize your work activities. For one week, any time you are stymied by a work situation, bring in one of these PowerHunch Tools to pull you out of the doldrums pit. For example, you can break through the fear barrier and learn the new computer system. To do this, look down and envision every key on your keyboard with a smiling face. Are you facing some routine clerical tasks that you would like to avoid? Have fun while doing these chores by wearing your kid's rabbit ears to work. The laughter from others will be contagious and will filter through to these tedious tasks.

Week 2: Let your intuitive mind help you bring more creativity into your social life. For example, shift your perspective to creatively resolve a relationship problem. Has a friend stepped out of your good graces by revealing a confidence to someone else? Bring up the cherished memories you once shared. Recall the times your friend provided unconditional love to comfort you during a trying time. Shifting this perspective will allow you to once again extend your friendship to this person. And don't forget to completely release the upset by talking it over with your friend.

Week 3: Invite some family members to join you in a brainstorming session to resolve a mutual concern. In addition, engage in a private brainstorming session as you let the intuitive mind flow through your pen to give you additional insight. Record what you have learned in your PowerHunch Journal.

Week 4: During this week, focus on the critical self-judgments that have prevented you from moving forward with any part of your life. Make a judgment adjustment. Have you judged yourself for not being more extroverted? Examine the roots of this. Perhaps you were told that "children should be seen and not heard" or a teacher repeatedly expressed disdain about your original ideas and told you to be quiet. Dig deep and uproot these limiting beliefs. Then replace them with more appropriate convictions. Resolve for example, that you will be both seen and heard.

Record what you have learned in your PowerHunch Journal.

5

The Fifth Secret
Learn from Your Dreams

The dream is an invaluable commentator and illuminator of life.
Listen to the wisdom of the dream.

— Dr. Carl Jung

Jenny vividly recalled her "lost locker" dream. She is back in college, cramming for a final exam. Then she can't find her locker, her textbook, or the classroom where the exam is being held. She wakes up in a sweat. As Jenny began to figure out what the dream meant, she thought it probably had something to do with how lost she feels at her new job. The dream mirrored her fear that she was inadequately prepared for her new position. Since she had always performed admirably in school and at work, she realized she had to cope with lingering doubts that she may not do as well this time around.

Dave's "lost locker" dream gave him a different message. In the dream, Dave went to basketball practice. But he couldn't find his locker, or even remember the combination. In waking life, Dave spent a lot of time working and not much time playing. When he thought about it, he felt his intuitive mind was telling him to reclaim the athletic side of himself that had been lost.

Every dreamer has at least one dream of losing something, and each dream is custom designed by the intuitive mind for that dreamer. You really are your own dream expert. So if your head is tucked away in a dream dictionary that someone else has written, please take it out! If you accept the challenge of working with the practices in this chapter for at least a month, you will notice how much easier it will become to understand what your dreams are telling you.

Dreams are a direct conduit to the intuitive mind. You can use your dreams as problem-solving tools in the waking world— but first you have to remember them and learn to decipher their sometimes confusing messages. Through the practices and examples in this chapter, you will learn how to use your intuition to retrieve, respect, and listen to the insights embedded in your dreams.

The noise of the day silences the intuitive voice, but that voice gets a chance to speak clearly through a dream, providing a warning, direction, or guidance. The dreaming mind is the same intuitive mind where impressions of all the events and interactions with others since the moment of birth, or perhaps even from the beginnings of time, are recorded. The mind has complete access to all this dynamic information and, like a computer, sorts through the possibilities and communicates to the individual via a dream. This point was brought home to me dramatically some years ago. I had a puzzling dream about a high school buddy, Carl Sloan, whom I hadn't seen in twenty-five years. "Why now?" asked my logical mind. Intuitively, I knew that the universal data bank must have been tapped for a good reason, so I waited to find out. Some weeks later, I met a man who looked exactly like Carl and we fell in love. From that moment on, I had complete respect for my intuitive dreaming mind, which had prepared me for this intense romantic involvement.

In this chapter, you'll learn:

- how to access the illuminating wisdom contained in dreams.
- how to use intuition to interpret your dreams.
- how to use the DreamShift process to learn from your dreams.
- how to turn negative dreams into positive dreams.
- how dreams come true.
- how to invite a dream to visit.

The Wisdom of Dreams

Dreams are full of wisdom—wisdom from inside you. For months, Ed harbored a secret desire to shift careers and become a professional speaker. He didn't share this longing with anyone else. Then, Ed had a dream in which he was searching for the best speaker for a meeting. Upon awakening, he realized that *he* was headed toward a career as a speaker. From that moment on, his talents and abilities as a speaker have been widely sought by others.

Other dreams can resolve seemingly insoluble problems. The staff at the Fetzer Institute in Kalamazoo, Michigan, was struggling with how to build community, and realized they needed a break space where everyone could gather. They consulted an architect, who gave them a costly estimate and told them the building project would take a long time to complete. One staff member was unwilling to wait for this much-needed social space. She solicited help from her dreaming mind by programming a dream, which gave her a simple and highly practical solution (you'll read about programming a dream later in this chapter). She dreamed that they had created a break space from an existing conference room, which none of them had previously considered. She told the group, and they acted on it. A great solution at minimal cost.

Dreams can also provide insights into puzzling relationships. Anita's husband hired some attorneys to help his mother through her messy divorce. They seemed competent, but for some reason they made Anita uneasy. That night she had a dream in which the attorneys appeared as gangsters with beady rats' eyes, who came to their house with guns to rob them, causing her mother-in-law great distress. In the dream, her husband was vacuuming and was nearly electrocuted when the gangsters spilled a vase of water on the outlet. Anita rushed to pull the plug, saved her husband's life, and told the gangsters to leave. She woke up thinking hard about these attorneys. In real life, she felt, the attorneys mirrored the dream gangsters because they held her husband and mother-in-law up for "ransom" by demanding her car, her certificates of deposit, and all her jewelry before they would go to her divorce hearing. This dream clarified for Anita why she was repulsed by the lawyers. As in her dream, she advised her husband to "pull the plug" on them and find some new attorneys.

Sometimes, dreams really can foretell the future. Vern had a dream that he and his partner Jamie had one chestnut horse. The next day, they responded to an ad for a horse and found that it looked exactly like the one he had seen in his dreams. He bought the horse, feeling that it was already a done deal.

You can thank the dreams that give you a red-flag alert to trouble up ahead. Years ago, I had a dramatic and crystal clear dream that probably saved my life. In the dream, I was driving a car, put my foot on the brake, and it went right to the floor. The car turned over, but I got out unharmed. A week later, I was driving down a heavily trafficked street in Washington, D.C., when I put my foot on the brake. The brake failed and my foot went right to the floor, just like it had in the dream image. The emergency brake didn't work either. My dream had alerted me to this possibility, and my intuitive voice told me to make a quick right. I did, and the car came to a stop between two clothing stores—the only area of safety.

Intuitive Dream Interpretation

Whenever I interpret a dream, I feel like a detective digging deeply to unravel the mystery embedded in it. Here are two ways to look at dream symbols:

- The dream *literally* provides an answer
- The dream speaks *symbolically*

The Literal Dream

If your dream is literal, what you see is what you get. When Bill Chada served in the Air Force years ago as a counterespionage and criminal investigator, he learned a self-hypnosis technique used to help the investigators concentrate on something they had witnessed: a conversation, crime scene, or any activity in which they had to be explicit about minute details. Most important, the investigators were able to put themselves to sleep quickly, which was especially helpful when they had only a short time between assignments to rest.

Bill continues to use this "quick sleep" technique to connect with his intuition. At one point, Bill was an independent sales representative. He had developed a reputation among his customers as a guy who could either provide an item or know where to get it. Everyone would say, "Ask Chada." Bill never thought that he was doing something worthwhile by securing these items as favors for his friends. Years later, Bill and his wife decided to develop their own business. They looked at a number of different situations including wholesale, distribution, retail stores, and franchises. They probably considered a hundred different businesses, but nothing really clicked.

After a troubled evening of equivocating about the business, Bill used his self-hypnotic technique to put himself to sleep. He was suddenly awakened from a sound sleep at around two in the morning. He still recalls the clarity of the dream image that led to the name, ASAP, that he gave his business, which focuses on advertising, specialties, and promotions. In the dream, the entire concept, including the name and logo, was displayed in front of him, as if he were looking at a slide projection. He started making notes on a pad he kept by the bed. He was so excited that he couldn't go back to sleep, so he went down to the office. He drew out his logo, which has remained unchanged to this day, and wrote out the entire business plan detailing the concept and the direction he wanted to go. Although the business plan has been modified and expanded over the years, it still contains the basic formulations presented to him in this dream.

POWERHUNCH TOOL

Ask for a Literal Dream

You may be surprised to learn that you can actually ask for—and get—specific types of dreams. A literal dream is a great shortcut when you are looking for a specific answer to a concrete problem: a new career, a theme for a speech, a name for your baby, a healing balm, words to amend a misunderstanding, or even a gift for a loved one.

Lois wanted to find relief for her aching back. She asked her dreaming mind to help her find a healing balm. Before going to sleep she said to herself, "I would like my intuitive mind to show me how to heal my aching back. I will fall asleep readily, sleep through the night, and awaken with the insight fresh in my mind." In her dream, she saw herself walking in the country, breathing the fresh air and feeling the blood circulate through her entire body, including her back. She began taking refreshing walks that day, and her back did indeed begin to relax.

You too can program a literal dream. Ask for insight into the issue and give yourself the strong suggestion that you will sleep through the night and awaken with the insight fresh in your mind. Be sure to record what happened in your PowerHunch Journal in a new section, Dreams.

The Symbolic Dream

It is more likely that the content of your dreams will be symbolic or metaphoric. For example, if you dream that a lion is roaming around your apartment, chances are this is a symbolic dream, not a literal one! As you dig underneath the dream symbol, you will find the true meaning. Dream symbols are fun to decode, but sometimes the symbolic content can be alarming. One of my students frantically told me that she had had a dream about her son being killed. Two weeks later, she understood the dream's meaning with some relief as she watched three boys tackle her son all at once at a football game. He wasn't actually being killed, but he was definitely put out of action. Later in the chapter, we'll explore the interpretation of seemingly negative dreams.

Any dream teacher or researcher will vow that every dream reverie is meaningful. In the thirty years I have been involved in dream work, I am constantly amazed how the intuitive mind provides penetrating insights through dreams.

I love to help people unravel their dreams but remind myself of the cardinal rule of dreaming, so I preface an interpretation with, "If this were *my* dream, this is what this would mean to *me*." In the final analysis, the meaning has to resonate with the dreamer, not with an outside interpreter.

With a one-shot interpretation, your intuitive mind dives down to the root meaning of a dream and effortlessly provides you with information. As soon as you record the dream or relate it to someone else, the underlying insight emerges immediately and just grabs you. For example, Howard dreamed that his friend Annie was in a house, along with some unwanted guests and animals. As soon as he asked his intuitive mind, "Why Annie?" he had a flash that the word for "I" in Hebrew is Ani. Howard realized that he had invited some unwanted "guests" into his inner household.

Jason worked at a dot-com. It's a fun and exciting environment, but the threat of layoffs was always in the air. Jason rarely remembers his dreams, but he remembered this one: He dreamed he was on a skateboard, sailed over the edge of the cliff, and landed on his feet. When he got to work, the meaning of the dream hit home: He understood that no matter how close he gets to the edge at work, even if he falls he will be landing on his feet. He felt reassured by the dream that he will survive the dot-com turbulence, and even if he gets laid off he will find another job.

The DreamShift Process

When instant clarity is elusive, and you want to delve deeper into a dream's meaning, use the DreamShift process—a slight variation on the PowerShift you learned in chapter 3. The following six steps will help you decode the underlying message in most dreams.[2]

1. Give the dream a title.
2. Become centered and receptive.
3. Identify the major symbols.
4. Interpret these symbols.
5. Engage the symbol artistically.
6. Implement your dream discovery.

Step 1: Give the Dream a Title

Just giving your dream a title can help you begin to understand its underlying meaning. Title the dream in eight words or less.

Example: Helen's teenage granddaughters, ages fifteen and seventeen, have just come to live with her. Helen finds herself anxious and a bit resentful about the loss of privacy and invasion into her daily routine, yet she loves having them with her. She asks her dreaming mind for an answer to this dilemma. Before going to bed, she writes in her PowerHunch Journal, "How can I adapt to Crystal and Erin living with me?" Before drifting off to sleep, she silently directs this query to her intuitive mind. The next morning, she has this dream:

> I was at a family reunion. Everyone was there, aunts, uncles, cousins, children, grandchildren—the whole lot. We were in a lovely park, and in the park was some kind of yellow building with a narrow catwalk along the side about midway up the building, leading to a very private balcony overlooking a beautiful valley of farmland. This is where I wanted to be, and began walking along the catwalk. Up ahead there were a couple of large gift-wrapped boxes blocking my way. I could see no way around them, over them, or through them. I turned and was complaining—whining—to my real-life partner, George. He said, "If you stay centered and focused, the way will open."

Helen titles her dream "The Gift at the Family Reunion."

Step 2: Become Centered and Receptive.

Engage any centering, breathing, or relaxation techniques to move your energy away from all that is going on in your environment to the peaceful confines of your inner mind. Review the Centering and Receptivity steps that were suggested in chapter 3, if necessary.

Example: Helen sat on the balcony and focused on the Canadian flag atop a downtown hotel about six blocks away, while listening to a CD of a bamboo flute. This was very peaceful and reverie-inducing. She pictured a fence lying flat on the ground, so nothing could act as a barrier to the flow of wisdom.

Step 3: Identify the Major Symbols

As you are in the quiet space, let the major symbol(s) come forward. This may happen in any number of ways: You may see them visually, hear the words, get a feel for the symbols, or of what symbol(s) is coming forth, or just "know."

Example: The three symbols that emerge are: gift-wrapped boxes, narrow catwalk, and private balcony.

Step 4: Interpret These Symbols

Use amplification or word association to analyze the most important symbols. These techniques have been defined and used in chapter 3. To remind you, with amplification, you start with a central image and continue to associate until you get to the "Aha" meaning. With word association, one word triggers another until you reach the intuitive insight. Be alert to any symbolic associations presented by your intuitive mind. For example, a "robbery" may represent a "hold up," signifying a delay in your life.

Example: Helen interprets the gift-wrapped boxes as the two granddaughters, the private balcony as her private space, and the catwalk as her narrow view of the situation, or even the narrow walk to privacy.

Step 5: Engage the Symbol Artistically

Capture any part of the dream artistically. You can make a drawing, let the symbol move you in a dance, speak to you in verse, or strike a musical chord. You are inviting the dream to speak to you in its own language. Connie had a graphic dream showing her living in a cul-de-sac. All of the houses were exploding with fire. She began drawing and noticed she had drawn a helicopter making an airlift rescue. She was encouraged to know that relief was in sight for any explosive situation in her life.

Example: Helen hums the melody the flute was playing, which infuses her with a feeling of peace about the girls' arrival.

Step 6. Implement Your Dream Discovery

96

After the dream analysis, let your logical mind figure out how to implement the intuitive information. If, for example, you missed your plane in the dream, the intuitive mind might provide the insight that you are behind schedule. You might take a look at your activities to see how you can realign your priorities.

Example: When Helen shared the dream with George, he interrupted her and said, "If you stay centered and focused, the way will open"—the exact words he said in the dream! Helen felt that the advice to stay centered and focused must be right. So when she finds herself getting pulled this way and that by her granddaughters, she remembers the dream, digs out her flute CD, and gets centered and focused again. This broader view of the situation helps Helen cherish the special gifts in her life—her granddaughters.

Interpretation Variations

Everyone's interpretation is different. What matters most in this example is how the dream symbols resonated to Helen. Here's another round of interpretation to help you familiarize yourself with the DreamShift process.

Helen asked her dreaming mind for an answer to her problem, but most people go to sleep without asking a question, and when a dream comes along it leaves them befuddled. Here's a way to head this off before it begins. If you don't have a question to pose, as Helen did, briefly describe your day in a section of your PowerHunch Journal called "Day Notes." Let's look at Dora's dream, below, to see how the DreamShift can be used in conjunction with the Day Note entry to get further insight into the dream.

> *I am driving with a woman. The car peters out. It slides into a parking place across the street from an Italian restaurant owned by Mafia guys. A little girl is missing. I go to a movie with a woman and a man. We go back to the Italian place. I know a bad guy chopped up the little girl and put her in the spaghetti sauce. A few Mafia types taste the sauce. I knew they'd be found out. I was the partner of the detective looking for the girl. I knew something they didn't about the death of the girl and what became of her.*

97

When Dora looked at her Day Notes, she read this:

> *Reading a book by Richard Price about a missing four-year-old boy. This evening I did a wine tasting dinner with Angela, Sue, Rod, and Jim. There was a sauce, and rich salad, and soup. I told them about a noodle/pasta restaurant up on the avenue. Had thought about getting a job at new café. Yet didn't want clients, colleagues to find out I'm working in nontherapy job. It would kill me! Yesterday, I was with Melinda who may go into bankruptcy.*

1. **Dream Title:** Dora titled her dream "The Little Girl Caper."
2. **Become Centered and Receptive:** Dora listened to her wind chimes and focused on the water in her table-top fountain.
3. **Major Symbols:** The three symbols commanding her attention were: The car peters out, little girl in the spaghetti sauce, and the death of the girl and what became of her.

4. **Interpret These Symbols:** These salient symbols all involved dying. She wondered if something was coming to an end. Dora wanted to probe further since the deeper meaning still eluded her.
5. **Engage the Symbol Artistically:** Dora put her favorite CD on and danced, hoping the movement would free up some associations.
6. **Implement Your Dream Discovery:** This had to be delayed until she had a deeper understanding of the dream.

Dora reread her Day Notes. Then she sat quietly and affirmed that her intuitive mind would help her see the connection between her daily activity and the dream. She realized that the first symbol of the woman's car petering out corresponded to her friend Melinda's potential bankruptcy. A car as a moving container can be compared to a person's container or holdings, which are filled or empty. The friend's bankruptcy and the failing car both lacked energy or momentum.

Her biggest insight was embedded in the written expression in her Day Notes, "I didn't want clients, colleagues to find out I'm working in a nontherapy job. It would kill me!" She actually wanted to get in the sauce by working in a pasta shop, which would lead to her demise if others found out. Now that this inner secret was revealed in the dream, she reexamined her attitude and realized that taking time out to shift professions could be refreshing. Reading her Day Note information allowed her intuitive mind to reach in and rapidly make this decision.

POWERHUNCH TOOL

Practice Interpreting Your Symbols

George's dream is rich and filled with symbols. Immerse yourself in this dream by reading it several times. What symbol(s) jumps out at you?

"I had just arrived home and walked into the kitchen and my friend Alan was in the living room. In the kitchen I noticed my shoes (one shoe at least) were full of mud and I realized I'd have to clean all my little rugs, which I'd done before. I was surprised to see how thick the mud was that had collected on my shoes and was sticking out on the sides all around for half an inch. I called out to Alan to check his shoes and that he'd have to take them off. I noticed as he walked to the front door that he was leaving tracks, not quite as bad as mine. He had a ginger soda half full that he gave me to finish as he headed off down the street telling me that I could finish it. I didn't really want it as I think those sodas aren't that healthy and took a sip for politeness and then I realized I could dump the rest as Alan was out of sight and wouldn't know."

The symbol that jumps out at George is "ginger soda." He does a word association and stops at the words "being careful." Ginger → tender → being careful.

George realized that he was always being too careful in what he said to Alan because he was afraid to offend him. George was now aware that this feeling put a constraint on his relating to Alan. He vowed to come from a more authentic space and speak his mind.

I'd like you to amplify to the words "ginger soda" to see what other interpretation you might retrieve. Return to one of your dreams and let one, and only one symbol jump out at you. After you do an amplification or word association, does it give you a different meaning of the dream?

99

Turning Negative Dreams into Positive Dreams

It is so easy to fall into the trap of taking a dream symbol at face value without penetrating deeper. This is especially so with negative dreams, those that seem to portend destruction by earthquakes or tornadoes, or the death of a loved one. I want to share a few of these seemingly negative dreams so you can see how the intuitive mind reaches into the dark cloud to find a silver lining.

The Silver Lining: Peace

I'll never forget the morning I awoke horrified from a dream in which I had just shot a man who (in real life) had been publicly denouncing my intuition work for five years. No matter how much someone angered me or irritated me in real life, of course, I would never do such a thing. Symbolically, however, I realized that my intuitive mind was showing me that I was putting an end to this untenable situation. My gift for transcending the initial negative impression of this dream was the tremendous relief I felt. The man continued announcing his opinion, but my soul had finally put this matter to rest in peace.

The Silver Lining: Hope

Vernis told me the following dream:

> *I dreamed that I went to drop some papers off in an office building. I got out of the car and left my pocketbook inside. When I came out, the car and pocketbook were gone. I was overwhelmed.*

A dream like this is alarming under any circumstances. First, a bit of background to help you understand Vernis's interpretation of this dream. Vernis was going through a transitional time. There were two prominent endings in her life. Her company was in the midst of downsizing, and she has just been given a pink slip. In the middle of this turmoil, a two-year relationship with her boyfriend ended. Now, reread this dream and see if you can turn it around to find the positive message.

From participating in a dream group, she learned that a pocketbook symbolically represents the dreamer's identity, since a wallet with a driver's license are the usual contents of a handbag. She felt that, as in the dream, losing her pocketbook symbolized giving up the old and being galvanized into a new identity. The car represented mobility, and this, too, was taken away with the loss of a job and relationship. Feeling more optimistic now that she understood the intuitive elements of her dream, she realized that the old was gone to make way for a new phase of life.

The Silver Lining: Compassion

Jerald, the CEO of a large company, asked me to help him decode a frightening dream. He said, "I dreamed that it was Halloween, and someone was trying to kill me. I didn't like the feeling at all." I asked him if he thought that a killing could represent putting an end to an issue or position. That provided the needed "Aha!" Jerald told me that he was facing the tough decision of terminating an employee. His dream was showing him that he was worried that the angry employee wanted to "assassinate him" for taking this action. He had been putting off the termination, and was pleased that the dream insight showed how much intense anger this disgruntled employee was harboring. With this clue, he became more understanding toward the employee and was able to defuse the bomb that had been waiting to explode.

The Silver Lining: Forbearance

Jennifer was having a difficult time in her relationship with her dad, and needed to share some issues she had been holding on to for a long time. In her dream, Jennifer was talking to her dad when suddenly he grabbed her hands tightly and put his own hands over her mouth. She awoke scared and shocked. In real life, her father would never do anything like this. After some thought, she came to understand that the dream was telling her that her father didn't want to hear what she had to say, and was binding her hands so she couldn't write anything to him either.

Jennifer decided that what she had to tell her dad might be too much for him to handle right now, and she began to rethink the approach she would take the next time they spoke.

A Warning of Death

Brittney, a friend I have known for years, shared with me a dream she had. "I'm a little girl again at home in my kitchen. I'm sitting at the kitchen table having tea and homemade Italian pastry with my parents. My mother tells me that if I leave the house I will surely die."

Brittney was very disturbed by this dream. Her initial reaction was thinking that her late mother was giving her the message that she would die soon, but on another level she really didn't think that was so. Wanting to delve further into this puzzling dream, she decided to center herself and ask her intuition, "What is the real message in the dream?" In her mind, she drifted back into the dream. Once again, she saw herself sitting at the kitchen table of her youth, laughing and sharing with her family. The house was filled with the fragrance of fresh baked goods, and the room was warm and inviting.

Instantly, she realized this dream was a *gift* from her mother, not a warning—a reminder to bring the good times back into her life. Her mother saw her dying with the weight of her adult responsibilities, and didn't want her to "leave" the playful and fun times. Her mother was telling her not to let the child in her die.

To implement the message embedded in the dream, Brittney began to allow herself to sit around the table with friends and family, enjoying good food. That way, she could experience the good memories and feel those warm feelings while awake. She also began to schedule some playtime for herself. The next weekend Brittney went to the park with her grandchildren and had a great time. Now, she loves having coffee and pastries with her family on Saturday morning.

POWERHUNCH TOOL

Just Ask

When you awaken from a bad dream, calm down, get centered, feel yourself connecting with the menacing dream symbol, and ask, "What are you really trying to tell me?" You will be amazed at how well this technique works. In fact, this is a most effective tool for helping children deal with nightmares.

How Dreams Come True

A precognitive dream is one that eventually comes true. Its function is to warn or prepare the dreamer for a significant event. You can't always prevent the event that the intuitive mind senses is coming, but you can honor the dream by being grateful that you were prepared.

103

How can you tell a precognitive dream from other kinds of dreams? Precognitive dreams are unusually vivid and unforgettable. These dreams grab you by the shoulders, give you a good shake, and demand to be remembered. I have learned that my precognitive dreams are unique, distinct from any others.

Precognitive dreams can be life-saving; can provide a warning about an accident, death, or health challenge; or can prepare us for calamities and natural disasters. One morning, I awoke with my heart beating rapidly, in a cold sweat. Even catching my breath was difficult. I looked around my bedroom for some trace of reality, something to tell me I was safely at home and not frantically running to catch a connecting flight at the airport. In my dream, I had lost my luggage and missed my flight.

I dismissed this dream as a mere reflection of my fear of flying, but I was in for a surprise the following day. This nightmare became a reality when I missed a connecting flight because the first plane was three hours late. I had to rush to another airline, catching a flight with a minute and a half to spare. As in the dream, my luggage was lost.

After ignoring many dream warnings about accidents and robberies that later came true, I began to honor my precognitive dreams as the best inside source of information I could find. Looking back at the flight, I realize that my intuitive ability was sending me a warning through the dream about the delayed flight.

Here's how a precognitive dream prepared Anita for a sudden relocation. One night, Anita dreamed that she met the previous owners of her house. They proudly showed Anita and her husband their new mansion and said, "Anita you want to move, too, and you should, because look how lucky it was for us!" This dream stuck with her, and she was already considering moving when—four days later—a tornado devastated her entire neighborhood. Although she suddenly had to pack up and move, her dream had prepared her.

Not all precognitive dreams are about bad things. They can be practical, reminding you of an upcoming appointment, or helping you remember to buy an anniversary gift. They can also be happy: You may see your impending marriage, a connection with an old friend, a new love affair, the healthy birth of your children, or an unexpected gift of money.

104

Precognitive Dreams Can Change Your Life

Often, we can access higher spiritual states through dreams. Dreams occur in *kairos*—sacred time, or the eternal now. The subconscious steps into this sacred time to bring wisdom, energy, clarification, and insight from sacred time into *kronos*—chronological time, our day-to-day lives. Out of this sacred space we can retrieve some powerful information that we can use to change our lives.

Today, Jeffrey Mishlove is the director of the Intuition Network. Years ago, however, he was a graduate student in U.C.

Berkeley's school of criminology, struggling to find out how to study the positive forms of human deviant behavior. He didn't seem to be getting anywhere, and after months of struggle, he said to himself, "Tonight, the answer will come to me in a dream." His dreaming mind promptly honored that request and sent him this dream:

> *I was visiting some friends who lived across town in Berkeley. I got to their home and no one was there. I knocked on the door and there was no answer. In the dream, I knew where they kept the key. I found the key, opened the door, and walked into the living room. In the middle of the floor I saw a popular magazine called Eye. I was paging through it in the dream.*

On awakening, says Jeffrey, "It was like, 'Eureka, I have really found it!' I was excited. I just *knew* that I had the answer—but I hadn't any idea what the answer was yet." He decided to act out the dream drama. He put on his sneakers, ran across town, got to their home, knocked on the door, and no one was there. He knew where they kept their key, so he let himself into the house. Sitting in the middle of the living room floor was a magazine. (In this wonderful example of dream distortion, the magazine was not *Eye*, but *Focus*). He began paging through this magazine, which literally brought focus into his life.

Focus magazine was about listener-sponsored radio and television programs in the Bay Area. Intuitively, Jeffrey realized that he could pursue his interests through educational broadcast media. This major shift in thinking was stunning—Jeffrey did not even own a radio or television, and purposely shunned anything in the electronic media because it seemed artificial and contrived. Nonetheless, he followed the "advice" from his dream advisor, got a job as a receptionist at a local public-interest station, KPFA-FM, and also offered to work there as a volunteer. After a couple of weeks, he was trained in producing radio programs, and soon began hosting his own show.

In less than a month from the time he had the dream, Jeffrey found himself sitting across the table interviewing leading figures in the consciousness movement, psychology, philosophy, spirituality, healing, and intuition, with 10,000 people listening.

Today, more than thirty years later, he is firmly in the forefront of the consciousness movement and hosts the nationally broadcast public television series *Thinking Allowed*. Jeffrey says, "When you make up your mind that you are going to live in the service of the higher consciousness, or doing something better with yourself, it is as if the heavens will open up to support that."

Precognitive Dreams Can Help You Say Good-Bye

Precognitive dreams can prepare us for the transition of a loved one. I learned this the hard way, when I had two precognitive dreams that I did not understand until it was too late.

I had a dream two weeks before my dear friend Victor Beasley died. This precognitive dream snuck through my dream doorway unattended. I dreamed that Victor and I were going away together for a business meeting. I noticed he left a jacket and a couple ties behind. I thought I would just give them to him when I saw him. I packed them into my suitcase. Then he came into my room and I said, "You really need to take this and pack it and be responsible for your clothing."

At the time, of course, I had no idea that Victor would die in two weeks. Symbolically, the jacket was there to keep me warm when I heard this numbing news. The ties he left behind were the ties to me and his other friends in the intuition community.

Edgar Cayce, the late "sleeping prophet," once said, "Nothing important ever happened to an individual which was not first previewed in a dream." These words rang in my ears one year. On November 18, I had the following dream, which I recorded in my journal:

I was at Lilia's. There were a lot of people around at a class or a meeting. I was surprised that I didn't know most of the people. Mom was in the next room—she was still sleeping when we got up. She couldn't get out of bed. A man came over who looked like Pat from the Bahamas. He was all upset about the break-up with his girlfriend.

A few days later, on November 21, my husband and I went to a comedy club with two other couples. The comedian, who looked like my friend Pat, was talking about his girlfriend breaking up with him. When I got home, there was a message from my father saying, "Your mother just left me." I called back the next morning and Pop related how Mom had pains and was taken to the hospital for observation over night. He was joking, in his own way, that Mom had left him. But the dream had referred to a break-up. The comedian's reference was one, and this comment from Pop was another. The part of the dream where Mom was sleeping and couldn't get out of a bed indicated that something was wrong. The dream's intent was to prepare me for her death on November 28. Just like the song fragment, "Are you going away with no word of farewell," which echoed in my mind for days before her passing, I was given this inside information to prepare myself for the actual event and so I could say good-bye. Again, I didn't heed the warning in this dream—perhaps because unconsciously I did not want to hear this message. Now, however, I am vigilant whenever I dream about a loved one being incapacitated.

One very good reason to record your dreams in your journal is that you will be able, more and more, to distinguish the true precognitive dreams right away, and act on them in a meaningful way.

How to Invite a Dream to Visit

If you are an avid dreamer, you now have a sharp new tool to cut through the text and clip out the penetrating intuitive insight. Perhaps your dream practice is intermittent or even brand new.

107

Use these guidelines to consistently connect with your intuitive mind and learn from your dreams. Here are the rules:

1. Set your intention.
2. Create your dream environment.
3. Record the dream in your journal.
4. Follow the DreamShift.

Set Your Intention

Setting your intention really has three parts: making a commitment, programming a dream for a specific purpose, and asking for an unprogrammed dream.

Make a Commitment: If you have trouble remembering your dreams, tell yourself several times throughout the day, "I will remember my dreams." If your inner censor is chiding you by saying, "You won't remember your dreams," remember the refrain you learned in the last chapter: "Yes I can! Yes I can! Yes I can!"

Program a dream: Ask your dreaming mind to attend to a specific request. Many people literally sleep on their problems, and find the answer is there when they wake up. Before Yvonne goes to sleep, she appeals to her intuitive mind by making the request, "I need an answer to this by tomorrow morning." When she awakens the next morning, she has the answer and a strong sense of what she has to do, even though the actual dream content remains elusive.

Cay Randall May uses the dream state to retrieve lost objects, create outlines for books and classes, and even formulate meeting agendas. You, too, can formulate an agenda literally while you sleep. As you go into the dream state, ask yourself for certain information when you wake up. You don't have to remember the dream. Just know that when you wake up, you will have the outline of the meeting and a clear idea of the agenda.

She also uses this technique to help her decide between two alternatives. For example, if you are trying to decide between two jobs, first ask for a dream in which you see the results of taking Job A. Then wait a couple of nights and ask for a dream in which you see the results of taking Job B. You don't have to remember the contents of the dream; just check in with how you feel when you wake up in the morning.

Remember: You are not always going to get the results you want in this way. Laila was trying to make a decision between two daycare centers for her son. Every night, she instructed her dreaming mind, "I will go to sleep and find the right answer." After three nights, however, no answer came. She finally realized that her answering dream was thwarted because her heart wanted to choose one daycare facility, while her head wanted her to choose another! She finally had to reconcile herself to the fact that she wasn't going to resolve that dilemma in a dream. Intuitively, she understood that she needed to do more real-world research before she could let her intuition guide her to the right choice.

Elicit an unprogrammed dream: I usually feel that the cosmic or intuitive mind knows what I need to receive. Before I go to sleep, I set my intention to receive a dream by saying, "I will fall asleep quickly, sleep peacefully through the night, and awake in the morning remembering my dreams." I fall asleep knowing that the dream will clarify any disconcerting issue in my life; or bring any buried concern to the surface so the smoldering embers of a potential problem can be addressed before it becomes hazardous.

109

Create Your Dream Environment

Bring comforting objects into your dream environment. Place flowers, a plant, a crystal, a spiritual picture, an inspirational saying, or an attractive art object by your bedside. For example, Pete gazes at a beautiful geometric rainbow crystal on his nightstand, and says, "My intuition speaks clearly to me through my dreams."

Have your dream journal and a pen or pencil near the bed. My journal is a small, three-hole, loose-leaf notebook. You can also use a standard size notebook or a spiral memo book that is easy to carry.

Be gentle as you approach bedtime. If stimulants such as alcohol or caffeine keep you awake, avoid them before sleep.

Open to a new page in your dream journal. Date it for both the night and next morning. This is also the best time to record your Day Notes. If you have a programming question, write it down under the date. If you prefer, you can speak into a tape recorder instead of writing in a notebook.

Record the Dream in Your Journal

Your dreaming mind is very fragile as you awaken, and can easily retreat if stunned by a blaring alarm clock, restless partner, or affectionate children and pets. Lie still as you replay the dream in your mind. You can start at the end and go through each scene until you reach the beginning. Don't move or even open your eyes until you are ready to write in your dream ournal. Stay in the same position you were in when you were dreaming.

If the dream is elusive, lie still until you can "pull up a thread"— any image that will help you elicit the complete dream. If you only remember a fragment, an intention, or a word, write that down. Later, that fragment will spontaneously trigger another memory, which will give you the entire dream.

Follow the DreamShift

A Yiddish proverb says, "A dream uninterpreted is like a letter unopened." How long can you keep a letter unopened? Not for very long. The same goes for dream interpretation—don't leave it for too long.

If possible, upon awakening, follow the steps of the DreamShift. If you only have a hot minute, at least give the dream a title. Make a commitment to spend quality time with your dreaming mind as often as you can. By honoring your dreams, you will become a prolific dreamer.

POWERHUNCH TOOL

Collect Your Personal Symbols

Allocate one or more pages in the dream section of your journal to collecting interesting symbols that come to you in dreams. After all, they have been personally crafted and designed for you by your intuitive mind!

You might want to keep track of symbols that are especially important in other ways. For example, Ruby had an especially vivid dream of a black bear rising from the bottom of a lake to the surface. She felt that this powerful image was especially important to her, although at first she was not sure what it represented. She decided to buy a small bear charm and wear it on a necklace. Over the years, she slowly added other important dream symbols to the necklace, to remind her of these messages from kairos to kronos.

111

POWERHUNCH WORKSHOP

Program and Then Interpret a Dream

Your Dream Journal entries can be in the fifth section of your PowerHunch Journal. As your dreams start coming fast and furiously, you might want to record your dream entries in a separate dream journal if you run out of room.

This workshop will give you practice programming a dream for all of the five core issues you will meet in part 2, Living an Intuitive Life. You will take five weeks to complete this workshop. Choose a quiet time to communicate with your intuitive mind. Each week you will ask a question of your dreaming mind:

Week 1: Program a dream about using your vision to see the big picture.

Week 2: Program a dream on taking a risk.

Week 3: Program a dream on being in the right place at the right time.

Week 4: Program a dream on how you can enhance a particular relationship.

Week 5: Program a dream on finding balance in your life.

Use the DreamShift to help you interpret the dream that gave you an answer to these questions. For each dream, complete these steps and record your answers in your PowerHunch Journal.

1. **Give the dream a title:** Honor your first impression for a title. Does this give you insight into the dream?
2. **Become centered and receptive:** What did you do to shift to the intuitive mind?
3. **Identify the major symbols:** Did the symbols come forward readily?
4. **Interpret these symbols:** How did you decipher the symbolism?
5. **Engage the symbol artistically:** Did you have fun drawing, dancing, or singing?
6. **Implement your dream discovery:** How are the insights helping you?

PART TWO

Living an Intuitive Life

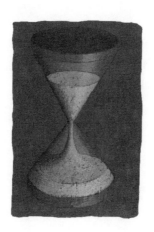

6

Vision
Seeing the Big Picture

*Vision is visualizing something that doesn't exist and saying,
This is what it is going to be.*

—Brian Maxwell, Founder, PowerBar

One day, Dan Gordon, budding entrepreneur and cofounder of
the Gordon Biersch Brewing Company, found himself staring at
a pile of dirt outside a Silicon Valley brewery that had gone bank-
rupt after only four months of operation. Out of the blue, he saw
this pile of dirt transformed into a bustling outdoor beer garden.
He saw people sitting outside in the hazy, warm California sunlight enjoying microbrews while they dined on the best in pub
food—crispy fried calamari, excellent burgers, mouth-watering
onion rings, even meal-sized salads for the health-conscious.
Immediately, his logical mind went to work figuring out exactly
how to make this vision a reality. A short time later, the transformation was complete: The pile of dirt became the second
Gordon Biersch Micro Brewery restaurant, the beginning of a
popular chain that now numbers twelve locations and is worth
tens of millions of dollars.

Gail had a similar empty-lot revelation while driving through
Houston with her husband many years ago. She "saw" the out-
lying areas developed—into housing tracts, shopping centers,
houses of worship—and suggested to her husband that they put
together as much money as possible to buy land there. Gail had a
PowerHunch: She knew this area was going to explode with

growth, and that investment would be highly profitable. Her husband looked at the emptiness and couldn't see what Gail saw, so the golden opportunity slipped by. Years later, Gail's vision came true, but her investment dream had long ago evaporated.

Yvonne Lo's father founded the Vitasoy company in Hong Kong sixty years ago. In 1980, Yvonne had a clear vision that she would successfully bring this product to the United States. At that time, most Americans still viewed soybeans as animal feed, and tofu as "hippie" food. Still, Yvonne's intuitive vision burned bright, and she met the challenge by identifying two separate markets: Asian Americans, who were already familiar with soy foods, and mainstream Americans, who were not. From these risky beginnings, the Vitasoy product line in the United States grew from soy milk to tofu, and Yvonne—now the company president— eventually saw her dream come true. Passing on the seeds of this rich visionary spirit, Yvonne says of her daughter, "If she believes in what she does and has vision, she can do anything."

Have you ever wanted to expand your intuitive eyesight so that you can see *more* than what is here right now? As these stories illustrate, vision is the periscope that lets you peer around the corner into the future. Cultivating your ability to see the big picture—the probable outcome of a course of action—is an invaluable tool for decision-making in everything from relationships to work to money matters to planning your child's future or your own retirement.

This sort of vision may seem extraordinary, but it is more common than you may think. Here's a classic visionary story I have always loved. Auto industry executive Peter Cook has always followed his powerful hunches. In the 1950s, he was an accountant in a furniture company in Detroit when he decided to explore the import car business. Why? Because he just liked foreign cars, especially sleek European sportscars. Cook started importing British sports cars exclusively—those now-classic Jaguars and Triumphs. Then, in 1954, after one of the biggest auto dealers in Detroit turned Volkswagen down, he took a highly intuitive—and, some said, suicidal—step: He became a Volkswagen distributor.

This awkward, homely car was no Jag. The tiny Beetle really did look like a bug. Where American cars of the 1950s were big, muscle-bound, flashy "land cruisers," the VW was humble. It also lacked fins, the essential stylistic feature characteristic of that era. Cook's decision to import and promote the Beetle was intuitive, but he also knew that the Beetle had some practical advantages. "You could get parts and service for it," Cook recalls. Bottom line? It was a car most people could afford to buy and own.

Cook had a strong hunch that this was the car America wanted. And he had a vision: He saw Volkswagen Beetles swarming along the streets and highways of America. Cook had to overcome many practical obstacles and conventional prejudices—against foreign cars in general, and ugly cars in particular. While he had mountains of statistical data showing the Beetle's wonderful benefits, few shared his enthusiasm for the homely Bug. Still, he persisted, following his vision. And then his luck changed.

One night, three enormous men were driven to dinner in a Volkswagen Beetle. One was football player Leon Hart, then with the Los Angeles Rams. When these three big men arrived at the restaurant, they couldn't find a place to park—so they made their own space. They simply picked up the car and put it on the sidewalk next to the building. You couldn't do that with a Ford or a Chevy! That did it for Hart. "He couldn't get over how roomy that little car was for its size, especially for how big these guys were," Cook recalls. "Hart came to Michigan and said he wanted to be a dealer."

Visions may come unbidden, but they don't turn into reality all by themselves. They are nourished by your strong desire to see the vision manifest. Sometimes, that desire can keep a vision warm until the time is right. Twenty years of patient waiting elapsed from the time film producer Stephen Simon first read the novel *What Dreams May Come* until the film was released. When he read the novel, he felt that it was an extraordinary piece of romantic afterlife fiction, and he envisioned a groundbreaking

117

movie that would make this world real. He had to wait for technology and society to catch up to him, and he did. In 1999, his film became a starring vehicle for Robin Williams and won the Oscar for special effects.

You can hold a vision about anything you want to achieve, and you can nurture it into reality. For many years, my business made me a frequent flyer in the friendly skies of United. I was drawn to its in-flight magazine, *Hemispheres*. Each time I held it in my hand, I had a powerful vision that I would someday write an article about intuition and publish it in that magazine. But I didn't leave it there. I strengthened my vision by affirming, "My intuition article appears in *Hemispheres*." Every day, in my mind's eye, I would "see" this article. Then I began the writing and research on which this article would be based. What happened? *Hemispheres* published my article, "Power Hunches," which described how top-level business executives got to the top by integrating intuition and logic into their decision making. This article, in turn, ignited the vision of *PowerHunch!*—the book you now hold in your hands.

With awareness and attention to it, your intuitive vision will:

- show you the big picture.
- inspire you to action.
- motivate you to persist through all obstacles.

Visions Show You the Big Picture

On a recent flight across the United States, I became so engrossed in the book I was reading that I forgot I was on an airplane. The shade was down over my window, and my little overhead light was focused on the page. When I finally lifted my head and looked out the window, I was startled to see the Grand Canyon spread out below me in its magnificent entirety. This is a wonderful metaphor to show you the big picture! When we keep our vision narrow and limited, we only see a small portion of the whole. When our sights are elevated, we enlarge the entire view. So often in life we become so taken with details that we lose our perspective; our heads are buried so deep in the daily to-do list that we just can't see the bigger picture. No wonder we so often feel blocked, uncertain what the next step should be.

Julie needed a broader perspective about her mother's health care. Her mother had just had emergency surgery for a brain tumor. Concern for her mother's life and health created tremendous stress and anxiety for Julie. On top of that, after twenty-five years of marriage, she had recently divorced and was focused on supporting herself and creating a new life. As the only family member who lived close to her mother, she was faced with this dilemma of how to care for her. All possibilities seemed dim, so Julie contacted her intuitive mind to make a PowerShift. Let's walk these steps with her so you can see how she was shown the big picture.

Example: Health Care for Julie's Mother

1. **Issue:** Julie asks, "What would be the best care situation for my mother?"
2. **Centering:** Soft acoustical music in the background calms Julie as she looks at the seashore picture on the wall.
3. **Receptivity:** Julie uses the abbreviated autogenic relaxation technique by telling each part of her body to relax. She starts with her toes and works her way up to the head. (See Appendix for the complete exercise).
4. **Imagery:** Two images come in response to Julie's silent question. One is the image of a private nurse who is crabby and difficult. In this scene, her mother is lying in her bed and wasting away. The second image shows her mother surrounded by music and color. The activity around her is fun and stimulating. Although she seems to be dying, she is comforted and amused by her surroundings.
5. **Deciphering the Image:** The image of the private nurse brings up old images of Julie's crabby father who was difficult to live

with. This private nurse idea is not acceptable as Julie senses that her mother has lived with her father's negativity for a long time. The second image of group living in a residential care facility is the desired choice.

This image also guides her as to the qualities of a care facility. The idea of music and color is something to consider. The words fun and stimulating suggest continuing to be amused to the end.

6. **Incubate:** After several days of contemplating the second image, Julie drove around to look at care facilities.

7. **Go Deeper:** One place she visits has deep rose-colored walls— the same color that surrounded her mom in the imagery. She also has the same impression of hustle and bustle or activity that she felt in the picture. Another place she visited had bright colored flowers all over but the "feeling" of the place did not match the original image she received. Now, she consciously uses the image as a reference for comparison in her search.

8. **Implementation:** Her mother was moved into the care facility with rose-colored walls. The first night, Julie saw her mother in bed surrounded by color and light and activity. Since this was an exact match to her PowerShift image, she came home very satisfied with her choice.

Through a vision, the doors and windows of your inner mind are flung wide open. Julie envisioned a health care solution for her mother that was invisible to the logical mind. In every example, notice how the mind is expanded to encompass a variety of resolutions.

Let's reverse the parent–child situation. As a parent, it is important to have a wider perspective, especially when manifesting a vision for your child's physical and emotional well-being. Catherine and her ex-husband had been divorced for five years, and she had had custody of their son, Jonah. At fourteen, he had become sullen and uncommunicative, refusing to do his homework or participate in household chores. Reluctantly, Catherine came to the conclusion that perhaps Jonah should live with his dad for a while. She mentioned this idea to Jonah, but was answered by his habitual nonresponsive grunt. She wanted to contact her ex-husband 2,000 miles away, but she just couldn't bring herself to do it. At her wits' end, Catherine felt that maybe there was something she was not seeing. She decided to let her intuitive mind help her out.

She got centered and relaxed, and asked her intuitive mind to give her a sign showing her what reflected her son's best interest. Then she went back to her household chores. As she started sorting through a stack of old papers, a card fell out and landed right on her feet. It was a valentine card that Jonah had made years ago—a big red heart saying, "I love you, Mom." This environmental cue showed Catherine the big picture of what was going on, and went right to Catherine's heart. And she began to cry with the realization that despite Jonah's hard shell, he still desperately needed her love and attention—maybe even more now that he was entering the uncertain years of adolescence. Sending him away to his father would only compound the resentment he felt. She made a plan to honestly tell Jonah how she felt, and to make a special effort to give him her loving attention. She knew he hated to talk right now, so she began by writing him a letter expressing how much she loved and appreciated him in her life. She was so grateful for the intuitive spark that rerouted their relationship onto a more positive course.

121

POWERHUNCH TOOL

Show Me the Big Picture

Ask your intuitive mind to show you the big picture for any situation or person in your life. In this exercise, find a time where you will be undisturbed for at least fifteen minutes, and decide on the focus of your vision: a situation or a person. Before you start, select an object that you will use for centering, and that also symbolizes a key to unlock your vision and show you the big picture. My personal centering objects or keys are several shells and amethyst crystals I keep on my desk.

1. Look at your key. Observe everything about it: shape, detail, color, weight, texture.
2. Take three deep breaths. Each inhalation cleanses and renews; each exhalation releases impurities and waste.
3. Imagine a calendar with today's date, and see what is happening right now for the person or situation you have chosen as a focus for your vision.
4. Turn the calendar pages in your mind's eye until you are one year in the future. What is happening for the focus of your vision now? Look at every detail, as if you were watching a movie.
5. In your PowerHunch Journal, describe in detail the vision you have received.

Vision Inspires You to Action

Having a vision is a good start, but, as Gail's story showed at the beginning of this chapter, it won't do you much good if you don't act on it! In my practice, I talk to many people who want to meet Mr. or Ms. Right. Most of the time they give lip service to this desire without taking action.

Dave was one of these—he described himself to me as more of a "relationship talker" than a "relationship seeker." At age thirty-five, however, he was getting pretty lonely. Together, we worked on a plan to use his intuitive vision to help him find the woman of his dreams.

Dave asked his intuitive mind to present him with a vision that would inspire him into action to reach his goal, which he described as "a long-term soul-fulfilling relationship with a special woman." Clearly, whatever he had been doing all these years wasn't working. He knew he needed to find a creative solution that would help him do something he had never done before, and he wanted it to be fun. In his mind he suddenly saw a flyer about a salsa dancing class followed by a dance that had come in the mail. He had thrown it away—salsa dancing was a very "non-Dave" activity. In the spirit of the fun and the different, he thought, "Well, maybe I'll go and see what happens."

Acting on his vision, he went to the class and found himself immediately attracted to Carla, one of his classmates. To his surprise and satisfaction, she seemed to like him, too, and they danced all night. As they got to know each other, Dave discovered that this was also Carla's first time salsa dancing—her girlfriend had talked her into trying something new—and they actually had many things in common. Dave was amazed at how quickly he was able to manifest his vision once he decided to take action.

Vision Motivates You to Persist Through All Obstacles

Not all visions are achieved as quickly as Dave's. I love to hear about people who persist against all odds to achieve their vision, whether it's to make a marriage work, to see a child safely through the teen years, or to achieve a career goal. One of my favorite stories is about how two young people stayed true to their vision and persisted, despite many obstacles, to create the PowerBar.

In 1975, Brian Maxwell's goal was to be the best marathon runner in the world. By 1977, he was third in the world and looking for food that would maintain his energy while he ran. He couldn't find what he was looking for. The quest, however, sparked a vision: a healthy and nutritious product for marathoners.

In 1983, he was still intrigued by the idea, and was directed to a chemist at the University of California, Berkeley. Together, they created a concentrated food that would solve the energy problems of long-distance runners. He also met Jennifer Biddulph, a twenty-year-old runner and Cal undergraduate studying nutrition and food science, who coached him for an upcoming race.

Eventually, she became part of the research team on his energy bar project and also his girlfriend.

In 1985, Jennifer and Brian began brewing batches of their PowerBar on the stove in their one-bedroom apartment, and testing the results on their athletic friends. They also surveyed the 1,000 athletes on their mailing list about what they ate before workouts. From these athletes, they found a common interest in having a digestible product filled with nutrients and energy to eat while engaged in the sport.

After three more years, Brian and Jennifer began filling orders out of their basement. They manufactured 35,000 bars for the initial run. It took Brian and Jennifer a decade to realize their vision, but their motivation was strengthened along the way by Brian's intuition. When the company was just starting, there were lots of problems. Chaos reigned and sales were lower than expected. Brian wondered if he was really on the right track. One night, however, he had a dream that he won the lottery. Intuitively, he knew that the dream was telling him to hang in there because he had a winner. He did, and today PowerBar manufactures more than 500,000 bars each day, and the company created by Brian and his now-wife, Jennifer, was later acquired by Nestle USA Inc. for approximately $375 million.

Having a vision is the necessary prelude to future accomplishment. Vision both guides and empowers our intentions. Are you wondering how anyone I mentioned so far actually "saw" their vision? This "seeing" evolves from the inner senses—it is not a manifestation of physical reality. As we saw in chapter 1, your intuitive mind communicates through the five senses: seeing, hearing, feeling, tasting, smelling. Yes, some people really do see a picture in their minds, but others may hear, feel, taste, or even smell their PowerHunch vision. Perhaps you have a sudden sensation of a pen in your hand, signing an important contract; or you have a "warm feeling" in your heart as you consider living the rest of your life with your beloved partner.

Denise Debaun is a successful entrepreneur in the cosmetics and fragrance industry. Some years ago, however, she worked for someone else. One day, while meeting with her boss, she suddenly had a vision that her life needed to go in a different direction. She describes her vision as coming in the form of "hearing." But what she heard was not a voice. "It was," she says, "a knowing, with every single corpuscle in my body, in my heart and mind—an opening that I heard totally with every experience that I had—that it was time to quit my job and start my own business." She acted on her vision and turned in her resignation—the first vital step in her blossoming career.

Why stop with just one sense? You can call on *all* your senses to create a vision. That was the case for Joe, one of my students. Joe was confused about his future. He had recently been laid off, and he couldn't imagine what kind of work he should go after. I asked him to review his talents and abilities, and he said, "I've always loved to cook." Suddenly, into his head popped a vision: a sort of retail "meals on wheels" service in a thriving downtown business area. It seemed like a fantasy. "How could I ever do that?" he asked.

I encouraged Joe to continue with the vision, creating imagery that would make it more concrete. To his surprise and mine, Joe turned out to have a talent for vision as well. First, he saw himself in his kitchen with an assistant. Then he imagined the food ingredients in front of him. He actually smelled the aroma of the pasta sauce, and tasted it to make sure it was right. He heard the phone ringing—someone was placing a sizable order. Finally, he brought himself back to sight: He saw himself driving his car through his future delivery route. In the end, he saw all the steps, from buying the ingredients to delivering the food. He even visualized many satisfied customers.

By the time Joe started putting his business together in real life, he felt it was a done deal. In fact, he had it up and running in nine months.

POWERHUNCH TOOL

Develop a Vision to Inspire Your Talent

You can open the door to any talent you would like to develop. Let your extended senses go to work as you envision yourself using the talent in a new way. Pick a talent and develop your vision in every sense of the word. See it, feel it, smell it, taste it, and hear it in your intuitive mind. For example, can you see yourself demonstrating the latest dance craze to a group of people? How does your body feel as you are moving? What sights are you taking in from the surrounding crowd?

Indulge in a Daydream

126

Like a night dream, a daydream allows you to enter the intuitive realm. In both, the pictures, symbols, and images come cascading out of the intuitive mind. You can call this progression of images whatever makes you feel comfortable—a daydream, vision, altered consciousness, or entering the future. It begins with setting your intention to use your intuition or active imagination to enter the future. Daydreaming is especially useful if you have trouble remembering your dreams.

Maris and her husband didn't want to stay in the town they had both grown up in but were not sure where to go. Maris, an experienced "visioner," decided to slip into a daydream to retrieve a clue about this move. To her surprise, she did not end up envisioning a new locale. Instead, she received important information about her approach to the move.

She entered the daydream in the same way she initiated the PowerShift. When she looked around her office, the silver doorknob on the door next to her desk caught her attention. She concentrated on the textured pattern until it filled her entire vision. The word "open" began to repeat itself while she remained focused on the doorknob. Then she closed her eyes and continued to visualize the doorknob while she repeated the word "open" until she felt her mind quieting and her body relaxing. She inhaled deeply and became aware of the breath filling her lungs with fresh energy and moving through other parts of her body. Then, on the exhalation, she felt her body exhaling all its waste energy.

In her daydream, she went to a beautiful beach. The weather was warm and she could feel the soft tropical breeze against her skin. She could hear the pounding of the ocean waves on the beach and see the beautiful tropical birds flying through the air. She could smell the salty tang of the sea, feel the grainy sand in her hands and the rough texture of the tree against her back.

An image popped up of a cruise ship, just offshore. She could hear soft music playing. Some people were engaged in activities on the deck; some were in deck chairs reading; others were swimming; and some were just lying in the sun. All the while, the ship kept moving effortlessly through the ocean waters.

The cruise ship moving effortlessly represented a smooth transition. Suddenly, it didn't matter when the move took place or where she went. There were many things she could do in the meantime. In particular, she could relax, enjoy the ride, and wait until she reached the port of call, which was her new home. After this daydream, Maris felt much more relaxed, ready, and willing to be "open" to the next stop.

POWERHUNCH TOOL

Indulge in a Daydream

Find a quiet place inside your house or in a natural setting. Wherever you are, make sure you will not be distracted by extraneous noises or disturbed by people interrupting your reverie. Use any of your centering and receptivity techniques to expand your awareness. If you are "a sleeper" and go into the void quickly, affirm, "I will not fall asleep." When you are receptive, let the pictures and images emerge spontaneously. You can also actively invite the flow with a query. Be sure to write your daydream in your PowerHunch Journal. Is there anything in that daydream that you would like to see become reality?

If you are a parent, consider inviting your child to daydream with you. This is a great way to gain insight into children's feelings, which they may be reluctant to share in the usual way. When Lizzie tried this with her son Dylan, they rested on the playroom floor together and closed their eyes. She explained to Dylan that they were going to get very quiet and see movies in their head, and narrate the movie so the other person could see it, too. The rule was, just listen to the other person's movie unfold—no probing questions! Dylan's movie was all about a little boy who does everything by dancing—including vanquishing enemies and saving planets from destruction. Afterward, Lizzie told Dylan how wonderful his dancing images were, and they agreed to play this game more often. Lizzie was stunned. She had no idea that Dylan had ever thought about dancing, and this was not an activity she had ever considered for her robust and active little boy. The next day, with his permission, she signed Dylan up for dancing lessons.

128

Visioning: Step By Step

Almost all of us can tap into the vision sent by the intuitive mind. First, use the PowerShift method in chapter 3. Just allow the vision to well up from your intuitive mind, and then assign your logical mind to organize the details. Why try to do everything with one hand tied behind your back? Use your whole brain to integrate your vision into your life and work. This partnership between intuition and logic creates informed and effective decision making and dynamic action. To begin your visioning, work with the following four steps:

1. Clearly describe your vision.
2. List the things that motivate you to achieve your vision.
3. Describe what your vision will provide for others: Who needs it? Why?
4. State what will happen if you abandon your vision. What is at stake?

This four-step visioning process is an introspective one. We want to develop a vision but first we have to look at what it is, what motivates us, what our vision is giving to others, and what happens if it is abandoned. The PowerHunch Workshop that follows these four visioning steps will help you anchor the vision to the outer world—your reality. It is designed to help you practice developing your vision.

Take plenty of time to write your answers in your PowerHunch Journal, and ponder them at length.

Step 1: Clearly describe your vision. A clear description and picture of your vision are prerequisites for accomplishing it. See it in your mind, feel it in your being, and write it down, with as much detail as possible. Now it is already becoming an inner reality, and will eventually become an outer reality in your life and in the world.

Step 2: List the things that motivate you to achieve your vision. Being clear on why you are attracted to this vision will help you stay motivated. What is it about your vision that inspires you to action and makes you feel good? Once you are clear about your compelling reasons, you can remember them and tap into them on a feeling level. This is a crucial source of motivational energy, and a key part of your visioning process.

Step 3: Describe what your vision will provide for others. This is the idealistic component of your vision. By now you already know what your vision offers you. Now examine what it offers to others. A true vision is rooted in something deeper than mere profit—it empowers you to succeed because it fulfills a real need or provides a real service to others. When you find the deeper meaning of your goal, you will find the fuel that will take you there.

At some point as you pursue and manifest your vision, you will probably need to involve others—as employees, partners, or customers. Drawing others into your vision requires that you be able to take these first three steps in a way that is as compelling to them as it is to you.

Step 4: State what will happen if you abandon your vision. This question reminds you why it is worth pursuing and manifesting your vision. Knowing what you have to lose and feeling the pain of that potential loss reminds you what is at stake. Positive and negative motivation are both valid, but don't beat yourself up with fears of failure. Judiciously remind yourself of the cost of giving up whenever that seems like an option.

130

POWERHUNCH TOOL

Look Through the Lens of Intuitive Vision

Take at least five minutes each day to go inside yourself and engage this four-step visioning process. Visualize the steps you must take to get from inspiration to manifestation. Make it a habit to see your vision fulfilled, in as much detail as possible. See and feel yourself doing exactly what you want to do successfully. At least once a month (or each time you fulfill one important step), work with the above four steps in detail and see if you achieve any greater clarity.

Inevitably, doubts, confusion, and mistakes will occur in the process of fulfilling these steps and manifesting your vision. Remember: They are only bumps in the road, not the end of it.

POWER**HUNCH** WORKSHOP

Directing Your Vision

In this workshop you will discover how a PowerHunch can direct the vision you have tapped into with the four-step visioning process. Do the following exercise in your PowerHunch Journal. Be thorough and detailed. You may need two or three half-hour sessions to complete this exercise, but it will be worth it. Set aside time over the next three days to engage fully. Persist with this process until your vision is clear.

Many people feel intimidated because they cannot close their eyes and actually "see" their vision. As you have learned, your intuitive mind speaks to you through your senses in your own unique way.

Before you begin, decide whether you would like to create a vision for your current job or business or go into an entirely new area. If you are in a transitional mode, you might first create a vision for your present position or business and then repeat the workshop to get insight into an entirely new circumstance. Or, you might want to create a vision for a member of your family. In any case, you will need to go through the following seven steps.

1. Find Your True Purpose.
Describe your activities at your worksite, or describe the activities you would like to do. Who will benefit from this work in the short term and how? Whom would you like to benefit and how? Or ask, who will benefit from this work ultimately and how? Whom would you like to benefit and how?

For example, James works at Circuit City. For the past two months, he's been assigned to the computer section and has become fascinated with voice-activated computers. He begins fantasizing about selling this product to the multitude of people who cannot type because of physical or other problems. Daily, his mind conjures up images of preschool children who could use this voice-activated computer to write a story or a letter to their grandparents.

These young faces transform into the arthritic elderly, who could more readily speak than type. Then he sees people who have lost the use of their hands due to illness or neurological problems. Spurred by this PowerHunch, he knows that this product can serve those in need.

2. *Analyze Your Interests, Desires, Abilities, Skills, and Experience.*

- What skills, strengths, or talents do you have? What do you do well? You've probably been laying the foundation for your vision with years of unwitting preparation. (Mrs. Fields was baking cookies long before she opened her first store.)
- Make a list of your most notable skills and talents: physical, mental, practical, artistic, and so on. Now list any special areas of interest, even if you have no special skills in that area. For example, you may love music without being a musician or enjoy art without being an artist. If you are actively looking for a new position or even contemplating a change, make a list of three fields (or business opportunities) in which you would love to work and make your living. Indicate what it is about them that gives you satisfaction, and what kind of work you would like to do in each.

James notes on this talent/skill list that he is gregarious and loves to convene social gatherings and be around people. He also enjoys traveling, watching sports, growing orchids, playing the guitar, acting with his local theater group, and working with children.

Three fields he would like to invest in energetically are computers because they are a tool of the present and future, organizing social events because he likes to bring people together, and entertaining children with his guitar. Like a magnet, the computer idea compels his interest.

3. *Call Your Vision.*

Whether you direct your call to your intuitive mind or subconscious, to your higher self or a higher power or to God, this focus on your mind and intention will activate the dimension of your being from which dreams, visions, and creative ideas spring.

Close your eyes, and see yourself on a bare piece of ground. Now start filling in the picture:

What kind of environment are you in? Let the images well up from inside you. You may see yourself inside a high-rise office building with many colleagues, traveling in your car, or even on a secluded beach.

- What are you doing?
- Who are you working with?
- What kind of business is this?

As soon as James closes his eyes, he sees his private office, on the ground floor of an office building. The gadget box in one corner of the office is beneath a big calendar on the wall. A laptop computer sits on his desk, and a larger state-of-the-art model he uses for demonstrations sits in a corner of the room.

James sees himself as part of a seven-person team selling computer software. His specialty is the voice-activated component. Although he shares secretarial services with one other colleague, he sets up his own calls and speaking engagements.

4. Call Your Intuitive Images.

What do you need to make this vision a reality? Instead of putting your logical mind to work on the problem, let images, thoughts, concepts, or feelings rise up from your intuitive mind. Record these impressions in your PowerHunch Journal. Don't analyze or judge them, just write them down.

For example, James wants to make a living as a successful salesperson. When he calls his intuitive images, up comes a podium, a Lexus, a toolbox, and a jaguar,

5. Unravel the Meaning.

Ask your intuitive mind to help you unravel the meaning of these images. For example, when James sees the podium image, he realizes he will make a sales pitch to a large audience. The Lexus is an interesting image for James, who likes fast, flashy sports cars. He probes further and realizes he needs to make a quality presentation for himself as well as for his product. From the toolbox image, he gets the message that he needs to present his product in a variety of ways. The jaguar image shows him that his presentation has to be swift, sleek, and incisive.

6. *Actively Create Your Vision.*

Now add more detail: Pay attention to your sensory impressions. Your success in manifesting this vision will escalate considerably when you include as many of these sensory impressions as possible. James can "hear" the thunderous applause, for example, and "feel" the warmth created by all those people waiting to hear him speak.

Now picture in detail the steps you need to take to bring your vision into reality: How will you get from here to there? Break your vision process down into a series of simple steps. Clearly visualize each step. Go through all the steps in this way. Here are the steps James visualized, culminating in his giving a successful sales presentation.

1. In his image, he goes into a toy store and picks up a variety of toys. Then he selects a few that feel perfect when he touches them. He knows these are ideal to represent his product.
2. James imagines himself in an upscale clothing store, trying on a variety of suits. He looks at himself in the mirror, and clearly knows which suit will project the right appearance.
3. Next, when James imagines the preparation for his talk, he sees a banquet before his eyes that stimulates his taste buds. The smell of gasoline abruptly interrupts the image, but sends a clear signal that he is all tanked up and ready to give the audience something to feast on.
4. Dressed impeccably, he imagines himself talking to a filled auditorium. His presentation is strong, pointed, and deliberate. He frequently takes the objects out to demonstrate the product.

5. The thunderous applause and standing ovation he envisions at the end of his sales presentation fill him with confidence.

7. *Rehearse Your Vision Daily.*

Rehearse your vision every day for two weeks. Sit or lie down in a quiet place and spend ten minutes mentally trying your vision on for size. See and feel yourself living this vision in as much detail as you can. See how it feels and how well it fits. By first modeling the vision in your mind, you attract the complete reality soon after. Note what is beginning to manifest. Perhaps you are feeling more confident and prepared for the new situation that is emerging.

For example, James was hesitant about speaking to a large audience before he began his visioning process. Eventually, however, he began to feel comfortable standing before the large audience in his mind. And when he did have to speak in public, it felt familiar and comfortable.

When you mentally rehearse your vision, seeing each step clearly, it becomes a reality in your body-mind. And the more real it becomes in your body-mind, the likelier it will become a reality in your life.

As you pursue your vision, you will inevitably encounter obstacles and resistance, both inner and outer. Be persistent! Making realistic, attainable goals a part of your step-by-step process will increase the likelihood of your ultimate success. Don't make unrealistic or impossible demands on yourself. Don't be harsh with yourself. Above all, don't worry. Simply take and complete the necessary steps. Each step completes a piece of your vision.

Remember: A vision is always changing because the whole universe is always changing. The right step today may not be the right step tomorrow. It doesn't make much sense to hold on to an old vision whose time has passed. Use your intuition as a reality check to make sure your vision is still on track.

7

Danger or Opportunity?
Knowing When to Risk

The risk is just in trusting yourself that the issue is important so you can commit to a project and stick it through.

—Teresa Tollini, Filmmaker, *Breaking Silence*

You don't have to go rock climbing or race cars to take a risk. Just living day to day involves a certain amount of danger. Some life decisions, of course, seem inherently more risky than others, especially those—having a baby, leaving a steady job, moving far away—that involve risking a sure thing for an uncertain future. Because so much seems to rest on such life decisions, it's easy to become paralyzed by fear and indecision, which clouds your ability to see whether the risk is worth taking.

But hidden inside every risk is a chance for growth. In fact, the Chinese word for crisis—*weiji*—combines two characters that separately mean *danger* and *opportunity*. The perfect image!

As you get better and better at risking, you'll discover the secret of successful people. When you're so in tune with your intuition that you know in your heart and soul you are doing the right thing—no matter how it looks to everyone else—a risk is not a risk at all. Here's a good illustration.

In 1985, Birthale Lambert, a young professor teaching senior nursing students at a university, grew tired of teaching and wanted to start her own visiting nurse business. She was filled with entrepreneurial zeal. Everyone told her she'd need at least $50,000 and probably $100,000 to start her new business. These figures were far from Birthale's scant $25 bank account, but she never doubted she could raise the money and she never doubted that she would succeed. Instead, she listened only to her intuition, which loudly shouted, "Go for it!" She never saw this new business as a risk, but as the opportunity of a lifetime. She knew she had the talent and was willing to work hard. While someone else might have focused on the risk to their reputation if they were to fail, or on not having the needed energy or funds to make it happen, Birthale seized the opportunity. Today, Birthale has parlayed her vision, The Professional Nursing Force, into a million-dollar business.

Remember: A risk-taker is like a skydiver who confidently leaps into the unknown, but has the skills it takes to stay alive and enjoy the ride. Unlike skydiving, however, risk-taking is for everyone! Here's your goal: to trust your intuition to help you take risks that truly pay off. Someday, the word risk may even disappear from your vocabulary!

In this chapter you will learn how to use the PowerHunch principles to make intuitive assessments that will help you act with bold confidence in times of crisis and opportunity. Here's what you'll learn about risk in this chapter:

- Take a leap of faith.
- Ride the wave of change.
- Use your intuition as a life raft.
- Make a change.
- Choose the right partner.
- Leap over obstacles.
- Be an intuitive antenna.

Take a Leap of Faith

Risk comes in many forms. In the following examples, note how the heart's response on the emotional level was the ultimate risk meter that encouraged the gamble.

After eight happy years of marriage and a solid career as a bio-chemist, Cay Randall May heard her intuitive voice announce, "Baby time is here." She was already in her mid-thirties, with an established and demanding work life. Motherhood, she knew, would be a great responsibility. She was concerned about what it would mean to her marriage, her career, and her health. Should she take the risk? Her heart, the repository of Cay's intuition, opened up with an enthralling feeling about bringing new life forth. That's all she needed for validation. Today, Cay says, "I learned more from motherhood than from any professional endeavor that I have undertaken."

Leaving a homeland is an incredible risk. When Roland Hoffman left Germany to visit the United States, he never thought of his move as permanent. But his intentions changed completely when he met the woman who would become his wife. Roland's biggest risk was giving up his highly successful career in Europe. Yet the love in his heart ignited his intuition and prompted him to leave his secure position behind and plant new roots in America.

139

When Martin Rutte lived in Toronto, his work as a manage-ment consultant took him all over the world. After returning from a sojourn to Hong Kong, he slid into a mysterious funk. This inexplicable depression startled Martin, who dearly loved his wife and business activities. Later that year, while spending time in an Augustinian monastery, he had a profound epiphany: He heard the phrase, "It's about God." Intuitively, he knew that the field of spirituality would be his next professional focus. This was a risky career shift, since his colleagues felt that anyone talking about "spirituality and work" was either proselytizing, dogmatic, or gone off the deep end. In fact, every single person he talked to advised him against this career shift. How could he risk it and delve into this new arena without being totally ostra-cized? Still, his intuitive mind prodded him to risk it. Today, seventeen years later, he is a leader in the emerging field of spiri-tuality in the workplace.

Risk taking means a total leap of faith: Even as you jump into the unknown, you know you will land safely. What makes some people actually jump out of the plane, dive off a cliff into the ocean, or even get up off the couch to see what's outside the front door? What prompts a person to leave the security of a career, home, or solid partnership and venture into the void? This usually happens when satisfaction fades from a formerly nurturing situation. As the green light flashes GO, the adventurous risk taker is off to search for a more pleasing job, place to live, or partner.

Many people were surprised when Carol Hegedus left her twenty-two-year position as a hospital administrator to join the nonprofit Fetzer Institute in Kalamazoo, Michigan. A year later, however, her friend Ann said, "Carol, I couldn't believe that you gave up the career that you were so successful in and took the risk to do this thing at Fetzer." And Carol replied, "Ann, if I had known it was a risk I probably would never have done it."

POWERHUNCH TOOL

Taking A Leap of Faith

People who worked at McMillan Publishing in the 1970s still recall "Friede's Folly." Editor Eleanor Friede was determined to turn a children's manuscript that had been rejected by numerous publishers into a successful adult book. Against advice, she took the risk to publish *Jonathan Livingston Seagull*, a book that has since sold over 10 million copies in twenty-seven languages. Her leap of faith has delighted readers all over the world.

Have you ever taken a leap of faith? Focus on a goal. It can be approaching a project in a novel way, confronting another person, or even instituting an innovative way to help your child learn a new skill. Taking a risk begins when you actually take the first couple steps. Let your intuitive mind give you a signal about what you have to do to take that first intuitive step before you leap. Let your intuitive mind speak to you in pictures, symbols, and images of your end goal to guide you confidently through those first steps.

Ride the Wave of Change

There's no doubt about it: We live in a time of rapid change. Many people complain of feeling overwhelmed and fearful, describing the world as chaotic, turbulent, and troubling. They want to know how to live, how to arrange their priorities, how to get back in balance in such uncertain times. If this is the world you perceive, taking a risk is probably the last thing you want to do. But what if you turn your perception around and describe these times as challenging, exciting, and creative? As the wave of change wells up, you can ride your intuition like a surfboard, letting it carry you to your next destination.

141

When you choose to ride the wave, you need clear vision to see it coming. Janet deliberated for a long time before deciding on a suitable preschool for her daughter, Michelle. Michelle loved the teachers and the other kids, and Janet felt like her daughter was in preschool nirvana. But when she heard the school was experiencing a financial crisis and might close, she started feeling overwhelmed. Steadying herself, she reminded herself to use her intuitive vision and look at the bigger picture: The school was great, but it might close. She needed to find other suitable preschools.

One day while she was grocery shopping, she overheard two women talking about how their young children loved the innovative playground at their preschool. Janet asked them for the name of the school. It was one she had overlooked in her previous investigations. She tucked the name away in her mental file, went home, and read her mail. The newsletter from her fitness club had a feature story about the school she just heard about!

Her intuition immediately recognized these two environmental cues and she picked up the phone. Her "risk" in finding a new school was nonexistent because she kept her vision clear, despite her initial worry, and trusted her intuition. Why worry? Remember, you *can* ride the wave of change and come to rest safely on shore.

POWERHUNCH TOOL

Change Your Language to Change Your Perceptions

The words we use to describe our lives really describe our inner state of mind. By changing the way we speak about a situation, a person, a relationship, or anything else, we go a long way toward changing our attitude. Like most of us, you probably use words habitually, without hearing what they imply—is it negativity or optimism? Fear or trust? If you don't like what you hear, it's time to get a new vocabulary!

It's hard to hear ourselves, so for this exercise, enlist the help of a friend to make you aware when negative words or phrases are slipping through in your speech. For example, C. J. noticed that her friend Syd started almost every sentence with the phrase, "I know it sounds crazy, but . . ." Syd was really surprised when C.J. told her this. She realized she really didn't have much faith in her own perceptions, and decided to make a change. She tried to pay strict attention to what she was saying, and replaced this phrase with another: "Here's what I think . . ."

Try this for at least a week. Every time your friend makes you aware of a word or phrase that you frequently use, write it in your PowerHunch Journal. Next to it, write down a new, more positive word or phrase. Practice using the replacement. The more you practice this exercise, the more you will become aware of your speech and the more automatic your corrections will become.

Has your mind changed in the process?

Use Your Intuition as a Life Raft

What would you do if you found yourself in dangerous waters? You can learn to use your intuition to save your life.

Jackie, a police officer, told me about what might have been her last day of service—if she hadn't trusted her intuition and used it to save her life. "The most significant intuitive event in my life is one that literally saved it," she says. "I was investigating a hit-and-run accident, and went to the home of the suspect to get his side of the story. His father answered the door, and told me the car we believed was involved in the accident belonged to his son.

"After inviting me in, the father called to his son to come downstairs and talk about the accident. The son did not come down. Generally, I would have gone upstairs to get the kid, but I had this strong gut feeling to be patient and bide my time. After about fifteen minutes, this feeling faded. I went up to get the kid and found him passed out on his bed, clutching a loaded hunting rifle. There is no doubt in my mind that he had intended to shoot me as soon as I stepped into his bedroom doorway. The only thing that saved my life was a little voice telling me to wait."

You don't have to be a police officer to be in a dangerous situation. Connie Grazanka, a lawyer, grew up in Detroit in a really bad neighborhood. She feels that her sense of intuition was developed in that city, where she had to be able to "feel the atmosphere" and know whether it was safe to walk on a particular street, get out of her car at a certain time, or even sense if the people on the street were going to harm her in some way. One night, returning home late from work, Connie drove up to her house. Sensing that something was wrong, she decided not to park her car but to drive around the block a few times. She was glad she did—as she drove, she saw some suspicious-looking guys hanging out in the shadows near the side of her house. She waited until they were gone before she parked and went in the house.

143

Like Jackie the police officer, Connie was glad that she heeded her intuition, which probably saved her life. Your intuition is always there to guide you in any fearful or anxiety-arousing situation.

POWERHUNCH TOOL

Sensing Danger

We sense danger in many ways: a chill down the spine, a sudden sense of alertness, a bad taste in the mouth, a clenching in the stomach. . . .Your body may sense fear before your mind does. Learn your body's danger signals, and learn to pay attention to them. These feelings are especially noticeable in the body's seven energy centers, known as *chakras*. Each chakra is associated with certain characteristics. For example. the throat chakra is associated with communication, and the heart chakra is associated with love. You can learn more about chakras in one of the many fine resources under Suggested Reading at the end of this book. For now, know that these energy centers are located at the base of the spine, lower abdomen, solar plexus, heart, throat, brow, and crown. Any of the chakras can alert you to danger. For example, when I sense danger, my solar plexus tightens up and my heart beats rapidly. When I am personally afraid, my throat tends to close up.

For this exercise, get centered and relaxed. Work your way up your chakras, from the base of your spine to the crown of your head, and see what intuitive image you get of each one. You may see that each has a color, or a certain feeling. Some may feel vital and open, others closed off. Ask each to give you a message about how it can help you sense danger. Remember to write your impressions in your PowerHunch Journal. As you go through your day, pay attention to the messages you are getting (or not getting!) from each of these energy centers. Does your heart start beating faster? Do you feel your stomach turn over? Does your chest suddenly tighten up? Is your throat suddenly scratchy? If so, your inner alarm is ringing.

Before long, you'll become instantly sensitized to your inner alarms. Soon, you'll be able to use them to help you evaluate many situations.

Make a Change

If you've ever had the sudden urge to quit your job and do something completely different, you're not alone. Especially today, when jobs seem to come and go at the speed of light, changing workplaces or careers is getting to be a national pastime. But how do you know if you're taking the right risk?

Healthcare futurist Lee Kaiser had been a tenured faculty member at the University of Colorado for thirty years in health administration when he got an intuitive message to go out on his own and develop a consulting and educational program. This was very risky, since he would be giving up his tenure and a full university salary. Lee said, "Whenever you use true intuitive insight, you have to be willing to let go—because the intuition will take you to a place you wouldn't go by yourself. That decision was risky for me. Could I make a livelihood? Could I support my family? Is this going to work? I was older and had been at the university for thirty years. It was making a major change." Acting on another powerful hunch, Lee realized that he didn't have to give up the teaching to pursue his dream. Today he is still a part-time faculty member, and also continues to develop his Kaiser Institute, which offers executive-level education on topics such as intuition and integrative medicine.

An environmental cue like a workshop flyer can point a person into an entirely new career direction. Paul, an attorney with a young family, first discovered he could communicate with his dog when he was a young lawyer. When he saw a flyer about an animal communication workshop, he was excited. Afterward, he felt energized by what he had learned and wanted to enroll in an

145

intermediate workshop. But there was one drawback: The instructor had four cats, and Paul was painfully allergic to cats. As he struggled with his desire to go to the class despite watering eyes and sneezing, his five-year-old daughter said, "Daddy, last night I dreamed that you weren't allergic to cats anymore!" Paul felt strongly that this dream was a sign, so he cast caution to the winds and went to the workshop. Two of the cats spent the entire workshop climbing all over him. And to his surprise and satisfaction he seemed to be healed of his allergic reaction. The workshop was so provocative that Paul decided on the spot to shift careers and become a professional animal communicator. After ten years as an attorney, acting as an advocate for those who needed a strong voice, he became an advocate for those whose thoughts and feelings are crying (and barking) to be heard. While Paul's logical mind might have resisted leaving the legal profession, his intuitive mind was totally supportive of his entering an entirely new field.

146

POWERHUNCH TOOL

Let Your Dream Help You Make a Change

Program a dream to help you take a risk with a career, family member, relationship, or even moving. You might ask your dreaming mind, "Show me how I can take the first steps to implement this change comfortably." Or you can program a dream to show you how to add an exciting new element to your professional or personal life to keep it from becoming stale and routine.

Cynthia's dreams have led her into many changes. For about a year before she opened her Southwest art gallery, she had a recurring dream of being in a room filled with amethyst crystals and other gorgeous minerals. On a trip to Santa Fe, she recognized some of the dream images touching her in real life. When she returned to California, she began making sketches of her new art gallery. This new career adventure was instigated by a dream that forced her to go out and be in a place that caught her fancy sufficiently to create this risky move.

Choose the Right Partner

Selecting a life partner is a time when you really need intuitive discernment. Unfortunately, being in love can blind us to our intuition.

Many happily married couples look back with amusement, delight, and gratitude at the intuitive connection that first brought them together. In her twenties, Diane shared a house with a girlfriend and enjoyed frivolous activities for several years. Then one night, going back to their car after dinner out, Diane's gaze was drawn to the sidewalk, where she saw a wallet. She opened the wallet to find $100 in cash, as well as credit cards and a driver's license. She remembers thinking how nice this was, because she was out of money. Momentarily tempted to pocket the cash and forget the contents, she had an overwhelming impulse to call Lou Parente, the wallet's owner. When she called, Diane told him, "I could leave it in the mailbox, I could hand deliver it, or I could send it to you in the mail." But Lou said, "No, I'll pick it up." After that first meeting, Diane and Lou dated. After only one month, they took the risk to marry. Diane's intuition confirmed that deep down they were meant for each other. They went up to Reno, got married, and have stayed together for the past thirty-four years.

Risking it to take a personal partner is no different than entering into a professional partnership. Stephen says the riskiest hunch he ever took was forging a professional partnership with Barnett. They met at a seminar, instantly became best friends, and decided on the spot to be business partners. They knew nothing about each other, yet they both trusted their intuition. Their partnership has worked out phenomenally well, as they continue to listen to intuitive messages showing them how to have a deeper understanding of their partner's needs.

147

Leap Over Obstacles

What keeps you from jumping into the unknown? What prevents you from acting on your intuition and taking a risk? Let's look at how you can put on your intuitive cape and fly over the wall of obstacles.

Fear and wishful thinking can readily douse the risk-taker's fire. You might have a brilliant scheme to implement, but fear that the presentation might not be treated gently or in the right way. Don't fear success and hold back by not honoring the answers that are within you. Are these fears real or imagined? In either case, let your intuitive mind help you devise the perfect plan to surmount the fear barrier.

Wishful thinking comes into the picture when you want to take a risk so badly that you don't listen to reality. For example, during chaotic times, burnout is prevalent. People depleted from incredible stress can't tell the difference between wishful thinking and intuition. Their intuitive circuits get jammed, so they fool themselves with their dreams and their wishes and make incorrect decisions and conclusions. The intuitive mind is challenged to take the fire out of the burnout and return to a balanced state of mind. Using your inner compass will show you how to come back to your work, family, and friends as a whole person who is not wasted away from the stress in your life.

148

POWERHUNCH TOOL

Create Your Obstacle and Destroy It

Remember the fear barrier that can block creativity, which you read about in chapter 5? A similar obstacle can stand in your way and prevent you from taking other kinds of risks. Here's an exercise to transcend the barrier or obstacle that prevents you from taking a risk.

First, draw or create the obstacle or obstacles that prevent you from taking a risk. Then, use your creative mind to show you how to "jump over the barbed wire fence" or if necessary, eliminate the obstacle. Here's an example. Jim wants to be more adventurous with his work projects. His obstacle comes from the endless papers where he has to justify too many procedures before he can risk implementing his new idea. He creates his obstacle by taking all the papers from his desk and putting them in a tall pile. Then he puts on the fan and lets the papers blow away until a couple remain. Handling these few paper constraints is now manageable, and he resolves to put fewer demands on himself the next time he has a good idea.

Keep It Light and Playful

It is difficult to be in the right frame of mind for risk-taking when any of the four quadrants of your inner being— body, mind, heart, and soul—are dysfunctional. Adapting playful strategies can be revitalizing and can help you find the needed balance so you can confidently take the risk.

From Confucious to Oz, by the late Vernon Crawford, is an excellent example of synchronicity. His story shows how two separate events can be intuitively connected to culminate in a meaningful conclusion, and how the dreaming mind will help you keep it light and playful with its punny associations.

As Crawford packed his bags for a trip to Singapore, *The Wizard of Oz* was on the TV in the background. The next seemingly unrelated incident occurred when Crawford was met by a close friend in Singapore. He asked what the news was and found out that the prime minister of Singapore had resigned and that the people were turning away from Confucianism.

What did the resignation of Singapore's prime minister have in common with Dorothy, Toto, and the residents of Oz? The intuitive connection became clear for Crawford as he read news accounts quoting Confucius, who had said, "One who has *wisdom* never lacks. One who has *benevolence* is happy. One who has

149

courage is never afraid." Crawford went to sleep and woke up the next morning with the "Aha!" connecting the virtues of the scarecrow, the tin man, and the lion to Confucius's quote. The association of the two distinct events provided Crawford with the intuitive inspiration for his first book, which he called *From Confucius To Oz.*

Relocating is a highly stressful experience during which all sorts of doubts and questions emerge. Making a move is very risky. You might ask, "Is the move something I will regret? What is waiting for me when I get there?" Attempting to interpret the unknown can make anyone a nervous wreck. Your playful antics from the very beginning of your moving adventure can relax your nerves. And the moving experience will be converted into a delightful opportunity to creatively reorganize your possessions.

George and Betsy Greer made a very intuitive move when they relocated to St. Augustine, Florida, from Virginia. After five days of vacation in this enticing locale, they suddenly decided to buy a house there because it "felt right." Although Betsy lacks a background in real estate, she responds to the "bee in her bonnet." To date, she has made five house purchases that have been highly profitable. Intuition sends a strong message to Betsy, driving her to take risks in situations that ultimately have brought her much success.

POWERHUNCH TOOL

Lighten Up and Have Fun

This is a creative way to make risk-taking fun and not scary. You just read about Betsy's adventuresome behavior. Step into her shoes. What would you do to entice your partner to go along with you on another risk-taking adventure? Betsy could have a special "bee in her bonnet" hat that she crafted or bought. Putting this hat on sends a signal to George — it's time to have fun and take some risks.

Be a cut up! Actually, cut up some colored paper and make a badge or adornment for your risk-taking adventure. Take a beach towel or curtain and fashion it into a super duper cape to help you launch your adventure.

Make a montage from magazine and newspaper articles showing what you would like to do. Would you like to have a career as a public speaker? Then cut out pictures of well-known people speaking and insert your photo on top of the speaker's face.

Trust the Process

A high level of trust comes from being strongly connected to your intuition. The absence of trust creates a climate where everyone expects facts without honoring intuitive thinking. Wanting and not settling for anything less than the facts usually leads to a "win–lose opportunity." You can turn this into a "win–win situation" by using intuition, especially if trust precedes it. Without trust there is very little opportunity for intuition to prevail.

151

Becoming a parent in midlife requires a high level of trust that parenting at this age is in the child's best interests. When MJ Ryan, co-founder of Conari Press, was thirty-nine years old, she heard a powerful story about a single woman adopting a baby from China. As she listened to this story, a voice said to her, "You are supposed to do this!" This surprised MJ, since she had never heard a voice before. Her intuition usually came from general flashes of "just knowing." Although the voice was loud and clear, she felt there was no way she could do this. She was still reeling from a break-up with her partner of fourteen years and had helped raise his two children, who were now ready to enter college. Eventually, MJ met another man and . . . five years after the voice first spoke to her, she adopted a baby from China.

Can you trust the intuitive process when you are dealing with money? Who takes the risk when a person advises another on how to invest money? As an intuitive advisor, Victoria Weston takes an incredible risk every time she gives investment advice.

One day, when a client was asking her about Pepsi Cola stock, she suddenly received an image of a Campbell's soup can. She was impressed to honor this image and told her client, "I know you are not interested in this, but I feel like the Campbell's Soup Company is going to be sold, a new CEO elected, and the stock will go up ten points." She gave other specifics to her uninterested client. Then Victoria surprised herself by calling her stockbroker and sharing this spontaneous intuitive vision. Nonplused, the broker gave Victoria news from the rumor mill that this family-owned company would be sold. Victoria honored her vision and took the risk herself by investing in the stock. Two days later, the CEO died, and within ten days, the stock went from $30 a share to $55, finally settling at around $40. Victoria Weston was a prophet who made a profit.

Develop a Strong Belief

Many times a risk involves making a judgment or evaluation about another person's character that is not as obvious to others. Contrary to appearances you know the person can succeed. For example, you might choose to hire a person who has been shunned by others in your department. Developing a strong belief about the other person helps you and them take the risk.

Letting your children know you believe in them can pave the way for gargantuan strides. Dorothy went from working full-time and living alone to living with a man and his three young sons. She needed to find the quiet to listen to her intuition, to find out how to handle the challenges she faced with the children. The oldest boy, age thirteen, almost failed English and became very withdrawn when he realized he had to go to summer school. The child wasn't developing in the area of personal responsibility and still needed to be reminded to do his chores and even brush his teeth. Feeling exasperated, Dorothy connected with her inner source of wisdom to find the right motivational words to say. She started telling the boy that she believed in him and knew he could accomplish anything he set his mind to. She asked him to imagine how she and his dad would feel if he made an effort to do his chores without constant reminders. The boy acknowledged that everyone would be happier and things would be easier for him since the frustration would lessen. Soon, he began doing his chores and even assuming extra responsibilities. Dorothy is so pleased that she took the risk to utter the right words. Taking this risk allowed her to befriend the young boy rather than alienate him and cause more tension in the family.

As the national sales manager of Barefoot Champagne, Randy Arnold sells wine throughout the United States. Letting people in the industry know he is gay was risky, but it worked extremely well for him. Randy not only projected a strong, confident belief about his sexuality, but his employers developed a strong belief in him as a superb salesperson. As a result of making this risky disclosure, his company donates to charity functions in the gay and lesbian community. When a distributor finds out that Randy is gay, they have a niche market for him to utilize and work with. For example, in New York distributors wanted him to go to Chelsea and Fire Island. When the Miami distributor found out that Randy was gay, they requested that he work in South Beach and Key West, where there were prime opportunities. Making the disclosure about his sexuality was easy once Randy heeded the go-ahead signal sent by his intuitive mind.

153

Be an Intuitive Antenna

By now you are regularly tapping into the PowerHunch source you learned about in chapter 1. Here's the rule for risking it. When your body feels smooth, then move! When you are free from any residual aches or pain, it is time to risk it. As you become attuned to your body as an intuitive antenna, you will know instantly whether to go forward with the risk or stay in place.

Doug retrieved critical information from his body during the following PowerShift exercise. After living in his house for two years, it was time for repairs and small remodeling jobs. He looked at the work, which could easily become expensive, and wondered whether he should undertake them or risk buying a new house.

Example: Doug's Home Repair Dilemma

1. **Issue:** Doug asks, "Should I risk buying another home?"
2. **Centering:** Soft music is playing as he looks at a plant on his desk. He affirms, "My intuitive mind will lead me to the right answer about buying a new home."
3. **Receptivity:** Doug breathes deeply by taking several "Total Breaths." On the inhale his stomach goes out and then collapses on the exhale. (See the Breathing and Relaxation Exercises at the end of this book for the complete exercise.) To relax, he does the Count Down Relaxation technique, where he imagines he is walking down ten flights of steps. With each step down, he feels more and more relaxed.
4. **Imagery:** Receiving an answer is difficult. There is some chatter in Doug's mind about the cost of repairs as compared to the down payment on a new home. Then he notices that his stomach feels increasingly full and his throat is very tight. His inner voice tells him to pay attention to this. Doug decides to use the symbol of a house to help in the decision making. An "X" over a house would mean the answer is definitely no. Unfortunately, because of the sensation in his stomach, he has trouble getting the image. He becomes very focused on the full stomach and tightness in his throat.
5. **Deciphering the Image:** The fullness in his body was significant, since it was well past mealtime and he should be feeling hungry, not stuffed. Intuitively, he interprets the fullness to mean that his plate is already full and he has enough to deal with now.

The tightness he feels in his throat triggers memories from his youth when he tried to learn how to smoke cigarettes or drink alcohol. His throat literally closed up and would not allow the smoke or alcohol to pass. They were stopped from entering his body. The result is that he eventually gave up and never developed a habit for either. This memory symbolically says, "Let go of moving. It is not the right time to buy another house."

6. **Incubate:** He is satisfied with the answer.

7. **Go Deeper:** Doug knows this is the right answer. As he associates to the word "fullness," the following words leap up: "abundance," "overstuffed," "bulimia," and "relief." He continues to feel so stuffed in his belly that he wants to vomit. He plainly sees that his overstuffed stomach is uncomfortably stretched to the limit.

8. **Implementation:** At this point, Doug has no intention of adding any additional projects to his life. He will continue to focus on his job and his health. He will now be more vigilant about the messages from his body. The fullness in his belly was pivotal, letting him know he was stuffed to the gills.

155

POWERHUNCH WORKSHOP

Use Your Body as an Intuitive Antenna

As you learn to use your body to validate your intuition, risk-taking will become less and less risky!

Allow three weeks for this workshop. During the first week of practice, focus on five or six minor—nonrisky—decisions you make throughout the day. For example, "Should I go out to lunch today?" "Should I eat Italian food?" "Should I stay at work a little longer?" "What can I get my daughter for her birthday?"

Be vigilant about observing how your body responds to each issue. Does any area feel unsettled after you pose the question? Sweep your body methodically in your mind's eye: from the top of your head to your toes, diagonally across your back, and from your inner organs to your skin. How are you feeling? If the sweep is complete, go ahead—then act. But if the sweep encounters some sort of block, ask yourself what the message is. Note in your journal the ways in which your body responds to these seemingly trivial issues.

During the second week, focus on issues that reflect an everyday concern—making home repairs, buying a new car, or taking a vacation—but that involve slightly more risk. Again, use your body as an antenna.

During the third week, let your issue center on a career or relationship matter, or something more emotionally risky. Your intuitive antenna should be tuned to a much finer frequency now!

8

Timing
Being in the Right Place at the Right Time

The guys that finally rise to the top are a limited group who run on their intuition and say, "Let's go, march!"

—Richard DeVos, cofounder, Amway Corporation

Timing, as they say, is everything.

How did J. K. Rowling and her publishers know the right time to introduce Harry Potter to the world? This book series about a wizard in training has been translated into forty languages and has captured the imagination of over 200 million readers. Rowling has said that the idea fell out of nowhere—someone zapped it into her head.

Fashion designer Donna Karan openly admits to running her company by gut feeling. At the beginning of each fashion season, she scans her wardrobe to intuitively assess what is missing, and then she knows if it's time to conjure up a particular design.

ClifBar became a $40 million company because co-owners Gary Erickson and Lisa Thomas had an intuitive sense of timing. Fifteen years ago, Gary managed a bike-seat manufacturing plant and made Greek pastries with Lisa as a sideline. One day in 1989, Gary was 150 miles into a 175-mile bike ride, when he realized he wanted something different than a PowerBar—the only energy bar on the market at that time. Just like lightning, the flash hit him: It was time to create a competing energy bar!

Gary and Lisa experimented in his mother's kitchen for three years until they found the right recipe, and named it after Gary's father, Clifford. When ClifBar was introduced to the public in 1992, it was an instant hit with cyclists and climbers.

Gary and Lisa worked patiently to make their PowerHunch a success, but sometimes we want something so much that we just can't wait two or three years to take action. Rita told her boyfriend she was in love with him after two dates, even though her stomach was churning. Thomas was so upset that his daughter wasn't invited to a schoolmate's birthday party that he immediately called the girl's mother to complain, only to be told icily that the invitation had just been mailed. Gina and Terry were so eager to launch their gift basket business that they rashly placed an ad before their products were ready for sale—and you can probably guess the outcome. When we act out of desperation or need, that's the logical mind overriding the quiet voice of intuition. At times like this, it's especially important to resist the tendency to rush in and act because we feel that "time is running out." Go to your intuitive timepiece to validate whether it is time to go forth or pull back.

Your Intuitive Timepiece

Years ago, I wasted a lot of time going outside and calling my cat to come inside. Finally, I realized that all I had to do was ask my intuitive alarm clock to let me know when my cat was *ready* to come in. As soon as I "heard" the bell ring, I would go out and call, and the cat would come in. Instant success and less wear and tear on my shoes! When my visual sense strengthened, I could just close my eyes and "see" the time on a clock.

Spending less time calling my cat may sound frivolous to you. Not to me! This is just a small example of how success means being at the right place at the right time. You can be meeting your soulmate, accidentally bumping into the person who hands you the perfect job offer, discovering the health professional who has studied your problem for years, or buying a house on impulse and selling your old house in under a week for a profit. Is it just luck?

Nope. The secret is in paying attention to your intuitive timepiece, the inner certainty that tells you when the time is right.

Your choice of intuitive timepieces is virtually infinite. Here are a few ideas you may want to try.

Emily needed to borrow her uncle's truck to move a bookcase she had just bought at a sidewalk sale. Sometimes he was very responsive to her requests, and at other times he was just too involved in his own business pursuits to even listen. She had to find the perfect time to call. She imagined looking at the electric clock in the bedroom. It read 1:22 P.M. Although it was morning and she was eager to call, she waited until that time. Bull's-eye: Her uncle was thoroughly receptive!

Matthew and his family had been trying to plan a time that the family could take a vacation to Chicago. Unfortunately, he was going to be incredibly busy for the next two months and didn't think this would be possible. After becoming centered and receptive, he posed his issue and sensed the pages of the desk calendar as they flipped through May and into June. They stopped at June thirteenth. He checked his calendar, and saw that day was an unscheduled Saturday. What a perfect opportunity for the family to take a weekend together.

Aaron had been wanting to ask Ariel out on a date for some time. His fear of being rejected prevented him from reaching out. He sat in front of the phone and imagined an hourglass. The sand was running and suddenly stopped. This was a clear signal not to call at that time. He would check in with his intuitive hourglass at another time. When all the sand ran down, he would call.

Rachel wondered, "When will I have a meaningful relationship?" Her timepiece was a bar graph, so she imagined the next five years on the horizontal axis. She labeled them one year, two years, and so on. On the vertical axis she imagined the twelve months of the year. The highest vertical bar indicated the time frame. As she watched in her mind's eye, she saw the next year filling up and stopping at May. Her intuitive mind had given her a signal that this period was ripe for a new relationship.

Ilene wanted to be sure she woke up in time to take her daughter to school. Unfortunately, she woke up in the middle of the night and had trouble getting back to sleep. Worse, the alarm on her clock was broken. As she was drifting off to sleep, she told herself in no uncertain terms, *"You will wake up at seven o'clock."* A few hours later, she had a dream that her cell phone was ringing so loud that it woke her up—just as her digital clock showed "7:00."

POWERHUNCH TOOL

Discover Your Intuitive Timepiece

It's handy to be able to access your alarm clock when you have a question about timing. Your intuitive alarm clock doesn't *have* to be a clock: Anything that helps you gauge time will work: a clock, a calendar, an hourglass, a graph, even a sundial. The first step is to discover the form of your unique timepiece. Here are some suggestions:

Start with something that's an issue for you—the best time to take a vacation, the best time to talk to your child's teacher about her progress, the best time to file divorce papers. Imagine standing in front of a large wall calendar that contains all the months of the coming year. You have a dart in your hand, and you throw it at the calendar. See where it lands and plan your activity for that date.

Do you need to reach out to someone with an apology? What is the best time for them to be receptive and forgive you? Imagine a clock on the wall. The hands are spinning rapidly and come to an abrupt stop. What time is it? To find out if this is in the morning or afternoon, create imagery again showing you if the setting is dark or light.

Practice using your intuitive timepiece. Can you see or sense a time? Start with basic questions like "What time will the mail come? What time will my first phone call come in?" As you begin to get better at this activity, graduate to more difficult questions.

What other kinds of timepieces appeal to you? Try them all out until you find the one that works best for you. Record all your time-piece discoveries in your journal.

Most people feel agitated or excited when the time comes to make a big decision. When we listen to our intuition, however, a peaceful feeling of confidence replaces the anxiety. In this chapter, you will learn how you can use your intuition to full advantage to show "the right time" to:

- make an important decision.
- implement a major change.
- reach out to another person.

Make an Important Decision

Sometimes, the right time to make a decision occurs in the moment. You don't have *time* to weigh the pros and cons. That's when you can rely on your inner alarm clock to guide you in making the best possible decision.

161

Making a Life Commitment

Choosing to spend the rest of your life with someone is a huge decision. Until you speak those words of commitment, waves of doubt may roll through your body and soul.

Bill and Patti had lived together for a number of years. Was it time to get married? This was a scary area for Patti, who had had some pretty rocky relationships before she met Bill. Whenever Patti even considered this question, her mind shut down and her stomach started churning. Patti decided it was time to ask her intuition for help.

To become centered, she had a cup of green tea and relaxed with some breathing. Then she asked her first question: "What is to come of my relationship with Bill?" She closed her eyes and sat there without receiving any imagery. Then she heard bells ringing outside. Was this environmental cue foreshadowing wedding bells? Just then, she heard the mail being delivered. She acted on a hunch to look in the mailbox for another clue. In an advertisement from a home store, her eye immediately fell on a garden arch for sale. This was the same kind of arch she had always imagined herself getting married under.

The thought of marriage was still scary, and prompted her next question: "Will I be happy if I marry Bill?" Again, no image. But outside, a car went by and she got an immediate mental image of a family in the car taking a vacation and having fun. It was clear to her that the answer to her question was that she could find fulfillment by marrying Bill. Yet, the fear and queasiness remained.

Then she asked, "Why am I afraid of getting married?" Into her mind floated an image of a prison and the fleeting thoughts no escape, torture, pain, unbearable suffering, sickness, Mother. Yikes! She associated marriage with her mother, who was very unhappy in her marriage. But because of societal notions about marriage and divorce, mother stayed in the marriage, unhappy and increasingly resentful toward her husband. Mother finally ended up getting sick and dying—which Patti always connected to her unhappy marriage. Though witnessing this link in the association chain was painful, Patti was pleased to unveil the fears she was harboring in her psyche that kept her from entering a lasting relationship.

Patti's final question on this subject was, "How do I resolve this issue about marriage?" The image she got was of a pregnant woman doing yoga. The associations to this image were: deep breathing, relaxing, letting go, surrendering, allowing fears to come up, talking to Bill, loving, and being loved. She sensed that she needed to be willing to be honest and express herself. She also needed to release the pictures that she had been holding of being imprisoned. Sharing these insights with Bill led to a cathartic discussion, and they decided to set a date for the wedding.

POWER**HUNCH** TOOL

The Right Time to Act

The rapid tick of your intuitive clock can signal immediate action. Or, if you hear a slow beat, that would suggest you slow down for a month or two until the time is right.

The question is, "How can you sense the beating of the clock?"

Let's use a transportation analogy to help you pace your action. Ask, "Is this the time to act?" and then let a transportation mode spontaneously come into view. This can be a rocket, plane, train, bus, bicycle, roller blades, or even a slow boat to China. As you imagine each of these transportation modes does one light up? For example, when you see a border of white light around the rocket, you know it is time for immediate action.

A Great Idea

163

Have you ever wanted to implement a great idea but felt the time wasn't right? Dan Stifter, director of new products for Jerome Foods, was sitting at his desk one day, trying to figure out how he could apply his past experience in the food business to a new Jerome turkey product. Suddenly, he made an intuitive connection between what his team did at Sargento with string cheese in terms of packaging and convenient consumption. Seconds later, the idea of GobbleStix was born as Dan envisioned this smaller, individually packaged hand-held turkey stick snack for toddlers and small kids.

POWER**HUNCH** TOOL

Time to Implement a Great Idea

I'm sure many great ideas come into your head as you are sitting at your desk or even watching TV. You've probably even said something like, "Fruit-juice flavored water? I thought of that *years* ago!" Why not implement one of them now? Start by writing down your great ideas in your PowerHunch Journal. Then read them over, and take them seriously. Which one could you actually put into practice?

A New Work Zone

How do you know the time is right to go into a new work zone? You can hear your intuitive timepiece ring out just like a blaring alarm prodding you to wake up and take action. Basketball coach Lenny Wilkens is legendary in sports circles. He is the only person named among the National Basketball Association's (NBA) top ten coaches and fifty greatest players of all time. I wonder how many people know that a gut feeling initially led him into the NBA.

When he was drafted by the St. Louis Hawks right out of college, he was a first-round pick. However, Lenny did not go out to see them because he had received an assistantship to work on his masters degree at Boston College. During that time, he went to see his first professional basketball game, which happened to be the Hawks playing the Celtics for the world championship. When he saw the Hawks play, he realized how good they were as a team and intuitively knew he could make the squad. He was right. He made the team and continued to play in the NBA for fifteen years.

Lenny found his right time for action when the Hawks moved to Atlanta. Following a strong dispute, Lenny was traded to Seattle. After his first year with Seattle, the coach was fired and the general manager wanted Lenny to become a player coach. Initially Lenny didn't want to assume that role, but then he had a PowerHunch: He realized it was the right time to try a coaching position. For twenty-seven years he coached in Seattle, Portland, Cleveland, and Atlanta. Recently, his intuitive time ticker propelled him away from Atlanta to become the coach for the Toronto Raptors. Listening to his intuition has been timely as he was always guided to the right place at the right time.

A metaphor for making a career change could be a revolving door. Many times people seem to go round and round until they finally stop when a clear cut decision surfaces. Sharolyn has been thinking about making a career change, but she's very unclear on when—even if—the time is right. To find out, she became centered and receptive. First, she asked, "Is this the time for a change?" and she got the green light. OK, the time was right. Next she wanted to find out, "What season would be best to make the change?" She was surprised to find herself visualizing four oil paintings on a wall, each depicting a seasonal change. They were dark, and she couldn't see too well. Then the lights went on above the Spring and Summer paintings. She took a break, and came back to visualize Spring, and then Summer. All of a sudden, again to her surprise, a rectangle entered the picture. What was that all about? She came up with associations: balanced, abstract, plain, geometric, parallelogram. And then ... board. Aha—she was very bored with her job. That was certainly true! Again she went back to the words "Spring" and "Summer." Summer was instantly illuminated. So, this coming summer, which is five months away, Sharolyn will begin a job search.

165

POWER**HUNCH** TOOL

Time to Go Into a New Zone

Is this the right time for you to go into a new work zone? Here's an opportunity to practice the solo brainstorming you learned in chapter 4. First thing in the morning, sit in silence for a few minutes and then ask, "Is it time for me to enter a new work zone?" Pick up your pen and start writing. By the third or fourth line, you will be getting excellent advice about this timely decision.

When finished, close your eyes and visualize a "yes" or "no" signal. This can be a traffic light going on and off, a "thumbs up" or "thumbs down," or a neon "yes" or "no" sign.

You can really have fun playing with images to get a yes or no. Bring in the other senses. Can you hear a bell ringing clearly, or is it barely audible? Do you get a pungent, stinky, or sweet aroma? Ask again, and lick your lips to get the taste of it. What does your body feel like after you ask? Is there a rocky feeling or a smoothness? You can also test the feeling sense out as you imagine someone handing you an offer. How does it feel? Hot or cold? Play around with the senses, and soon you will be doing this automatically.

Leaving Security Behind

How do you know when it is time to leave a secure job or home or relationship or lifestyle and go off to something new?

Ellen's husband was offered a great job in a small town in Louisiana. All the job offers he received in California had not even come close to this offer; yet she and her husband were reluctant to leave their favorite state and all of their friends to live in a small town in the deep South. They were both tired of losing sleep over this decision.

Ellen posed the issue to her intuitive mind: "Is it time for my husband to accept the job offer in Lake Charles, Louisiana?" To find an answer, she went outside and did a walking meditation. She kept her eyes softly focused on the ground ahead of her. As she moved in this slow and deliberate manner, her focus became concentrated on the movement of her body, the air as it moved past her, the expansion and contraction of her lungs, and the gradations of the pavement. She relaxed by softening every body part consciously. So mesmerizing was the movement that after a while, she felt almost as if her body was standing still and the world was going by.

The road Ellen was walking on seemed to narrow, and she saw a golden glow shine on the path. She experienced a sense of well-being in her body and felt that all was right with the world. She felt that she had her message: The way forward narrowed. It was no longer the wide path of California, where all the support that she could want, in every form, was readily available. Yet Ellen had a strong feeling that it would be good, and this was the time to accept this golden opportunity. She associated to the word "golden" and got: lucky, blessed, filled with good things, rich, and never decaying.

Ellen shared her intuitive insights with her husband. They decided that if it still felt right in the morning, he would accept the job offer. When he called the next day to accept the job, he was immediately told they would give him a $12,000 signing bonus in addition to paying his relocation expenses. For Ellen, this was the right time and it immediately looked like gold.

Let me remind you of the chapter 3 credo: Shift needs to happen. This shift is so needed to sweep the weary decision-maker out of the indecisive waters. Carmen felt that it was time for her three-year-old, Peter, to enter preschool. The catch was that he was still in diapers. She was torn between two schools. One was a Montessori school, which had an excellent reputation, a small student body, a neat and clean playroom, and staff that would help with potty training. The other was called the Farm School. It was older and more relaxed, with a little barnyard of tame animals and well-used play equipment. They preferred incoming three-year-olds to be already out of diapers. Carmen thought the Farm School looked like a lot of fun. The new term for both schools started soon, so Carmen needed to make a decision. She used the PowerShift for added insight.

167

1. **Issue:** The question is, "Which preschool is best for Peter right now?"
2. **Centering:** She affirms, "I intuitively know which preschool is best for Peter." She listens to the ceiling fan hum rhythmically as it slowly spins.
3. **Receptivity:** Carmen progressively relaxes her body, starting with her toes, letting them get warm and heavy, and moves up her body until she is very relaxed. (See Appendix for the complete exercise). She visualizes herself lying in the sun on a

tropical beach. The fan becomes the sound of the waves and the ocean breeze.

4. **Imagery:** First she sees a large field of plants. This is a peaceful scene, and then a group of children appear from under the leaves and they begin playing. Now the scene is rollicking and joyous. A clown appears, and the kids applaud enthusiastically. This feels like the key image.

5. **Deciphering the Image:** Carmen is not a clown fan, but she is drawn to the image. This isn't a regular circus clown. He is more like the guy in the McDonald's commercials. This feels right—it's Ronald McDonald. And then it hits Carmen—"Old McDonald had a farm." Aha! The Farm School. The field of plants was a "nursery" for nursery school. The children coming out of the leaves signified growing. The Farm School would be the place for Peter to grow, peacefully and joyfully.

6. **Incubate:** She is satisfied with the answer.

7. **Go Deeper:** Not needed.

8. **Implementation:** Carmen calls the Farm School and explains that she would like to enroll her son, but he is still in diapers. The director kindly replies that would be fine. Her own grandson hadn't been interested in using the potty at three, but when he started preschool and saw the other kids using the potty and wearing "big-kid" pants, the problem resolved itself in a few days. Now Peter is enrolled and ready to start in two weeks.

Buying a Car

Many people approach car buying time with their logical mind. Making the rounds of dealers and reading through *Consumer Reports* are only two of the time-consuming activities related to the car buying ritual. In contrast, the intuitive mind sends the "buy now" signal and sends up an image of what car to buy.

A new car was on the agenda for Celia. Though her intuitive mind immediately sent her a picture of a sports car, her logical mind directed her to review *Consumer Reports* findings to determine what kind of car she *should* buy. Celia really wanted a sports car, but her logical mind kept telling her to be practical.

As Celia tried to make a decision, she suddenly began reflecting on her lifelong love for cars, and the times she and her dad would go to buy cars together. For Celia, cars were not just a means of getting from here to there. She really loved their shape and beauty, and remembered growing up in the 1950s when seeing how the models looked every year was something to anticipate with excitement. In the end, Celia spent a year looking at cars and analyzing their pros and cons. Finally, she knew when it was time to act and honored the picture sent by her intuitive mind: She bought a sports car and fulfilled her heart's desire.

Canceling a Vacation

A considerable amount of time and energy is expended in planning a vacation. When an unexpected event arises, the reality of taking a vacation becomes questionable. This is the time to rely on the far seeing ability of the intuitive mind to know if a cancellation is really necessary.

Estelle and her husband Ted were alarmed: Ted's eighty-year-old father, who lived three hours away, had just been taken to the hospital with chest pains. They were scheduled to fly off in two days for a long-anticipated vacation to the Caribbean. Estelle was in a panic. She couldn't make a rational decision, so she sought an instant answer from her intuitive mind.

After making some bodily adjustments with the PowerShift, she asked, "Should we cancel our vacation?" The image that came to her was a car. That was puzzling, since they were planning to fly. As she freely associated with the word "car," she retrieved the following associations: drive, flexibility, go, stop, and change direction. The words "flexibility" and "go" were lit up in green. She quickly realized that her husband had a great deal of "flexibility" in his schedule the next day and he should "go" and visit his father. The next day, Ted made the three-hour drive to the hospital. He spent the day there with his mother while the tests were being run, and actually sensed improvement in his father throughout the day. Both father and mother encouraged Ted and Estelle to go on their planned vacation. Later, it turned out that the pains were angina—something for Ted's dad to take seriously, but not life-threatening.

Implement a Major Change

Career changes can be riveting. Whether you are leaving a business voluntarily or involuntarily, the logical mind wonders, "Is it really time to change?" Many people shudder when they hear the word "transition," and automatically assume they will be catapulted onto the rockiest road or stormiest sea. For many, this fear is justified— especially when downsizing forces employees to leave seemingly secure positions. Many do make a successful transition simply because they knew it was the right time to make the change.

Since work occupies a majority of our time, it is not surprising that most of the transition decisions have to do with work. In this section, you will find examples of the right time to look for a new start and to retire.

Time for a New Start

Deciding whether to start a new business can present quite a challenge. Karen Sterk was intuitively led to acquire her Grand Rapids, Michigan, fitness studio, "Change Of Heart." After four years of involvement, her partner Chris, who owned the studio space, wanted to dissolve the company, and sell the memberships to an interested athletic club. Karen was perplexed and dismayed because she was told to vacate the space in six months. She struggled for a week over what to do next. Her intuitive connection knew it was definitely time to attract new business and keep the studio. So for two months Karen affirmed daily, "I will own this studio," although she had no idea how this would be accomplished. Just before the six months were up, Chris came to her and said, "I'm going to let you buy me out." He even agreed to finance the buy. This all happened twelve years ago, and today Karen's Change Of Heart studio is a thriving fitness center.

A business owner was the last thing Ken Rose thought he would be. He had been there and done that for almost twenty years, and for the last five years had been content to be an employee, designing and installing kitchen cabinets and counter tops for someone else. One day, a flyer addressed to Ken's boss literally fell into Ken's hands as he was picking up the mail in the morning. A kitchen cabinet business was for sale. Although Ken was not looking for change, he called on a whim and made an appointment to meet with the broker. The price was right, and Ken suddenly knew it was time to become a business owner again. His business, Great Kitchens, is now thriving. As Ken described his story to me, he said, it was "a coincidence" that he saw the flyer. Was it a coincidence, or an environmental cue that led him onto a new path?

POWER**HUNCH** TOOL

Looking for a New Start

Become vigilant to the environmental cues that are all around you. They can be found in a flyer, neon sign, or even eavesdropping on a conversation. First, become clear that you are looking for a new start in a career, relationship, or participation in a new extracurricular activity. Then, pose the question to your intuitive mind about how to make this new start. Begin to notice the environmental cues that can point you in the direction of your next job adventure, for example, or even show you how to tweak your current job to make it more interesting. After finding your cue, does something tug at your heart saying, "This is the time for a new start?"

Time to Retire

At age fifty-five, Jenny had a strong desire to retire from her stressful job. She seemed a little young, though, and she wondered whether that was the right choice. Would she have enough income to be able to live comfortably if she retired at fifty-five?

She was thinking about this while lying by the pool during her vacation—it was either take a vacation or have a nervous breakdown. Feeling very relaxed, she decided it was a great time to ask her intuitive mind what to do: "Should I retire at age 55?" Right away, she smelled the lovely aroma of roses. Then she saw herself sitting in her office with lots of work, but she was still smelling this fragrant rose. She smiled, realizing that what she needed was not retirement, but creating more time to "smell the roses." She decided then and there to take advantage of her paid vacations and get out of town to relax more often. This would allow her to periodically escape the stress, take the focus off the need to retire immediately, and allow her to work until she felt financially secure enough to retire.

172

POWERHUNCH TOOL

Time to Retire

Here's where you can have some fun eliciting images to help you decide about retirement. Pose the question to your intuitive mind as a baseball question: Should you stay in the game, or retire? When you step up to bat, see how you do. Will you get a hit, even a home run, or strike out? A strikeout or a walk may signal it's time to think about retiring.

Reach Out to Another Person

As manager of human resources, Cori counsels employees and mediating groups through the changes the company experiences.

One day, she suddenly felt it was time to call Gerry, a co-worker in the building. When Cori got her on the line, Gerry said she was just thinking about coming down to her office for some assistance with a difficult situation. They met and resolved the matter right away—perfect timing. While this type of encounter is subtle and not earth-shattering, the right timing connection kept a potentially messy situation from escalating.

Our dreams are wonderful informants, telling us when to reach out to another person. Pat Sullivan had a brief but crystal clear dream. In the dream, she was tearfully embracing her ninety-year-old grandma in North Carolina. This dream image showed her that a visit to Grandma was imperative. This wasn't exactly the timing her logical mind had planned, which was to drive from Washington, D.C., to Boston the next day with her fiancé, John, to visit his folks. To her surprise, John agreed to the change in plans. Pat called her grandparents. One of her cousins answered the phone and said, "Grandma is even more feeble than she was. She probably won't know you because she is pretty much out of it these days, but come on down." So Pat and John drove south instead of north as planned. To everyone's amazement, Grandma was really alert. She knew Pat, and she even knew John, whom she had only met once before, years ago. Pat knew this moment of clarity with her grandmother had been a gift, and the next day she and John continued on to Boston feeling warm and loved. Two days later, Grandma died. Pat was grateful she had listened to Grandma calling out to her in the dream so she could see her in person one last time.

173

POWERHUNCH WORKSHOP

Time to Use Your Intuitive Timepiece

The benefit of working with the intuitive mind is that answers to questions often come quickly and in a punny way. Before you begin this workshop, listen to this example of what I mean:

Zoe wanted to know, "When should I take my trip to DisneyWorld?" When she got centered and relaxed, her intuitive mind presented her with the image of a toy soldier. She associated with words like uniform, army, bugle, and drum and suddenly blurted out the word "march!" Of course! She would take the trip in March.

Week 1: Play with eliciting imagery for your intuitive timepiece, as we did at the beginning of this chapter. Have a good time, and don't worry about finding out if the "time is right" for anything in particular. Try to become familiar with as many modes of intuitive timekeeping as possible—each one can help you in a slightly different way.

Week 2: Work with your intuitive timepiece and learn how it communicates with you. Use those timepieces that you feel most comfortable with. Again, have fun with simple matters.

Week 3: Use the PowerShift to help you find answers to your serious time quandaries. Pose your questions carefully. Act on those answers that resonate deep within you. Record what happens in your PowerHunch Journal. Was your timing right?

Week 4: Work with your dreams. Begin to notice the references to time that unexpectedly pop onto the screen of your awareness. For example, suppose you dream, "I was in Paris and had to get to the airport to make a 4 P.M. plane. The time was 3 P.M. I felt rushed and concerned that I wouldn't make the plane." What is this telling you about your timing? Perhaps you are not quite ready to make the "French connection," or travel abroad, or simply go forth on a project. You can also program a dream about time. Simply ask, for example, "Is it time for me to move?" "Should I start a new business now?" Remember to tell yourself to remember your dreams when you wake up.

9

People-Smarts
Enhancing Your Relationships

As I sit and talk with people and react with them, what I should say next and how I should behave in this situation is all done intuitively.

—Barrie Bechtel, Rapistan Demag Corporation

I look back at my dating escapades with amusement. Many of the guys who seemed seriously interested in me never called back. I would play the daisy game to find out what was really going on. Irreverently mutilating nature's finest work, I would peel the daisy petals back and say, "He loves me. He loves me not." In those days, I had not yet activated my intuitive antenna. Now I know that I can use my inner radar to reach into another person's mind and heart to assess their true thoughts and feelings.

Relationships are complex! We need all the help we can get to unravel the perennial mystery "What makes Josh or Jenny tick?" Intuition is the inner barometer that provides an accurate read about how people really feel.

Shannon's relationship with Alex is very confusing. They enjoy going out to shows and dinner, but he refuses to bring her home to meet any of his family. Her logical mind tells her to look at his positive attributes—he has a stable job and earns a good living. Meanwhile, she ignores her intuition's loud pleas to "Leave now!"

She could take a lesson from Harriet, who says, "Today I was talking with my father, who is in a conflicted relationship with my brother and his son. There is a lot of anger and hurt in this relationship due to my father's controlling personality. I seem to be the only one who can talk to my father without getting him upset. I wanted to help, but didn't want to interfere. I asked my intuition if I should say something about this situation. In a few moments an easy opportunity opened to lovingly suggest a different course of action. It averted more pain and hurt."

Joe used his intuition when interviewing job applicants. The skills one candidate possessed were perfect for the job and her references were great, but Joe had a lingering "feeling" that she wasn't right. To everyone's surprise, Joe rejected her. Days later, his mysterious veto was validated when she admitted she was having great personal challenges and her performance at her current job was problematic. Joe was grateful that he listened when his intuitive voice said, "Not now."

For days, Michael was having flashes about a friend. Her name would come into his mind from nowhere in particular. Finally, Michael called to check on her. She immediately burst into tears and told him she had had several upsetting events over the past couple of days, and she was so glad he had called.

Your PowerHunch tools will help you read others and respond appropriately so you can get the most out of any human relationship. You can deepen your understanding of potential partners, family members, friends, work associates, potential employees—virtually anyone. Intuition can help you figure out an individual's perplexing dynamics and anticipate his or her unspoken needs. As you listen carefully to what the person is saying, you will become more attuned to what really lies underneath the words.

Your People-Smarts meter can help you get past any fear or posturing that prevents authentic communication. Bonnie expresses this so well. She says, "I have discovered some blocks to using intuition and hearing my inner voice. All of my life I have been conditioned to meet other people's needs. My dad needed me to be good in math; my mother needed me to be soft spoken; my boss needs me to be assertive. I got so good at listening to other people and determining what they want from me, that I forgot how to listen to myself. Developing my intuition is a joyous

176

opportunity to quiet the needs of others and gain inroads on knowing what I want."

Leo Buscaglia talked about his deep desire to communicate authentically when he was standing before an audience, and to express what he was feeling in the most entertaining and simplest way possible. In order to do that, he had to get in touch with himself. When he was, he found that his audience understood him in an intuitive way. He didn't have to use the brilliant words. Leo found there is no better way to communicate than to get in touch with our true humanity. In so doing, we become aware of the humanity in others. Then, Leo said, you can fall on your face, you can slip and fall off the stage, you can do anything, but everybody understands it because we are relating to each other, human being to human being. By going with the flow, the intuitive mind becomes available.

The key to communication is understanding how each individual is thinking and feeling. Beginning with your family, through school, work, dating, life partnership, parenthood ... you are significantly relating to others. The exercises in this chapter will help you use PowerHunch Principles to find the best way to communicate and get the most out of your life relationships. We will explore:

177

- intuition and social relationships.
- intuition and family.
- intuition's role in the workplace.

Intuition and Social Relationships

The ever-burning intuitive light can provide clarification during friendship, courtship, marriage, and divorce.

Friendship

Let's go fishing again for a symbol to clarify a puzzling personal dynamic. You'll cast your line into the ocean of intuition to net the enigmatic image. Renée is thinking about a budding friendship with a woman she met through her social club. She would like to interact more with Sharon, who seems somewhat reserved. To discover the potential of this friendship, Renée transports herself mentally to her special place by a river. She imagines herself sitting on a beach towel looking at the moving water. The sun warms her face, and the river and surrounding trees give off a fresh scent. As she begins to think of this budding friendship, she gets an image of a crab. This immediately reminds her of many things, including the crab's sharp claws and hard shell. Slow moving also comes to mind. She realizes that, like the crab, Sharon has a hard shell that makes her difficult to approach. This image shows Renée that trust is needed, and trust comes with time. If she waits, Sharon will reveal more of her needs and desires.

As you discovered in chapter 5, dreams do reveal what's going on. Roz was questioning her wavering friendship with Nelly. They had been friends since college, eight years before. Now, however, Roz felt uncomfortable in their relationship, and could not quite figure out why. Here is her illuminating dream.

178

> *I was in a social setting and Nelly was being strong and intimidating. She pulled out a gun and shot someone. Then she pointed the gun at me and was going to shoot me. Then Nelly said she'll decide whether to spare me. I wasn't completely afraid. Then another woman came along who held a gun over Nelly.*

When she thought about the dream, Roz immediately saw how controlling Nelly was in their relationship. She was the one who called "the shots." Roz was uncomfortable with this one-sided relationship and planned to talk to Nelly about creating more give and take interaction.

Courtship

Here's a brief dream that was eye opening about a relationship dilemma. Carol had a serious conflict with her boyfriend that lasted two days. She invited her dreaming mind to reveal the best way to resolve it. The next night, she dreamed she was playing tug-of-war and dropped her end of the rope. Game over. Upon awakening, she knew she had to give in and apologize. Feeling peaceful about initiating action, she and her boyfriend had a loving, understanding conversation, and the conflict ended.

Have you ever noticed how a strong bodily cue can literally push you into an introspective posture? Charlie periodically got upset with his girlfriend because she sometimes read in bed in the middle of the night, waking him, upsetting him, and setting off a string of negative feelings. One night, he decided that instead of getting agitated he would ask his intuitive mind, "What can I do to work with this issue in a positive way?" He felt his head nodding back and forth, although, in reality, he was laying still. As the rocking grew more pronounced, he free-associated to the feeling. Aha! Being rocked. He realized he needed to cradle that part of himself that gets upset. He needed to restore his own balance and clarity before he said or did anything. He fell back to sleep. Upon awakening, Charlie knew what words to use to address the problem and to maintain equilibrium in this relationship.

179

Here's another dating dilemma. Jerry, the office manager of a physical fitness studio, was good at his job: maintaining the records, supervising a staff of ten, and relating to customers. But he was less adept in his personal life, and couldn't decide if he should enter into a more meaningful relationship with Andrea, the woman he was currently dating.

He closed his eyes and imagined himself walking in a wooded area until he came upon a stream. Stopping to take a sip, he noticed several objects in the water: a tent, a bike, a doll, a cocktail glass, and a photo of a beautiful woman. He realized that his intuitive mind was highlighting the attributes in Andrea that appeal to him. The tent signified their mutual love of the outdoors; the bike showed a desire to bike together; the doll represented children, which they both wanted; the cocktail glass reminded him they like to go out occasionally; and the photo showed him how attractive he finds Andrea.

POWER**HUNCH** TOOL

Getting to Know You Better

Here's an opportunity to practice retrieving imagery to help you better understand the object of your affection. Sue practiced this before every new date. She asked, "What will happen in my relationship with Tom?" She saw the image of a rising yellow sun. This seemed to her to represent a relationship that was just rising or coming into view. When she asked, "What will happen with Vince?" an igloo appeared. This image was too frozen for comfort.

You can also create imagery. By now you know if you can't inwardly see the imagery, you can find a way to sense the pictures and symbols. To find out if you have found the right person, imagine the person as a flower. Does the flower stand up or wilt? What special care does it need to survive? Or imagine you are talking to the flower. What does the flower tell you about caring for it so it can survive?

Do you want to get to know someone better from the inside out? Then play the imagery game. But remember, first take the time to become centered and receptive.

Marriage

When Tina Rosato went to buy stamps at the post office, little did she know that the man who sold them to her would become her husband. The day they met, she was captivated by his smile. The next time, when he recited two lines of poetry, she mentioned that she loves poetry. That did it! He gave her a book of his poetry on her next visit. After she read some, she responded by telling him he was a brave human being. The content astounded her. Their relationship began because she honored her intuitive mind, which prompted her to go back and talk about his poetry.

How well do you know your partner? Your logical mind might say, "I know all I need to know!" but your intuitive mind would reply, "Not well enough." No matter how long you have been together, there are still some surprises. Terri wanted to know how to improve her relationship with her husband. Although they got along well, they were more like roommates than husband and wife. Both were super busy, with many responsibilities that precluded spending time together. Terri wanted to know how to approach him so they could deepen their relationship.

Terri closed her eyes, became receptive, and heard a song from her childhood about a little "toy car." Using word association, she made a train of associations. Toy car → real car → travel → time together in a car. Terri knew that her husband enjoyed taking long weekend drives. She would suggest this and support doing it more regularly, which would provide them with special time alone.

181

Karen wanted to know if she and her husband should start an event planning business together. She wondered how her husband felt about this new venture. At that moment she looked up at the sky. Suddenly, among the puffy white clouds, a bolt of lightning and a heavy storm cloud appeared. She saw her husband's face, not in the puffy whites, where she would have expected it, but in the center of the storm. That was a strong sign not to begin a business together. They have been happily married for twenty-eight years, and successful in their separate careers, but this sign made it clear: Trying to work as partners could lead to a competitive rather than a supportive relationship. Her intuitive mind was very clear about showing her that underneath the surface, her husband was not receptive to starting a business partnership.

POWERHUNCH TOOL

Unmasking a Partner's Thoughts

This is an easy and fun tool. Just as Karen did, look to the cloud formations to understand what your partner really thinks. Pose the question, get receptive, and watch the moving images unfold. Remember: Your intuitive mind is doing the interpretation.

Divorce

What happens when the dance with the dream mate has terminated? How does the intuitive mind forge through the bitterness and recriminations to provide the spark that enables us to reinterpret the situation and see the person we once loved in a more neutral light?

Roger said that intuition helped him relate more successfully to his ex-wife. One day, he realized that his ex-wife had another role besides his personal antagonist: the mother of his children. He thought, "I can honor her and love her as their mother. Personally, I want nothing to do with her. But intuitively, I know I can relate to her respectfully as the mother of my children." Now, whenever he begins to react negatively to something she does, he focuses on this intuitive awareness and lets the negativity fade.

Susan was in a long-distance relationship with Ernesto, a man she thought was her ideal partner. One day he called to tell her that he was moving in with a woman he had recently met. She was shocked. Six months later, she wanted to move on and release the grief she felt every time she thought about him, so she used the PowerShift to get a deeper understanding of his character.

1. **Issue:** Sue asked, "How can I let go of a lost love relationship?"
2. **Centering:** Susan sat on a couch facing the cascading green oak leaf vines that had grown across the patio walls. She

noticed that each oak leaf had three lobes, which signify to her the balance of body, mind, and spirit.

3. **Receptivity:** As she began to trace the outer points of the leaves with her eyes, she used the Hang-Sah breath to relax her body. (See the Breathing and Relaxation Exercises at the end of this book for complete instructions.)

4. **Imagery:** As she began to elicit the image of Ernesto, he turned into an armadillo with a hard protective shell. She felt that this man wanted to hide or protect himself from her. She knocked persistently on the thick bony shell of the armadillo until two eyes peaked out, looking annoyed. She asked the armadillo what she could do to give up her attachment to him, so that she could go on with her life. Unemotionally, he told her to "get over it." She extended her arm to shake hands with him in a sign of friendship. While he accepted her handshake, he kept his arm stiff, to keep the distance between them.

5. **Deciphering the Image:** This graphic interpretation of keeping the distance was obvious. Susan had hoped for a more supportive and helpful response.

6. **Incubate:** She went to bed and slept on it.

7. **Go Deeper:** Later that week Susan researched the armadillo on the Internet, and was surprised to find out that it comes from South America, which is where Ernesto was born and raised. She realized from her conversation with the armadillo that it was her problem to resolve, and she did need to get over it on her own. She needed to forgive, and that was her responsibility and work—not his.

8. **Implementation:** She realized that she had held onto this bad situation by refusing to forgive. At that moment, her Bible fell open to Psalm 108. When she read the line "O God, my heart is ready," it was a clear sign to move on. Intuitively, she felt that she was now ready to let go of this hurtful relationship.

POWERHUNCH TOOL

Have a Parting Resolution

Is there someone you would like to release? Let the environment help you. Reach out for the first object that commands your attention. You may look up and see this object or even hold it in your hand. It can be on the table, in your jacket, from your purse, or in another room. Let the object speak to you intuitively. What is it telling you about letting go? For example, Joe didn't know how to release his ex-wife. He looked up and saw a vase of roses. Some were dying—the bloom had fallen off that rose! As he focused on a bud about to blossom, he knew a new relationship was waiting to bloom when he finally let go.

184

Intuition and Family

Have you ever felt so frustrated and angry with a parent that you wanted to shake him or her by the shoulders and say "Wake up!"? Kevin was upset with his father, who was planning to marry a woman his dad hardly knew. Dad was going to sell his house in order to join assets with his new love. Kevin knew he had to turn his negativity around, so he accessed his inner voice for guidance and heard the words, "Just let it be, just love your dad." Kevin then realized what his logical mind couldn't say: His dad needed his love more than his judgment or anger. By understanding these latent needs, Kevin and his dad both came through a challenging time. In this section you will learn how your intuition can deepen your understanding of your children and parents in order to strengthen the relationship.

Children

Madeline was getting married again, and her teenage daughter, Sarah, insisted on making her wedding gown. Unfortunately, she didn't know how to sew! To help her learn, Madeline let her stitch the easier pieces. One day, shortly before the wedding, she was startled by an inner vision of Sarah sewing two of the skirt panels together backward. Madeline dismissed the thought—she certainly did not want to offend her daughter by sharing this intuitive flash. The wedding was soon, and her daughter was sensitive to criticism, so she let the hunch go. A few minutes later, however, she heard a mournful, "Oh, no!" and knew exactly what had happened. Her daughter had stitched the panels together backward and had to rip them out. Madeline was sorry the sewing wasn't going well, but she was glad she hadn't said anything. Her daughter would learn eventually—criticism from her mom, intuitive or not, wouldn't help! Recalling the inner vision of the panels sewn together, she acknowledged that her intuition gave her a clear preview of upcoming events.

Jim came to acknowledge the power of intuition after it helped him resolve a problem between himself and his youngest daughter. They just couldn't communicate beyond surface matters. In fact, they rarely talked at all. Using the PowerShift, Jim became centered, receptive, and was able to use imagery to "get into her shoes"—literally. She had about fifty pairs of shoes. As soon as he mentally opened her closet and started going through her shoes, it became clearer to Jim that she didn't know her role or whose shoes she was supposed to fit into—her mother's or her father's. This was just the beginning of intuitive input that healed their relationship. By feeling his daughter's anxiety, Jim started letting her know she was unique. He started listening to *what* she was saying, rather than responding to the words she was using. Her compulsion for buying shoes diminished, and talking to each other became easier. If Jim hadn't connected with this powerful intuitive imagery, they would still be two total strangers connected only by their bloodline.

Pete was going to be a father for the first time, and felt apprehensive about this new role. He wanted to understand, "What is the key to being a good father?" As he relaxed into receptivity, he smelled the fresh scent of new-mown grass, which suggested to him "a newly seeded lawn with grass sprouts beginning to grow." Associating to his "new lawn" image, he elicited the words "sprout," "grass," "sod," "seed," "fertilize," "water," and then felt moved by the words "tender care." At "tender care," he associated to tender loving care and then to nurturing. He decided that the key to being a good father is to be a nurturing parent.

The role of step-parenting is a delicate endeavor—no matter how old the children are. Meg felt emotionally abused by her thirty-two-year-old stepson, Michael. The pain and anger were so intense, she couldn't make a rational decision about him. She turned to her intuitive mind to help her resolve this family affair.

1. **Issue:** Meg asked, "How can I heal my relationship with my stepson?"
2. **Centering:** Meg affirmed, "There is a perfect solution to heal the rage and resentment Michael holds for me." She focused on the image of a candle flame and noticed it expanding.
3. **Receptivity:** She used the Reenergizing Breath. (See the Breathing and Relaxation exercises at the end of this book for complete instructions.). Angry thoughts kept rushing in to invade the peace she felt from this breath work. She continued to breathe and went back to the centering affirmations.
4. **Imagery:** The image of a large dog came up.
5. **Deciphering the Image:** What were the qualities of the dog? First she saw it as loud and vicious—very frightening. This was how she saw Michael when he lost his temper. Then Meg noticed the dog was strong, and realized how she appreciated her stepson's strength and capability. She also saw the dog as well groomed and attractive, which corresponded to Michael's appearance. The dog lay down, and Meg noticed that it was lovable. Michael could show love when he felt grounded and confident. Meg found it easy to stroke the dog when it was in this nonthreatening posture.
6. **Incubate:** Not needed.

7. **Go Deeper:** An image of a computer appeared near the dog. The computer brought up the idea of e-mail, which Meg loved to use. She could be honest and open expressing her thoughts and feelings with e-mail, and decided she should communicate with Michael in this way. She needed to release the anger and hurt feelings that still lingered from Michael's verbal attacks. They had not talked because Michael became enraged, abusive, and unwilling to listen.

Meg noticed that the image had a distinct black border, flashing on and off, demanding her attention. This represented a boundary. She would find an appropriate way to set reasonable boundaries for her well-being. In the imagery, the border suddenly jumped out of the screen and encircled Michael in a loving way, then dropped, and encircled his feet to help him feel more grounded.

8. **Implementation:** Meg sent a healing e-mail to her stepson. Before she did, she felt confident that her intuitive mind would know the right words to help heal the pain within Michael that caused him to strike out and project his rage on her.

187

The Telepathic Bond

Sending nonverbal messages from one mind to another is called telepathy. This bond is especially close between parent and child. After my car was totaled in an accident, I stumbled into my apartment and heard the ringing phone. My mother's first words were, "How's your car?" My mother lived 300 miles away! Yet, her intuitive radar instantly picked up that I had been in an accident.

When I teach my students how to listen to their intuitive mind, it is exciting to witness those moments when a person literally flies into action in response to an urgent inner message. In one class, Brian, a senior accountant, suddenly ran out the door. The class and I looked at each other, stunned. When Brian came back to class the next day, he was eager to explain his erratic behavior. He had a pressing gut feeling that his son was in danger, and had fled the class to call home immediately. Upon calling home, he learned that his son had been in an accident and had been rushed to the hospital. Brian's wife was doubly frantic when she was told the boy couldn't be admitted until the insurance papers were completed. And who had the insurance card? Brian, sitting in class, had this card safely tucked away in his wallet. Fortunately, he heard his wife's urgent but telepathic plea, and took action. Brian admitted he would not have listened to this inner prompting if not for the continual emphasis in class about attending to the signals sent by the intuitive mind.

Telepathy happens all the time between people who have a close relationship. Gail had been thinking about her seventeen-year-old granddaughter all morning with an uneasy feeling in the pit of her stomach. Hours later, Erin called and told Gail she had been fighting urges of wanting to hurt herself ever since she woke up that morning. Instead, she chose to reach out to her grandmother. After talking for a while, she felt better and phoned her counselor for an appointment.

How does the telepathic bond help us understand one another? Simple! When someone sends you a telepathic SOS, as Erin did to her grandmother, you'll know that underneath any seemingly calm exterior beats a troubled heart. I suggest you begin recording telepathic moments in your PowerHunch Journal. This will show you how frequently the connection is activated between you and your loved ones.

Parents

How about trying to understand your father's unspoken needs so you can improve your relationship with him? Phyllis, a freelance writer, was gifted at words but couldn't mend a severely deteriorating relationship with her father. As she became receptive, the image she received was an "antique pewter watch." There were many associations including clock, schedule, numbers, old, refinished, which led to the word "refurbished." That was it! The relationship, like the antique watch, needed to be repaired and refurbished, and time was running out because of her father's health and old age. Letting this incubate, Phyllis realized that she could begin to repair the relationship by writing him a letter along with making a personal visit to his house. When she followed her intuitive directive she felt comforted by knowing that the healing had begun.

Our parents' influence on our lives is unending. Deceased parents can reach out to us through dreams and leave poignant messages. One insight Connie received through a dream focused on a childhood abusive trauma with her dad. Connie's dad, who had passed away years before, was currently being "overhauled." In this new realm, her dad's consciousness expanded so he could see things from a broader perspective. For example, he never acknowledged Connie's trauma with him when she was eight years old. In the dream, his spirit offered her a book. Connie knew that the book was about what was going on in her life. She rejected it that night and asked for it to be re-presented more clearly, which happened a few nights later. The insight carried in this new big book led Connie to break some huge barriers, freeing her to do the big things she really wanted to do, like using her creative talents.

Jana loved teaching high school students, despite the challenges of teenagers. One day she walked out of the classroom for a moment. When she returned, her purse had been stolen. That incident seemed to trigger a series of similar indignities, which culminated in her car being stolen and then set on fire. Jana was distraught and needed assurance that things would get better again. After these events, her friend Ann shared a dream she had had the previous week. In it, Jana's mother said to Ann, "Jana is in trouble and needs your help, but she will get over it." Ann was puzzled by the dream and never mentioned it to Jana. But when she stood with Jana by the burning car, she told her about it. Synchronistically, the dream came exactly four years to the day after Jana's mom had died. For Jana, this event helped her learn to trust and embrace the next step of her spiritual journey.

189

It can be hard to penetrate the silent façade of a strained family to understand its inner dynamics. Taking a step toward healing this relationship is essential to opening the lines of communication. Stacey grew up thinking her grandparents were her parents. Not until she was twenty-four and pregnant did she learn that her older sister, Sal, was really her mother. Shocked and hurt, she cut off their relationship completely. Later, she wanted to heal the schism. Stacey did a PowerShift to get clarity about how to take this first step to resolve the strain.

1. **Issue:** She asked, "How can I heal the relationship between me and my mother?
2. **Centering:** Stacey listened to a lovely CD with the sound of ocean waves.
3. **Receptivity:** After doing yoga breathing and progressive relaxation, she felt as limp as a dishrag. (See the Breathing and Relaxation exercises at the end of this book for complete instructions.)
4. **Imagery:** She recalled the TV show *Forgive and Forget*. In it, someone who has wronged another person tells their story, and the person who has been wronged listens backstage. At the end of the story, the one who has told the story is led to a door. If the person waiting backstage is willing to talk to them, that person is standing behind the door when it opens. If not, the door opens to reveal nobody, and the speaker is left to deal with the void. Stacey got an image of a door slowly opening to reveal her mother.
5. **Deciphering the Image:** Stacey realized that her mother, the wronged party, had been waiting backstage. Stacey no longer saw herself as the victim but as the one causing the pain. She knew healing was possible. A lot of emotion came up for her and she decided not to go further.
6. **Incubate:** She let the issue go for a week.
7. **Go Deeper:** Stacey was wandering around a jewelry store, looking at bracelets with words printed on them, such as

serenity, strength, and so on. Stacey bought the "Success" bracelet for herself and then heard a voice say, "Buy one for Sal."

8. **Implementation:** Stacey went back to the bracelets, closed her eyes, and held her hand over them. She reached for one. It said, "Healing"! This was the perfect gift to give her mother. Hopefully, this bracelet would open the door to communication so they could begin to understand each other.

POWERHUNCH TOOL

Reach Out to a Parental Figure

Reach out to a parent, or a parental figure who is at least ten years older than you. After you are centered and receptive, ask for an image that represents how this person is feeling right now on their life path. Are they in rugged terrain? Feeling overloaded with a full plate? Or bright as sunshine?

Ask for another image representing a gift you can give him or her as the journey in life continues.

Carrying the weight of the world on his or her shoulders? Use this intuitive input to guide you in relating to this parental figure. For example, let the image of them carrying the world on their shoulders guide you to help him or her with chores for at least three hours each week.

Ask for another image representing a gift you can give him or her as the journey in life continues. The image of a telephone might suggest giving the gift of making frequent phone calls.

Intuition's Role in the Workplace

Work occupies a significant amount of your time. That is why understanding the people in your work environment is vital. People issues in the work setting really need the intuitive touch.

The examples in this section will reinforce how you can use your PowerHunch tools to decipher the actions of people you meet on all levels of the workplace:

- supervisors
- support staff
- co-workers
- people waiting to be hired

Supervisors

As you have been learning, the intuitive mind will deftly reach into your personal computer to retrieve exactly the right image to clarify a situation. Bob wanted to know how to improve his relationship with his boss. His intuitive mind sent him the image of a "spinning pinwheel-like object" that started to emit water, like an automatic sprinkler. When he associated to this enigmatic image, he got words like "fire," "spinning," "fire extinguisher," "escape," and "alarm." Finally, he hit upon the words "jet engine" and "water." These images were simply telling him to "cool his jets" and slow down. He tried to be more patient and adapt to his company's philosophy, and he realized there is a value in a more subtle business approach with emphasis on long-term goals instead of short-term rewards.

If you are a visualizer, you can readily use your inner sight. If not, you can still activate your imagination or sense the action. With this alpha to omega technique, you create your own imagery starting with the current status of the problem and continue until you reach the desired outcome.

When Kathleen started her new job, she was blessed with a gifted manager who inspired the devotion of his staff. Unfortunately, he was promoted to another position. Her new supervisor was cold and disapproving to Kathleen. Her life was miserable. She wondered, "How can I improve the relationship with my supervisor?" Kathleen used the guided imagery tech-

192

nique to help her address this issue. She visualized herself talking to her supervisor, with conversation that was polite but strained. Then she visualized the supervisor in a more sympathetic light, and talked to her in a pleasant, conversational way, sharing some nonthreatening personal information with her. Kathleen visualized her supervisor responding with interest.

At work, when Kathleen was scheduled for a conversation with her supervisor, she would prepare first. After taking a few deep breaths she would smile in anticipation of a friendly meeting, with her supervisor smiling. She continued to visualize a positive and sympathetic relationship and to see her supervisor as warm and friendly. Consequently, the relationship improved immensely and was no longer a problem.

POWER**HUNCH** TOOL

Use Alpha to Omega

Practice the visualization technique that Kathleen just used, which I call "Alpha to Omega." Start by visualizing your current predicament and fill in the script until you reach an acceptable conclusion. After a few days, or even sooner, you will notice that this reverie has become a reality. Don't forget to record these startling revelations in your PowerHunch Journal.

The intuitive mind will clearly illuminate the underlying reason behind a person's irritation. Lately, everything Dana says to her supervisor, Lynette, seems to annoy or agitate her. Lynette is crabby and unpleasant, and Dana is beginning to become concerned.

1. **Issue:** She asked, "How do I find out what is agitating my relationship with my boss?"

2. **Centering:** Dana used the affirmation, "My intuition gives me strong and clear signals." Then she visualized walking along her favorite stretch of beach where the ocean is so blue and the sunlight just dances along the tips of the waves. She could feel and see and touch the beauty here.

3. **Receptivity:** She used the Ha Breath technique (See the Breathing and Relaxation exercises at the end of this book for complete instructions.) and became light-headed and a little dizzy. She then asked the question.

4. **Imagery:** Dana closed her eyes to bring up an image of Lynette. She was a big woman, and in the image she looked like "A bull in a china shop," a dangerous beast twisting and turning in a small fenced and confined area. She was damaging things and getting angry and frustrated because she could not find her way out. The harder she tried, the more mess she made. In the visualization she was saying emotionally to anyone who would listen, "Tim is going to make me do all his work."

5. **Deciphering the Image:** Dana realized that Lynette was angry about her own boss, Tim, giving her some of his workload. She did not know how to get out of doing his work as well as her own. The harder she tried, the angrier she got about everything. It seemed that she was not upset with Dana personally, but felt caught in the situation. Dana also realized that her supervisor was trying to get someone to notice her predicament

6. **Incubate:** Dana let the weekend go by, aware now that Lynette might be angry and out of sorts because she felt overburdened with her workload.

7. **Going Deeper:** Not needed.

8. **Implementation:** On Monday, Dana told Lynette that she had some time to help her with any of her unfinished work projects. As Lynette assigned Dana a project, she gave an audible sigh of relief. Lynette seemed to relax a little as they talked about the project.

Support Staff

I have always found the metaphor technique an invaluable tool for penetrating into a person's character. You can compare the person to an animal, a well-known person, a character in a book or song, a car, a color, a piece of furniture, or a plant. Then, as you have been doing all along, unravel the meaning of this imagery with amplification.

Kelley had an employee, Jena, who had been a challenge for over a year. She had previously spoken to Jena about her attitude and divisive behavior. When Jena displayed insubordinate behavior in a meeting, Kelley gave her a strong warning and explained that this negative behavior was getting in the way of productivity. To have a deeper understanding of this puzzling behavior, Kelley used the metaphor technique.

Kelley thought of Jena and immediately the image of a bear surfaced. As she associated, words came up like "large," "ferocious," "fierce when threatened," "retreats when not threatened," "beautiful," "majestic," "protective," "loud roar," "mother protecting young," and "keeping them safe."

This described Jena, who had the potential to develop into a terrific employee. Yet, she came out of nowhere and attacked with a disturbing loud roar. The bear faced the intruder when it felt threatened and retreated when there was no longer a threat. Most of the time Jana was pleasant and compliant and only "roared" at change. Kelley realized that Jena was reacting to change and was probably frightened of it. Kelley never would have come to this conclusion with her logical mind. This new insight was implemented immediately. She told Jena that her input was valued and would be incorporated in any final decision. Kelley decided to increase her communication with Jena because she now realized that she just wanted to be heard and not surprised. Jena was very supportive at a subsequent group meeting where new procedures were introduced. This big change for Jena occurred as a result of Kelley's intuitive insight.

Helen, a nursing supervisor, felt she had been too strong in confronting an employee about her behavior. As she thought

195

about the situation, a mule standing in a field spontaneously appeared in her mind. What came to her was an old joke about a stubborn mule that wouldn't work. The farmer cajoled and pleaded with the mule. When that didn't work, he threatened and yelled at it, which also didn't work. Finally, he picked up a two-by-four and whacked it on the head. A passerby stopped and asked why he was beating the poor animal. The farmer replied, "I'm not beating him, I'm just getting his attention." Helen then realized that she wasn't being too hard on the employee, but was merely getting her attention. She appreciated how her intuition was using humor, which relieved the tension and made her chuckle.

Co-workers

Have you ever been caught between two parties in a dispute? Two co-workers were making negative comments about each other behind their backs. Perplexed, Ty watched from the sidelines. He wanted to gain insight into this situation in order to improve the teamwork in his unit. When he invited imagery in, he received a brief sequence rather than a fixed picture. First, a cat played in a room alone. Then another cat entered the room. They sniffed around each other for a while, and then the first cat started a fight with the new cat. They wrestled, bit, and hissed at one another. From this imagery, Ty received the insight that the two employees had large egos and both wanted to be the "top cat" in house. By putting the other down, each was attempting to elevate their stature and influence. This insight helped Ty act as a mediator so the fighting cats could work out their differences and create a team.

People Waiting to Be Hired

You may not be a human resource officer, but you probably have hired many people in your business of living: a housekeeper, a baby sitter, an auto mechanic, or an accountant. Your intuition can always be called upon to assess another person's capability. And here's the good news: I sense that as a result of exposure to this book, you will be using your intuition more regularly and reliably!

POWERHUNCH TOOL

Using Intuition to Hire

You want to hire someone to assist you. To get a sense of who this person is, in addition to getting the facts, ask, for example, "What have you been doing the past five years? Where do you see yourself in five years?" As the person responds you can listen for an unspoken parallel script and determine, "Who is this person? What really turns them on? What are they passionate about? What is it about them that will really key into a job?"

If a person is hard to read, probe further to get a little more of an emotional response. You can ask, "Where did you go to school? What do you enjoy doing?"

197

Throughout this chapter, you have seen how the intuitive light illuminates any relationship to provide clear insights into people's character and motivation. These connections with others are invaluable. Putting the intuitive spark into each interaction will deepen your understanding of the inner dynamics, which will then strengthen and harmonize these unions.

POWERHUNCH WORKSHOP

The Metaphor Technique: Using Intuition to Understand Relationships

When I lived in New York City years ago, I loved to play the "subway game" to pass the time during my commute. I would look at a stranger near me and develop character sketches about him or her. Perhaps this activity was a precursor to my Metaphor Technique.

You can practice the Metaphor Technique on anyone. Try it on your partner and notice how images shift throughout the day. At one moment you may see a beaver, busy and capable of doing many tasks and responsibilities at once. Later, you may see a cow—udderly bored. Now select a character in a book. Perhaps you see your partner as Sherlock Holmes searching for clues to solve a mystery.

Now apply some of the other PowerHunch Principles you learned in part 1. Let the *environmental cues* around you guide your understanding of your family members as well as your relationship partners and people at work. For example, you are trying to understand your niece, and an advertisement comes in the mail about a "charm school." Suddenly, you realize what bothers you about her behavior. She is rough around the edges and needs to be more charming.

Are you puzzled by someone's behavior? Turn it around as you learned to do in chapter 4. Step into this other person's skin: what are you thinking and feeling?

Pay attention to your dreams and actively ask your dreaming mind to send you insights about the people around you. Do you see someone giving you a floral bouquet or tripping you up so you fall down?

Formulate three relationship questions, one for a family member, one related to a personal or social relationship, and the last related to someone at work. Go through the PowerShift to arrive at a penetrating answer to these concerns.

10

Finding Balance and Healing

If my intention is to live in harmony with my environment,
my single best indicator of success is
my body's feeling of comfort.

—Deepak Chopra

Imagine the miraculous power of a parent's kiss: A child falls down, gets a boo-boo, and with one magical kiss mom or dad makes it all better. This is balance and instantaneous healing in action. You, too, can get or give intuitive healing "kisses" to restore equilibrium and feel refreshed and renewed.

Two people can have the same work or family responsibilities. One feels stressed, and the other infuses every situation with passion and enthusiasm. It is not hard to see which person courts balance and healing. Jerry is a good example of the stressed person. He is suffering from depression and can't sleep at night. He turns to his intuitive mind for a remedy and gets an image of children playing. The meaning is clear: The children are showing him that life is fun—all areas of their lives are an amusement park. He realizes that he needs to feel this kind of uncomplicated joy. At some level, life really *is* that simple: Don't worry, be happy, and make your life a continuous activity of play.

Back to reality: It's no secret that we are living at top speed and intensity, and our lives—even our children's lives—are filled with tension and stress. We can't stop the world, but we can create a balanced life in the midst of it. The logical mind may tell us to take a vacation or get a massage, but it doesn't have all the answers. The exercises in this chapter will help you use your intuition to find out how to:

- create and maintain the needed balance in your life.
- manage and alleviate stress by changing habitual ways of thinking.
- create healing remedies that flow naturally from deep intuitive wellsprings.

Notice the circularity of the balance, stress, and healing cycle. When you are out of balance, stress sets in, which escalates to cause dis-ease, so healing is needed. You ask, "What brought on this dis-ease? How can I get back in balance?" Stepping out of this cycle is the best way I know to find balance and healing.

Finding Balance

You begin to find balance when you answer the question, "How do I want to live?" This question alone places value on determining the quality of life you want to maintain. You will discover more about finding balance as you learn to manage your time and identify your priorities.

Quality of Life

You may be an accountant, a teacher, an engineer, a restaurant worker, a dentist, a mechanic, a CEO ... your work is secondary to your purpose in life. The real issue is finding out what fabric you want in your life's tapestry. How do you want to live your life?

Annie asked for an image to show her what this time of her life was all about. When she became receptive, the image of a bumblebee flew into her mind. This puzzled her until she overheard a conversation during which one person told the other, "I don't know how to rest ... I feel like I'm always flying around and never getting anywhere." Bingo! Annie realized that this time of her life is just like the flight of the bumblebee flitting from one thing to another without getting anchored. Rather than staying in constant flight, she prefers to pursue a more pointed focus at work.

Many of us know our constant sense of exhaustion comes from a continual outpouring of energy. Still, we need to understand *why* we push without a break. When Sherry asked, "Why am I feeling so tired?" she got the image of an army of ants, carrying tiny burdens around in a busy little ant community. She realized that the ants' busy activity comes during summer so food and energy can be stored for winter. Sherry then recognized that she is planning to close her business and needed to work hard in the summer to save money for the leaner winter times when she will not be working as much. This imagery showed a very lopsided quality of life. Sherry realized that she doesn't have to go to these extremes that make her tired all the time.

Managing Time 201

Here's one way to manage time effectively: Stop the clock! Periodically, throughout your day, take the time to be still. To remind you about how to court quiet time, review the section on "Learning To Be Quiet" in chapter 3. Taking quiet time before plunging into all your activities is essential to readjusting your internal thermostat.

Where and how you find quiet time will be an interesting discovery. I frequently find quiet time when I stand in line at the grocery store checkout in the midst of all the activity. Away from all the outer stimuli reminding me of work and family responsibilities, I can feel so quiet.

Here's Sylvia's journey into the silence. It may be different from yours, but it works wonders for her. She has a strong need to just sit and watch her two box turtles, Caroline and Duke, eat for a half hour or so. At first this practice felt bizarre and then guilt set in because she was taking time from her busy schedule. Here's what she learned from the turtles. She noticed that when they got scared, or challenged, one of their great lines of defense is to pull their heads, feet, and tails inward. This image of pulling inward when confronted with life's challenges was an enlightening metaphor for quiet time. Like the turtles, when she is frightened or concerned, she can seek her quiet refuge inside. Also like a turtle, she carries a home on her back. This is her spiritual home, which is always with her. Sylvia can always go within and return to this sanctuary.

This process of taking quiet time with the turtles helped Sylvia manage time effectively. She now knows that taking time to simply sit, observe, and let go of guilt is well spent. Aside from taking this invaluable time for respite, she is continually reminded that she can turn inward and listen to her intuitive voice.

Do you ever find that you don't know how to manage that quiet or spare time even when it is handed to you on a silver platter? Your intuitive mind will tell you just what to do with that time. When Kim's husband and son left to go on a special camping trip, that gave her free time to spend with her fourteen-year-old daughter. Their ideas for how to use this time were quite different. Kim wanted to clean the house and unpack the last of the boxes from their move a year ago. Her daughter thought they should go on a "girl trip" to balance the "boy trip." Kim found herself torn between the practical housecleaning chores and having fun. It may not seem like a dilemma to you, but for Kim, straightening up the mess would actually relieve a lot of stress. She turned to the PowerShift to help her manage this time dilemma.

1. **Issue:** Kim asked, "How should we spend our free time while the men are gone?"
2. **Centering:** She focused her attention on a poster that has concentric golden circles on a solar-system background. The poster was very soothing and she affirmed, "My intuitive skills are strong and reliable."
3. **Receptivity:** She sat quietly with her eyes closed and used Pranic Breathing. To do this, she exhaled completely, held for

a count of one, breathed in slowly to a count of seven, held full to a count of one, exhaled slowly to a count of seven and held empty for a count of one. She repeated this for nine breathing cycles.

4. **Imagery:** Imagery came instantly: It was Elvis Presley singing "Viva Las Vegas!"

5. **Deciphering the Image:** Kim knew what this meant right away. Her message from the King was to lighten up and take the Vegas trip. The housework would wait. She wanted to seize the opportunity to have some fun. She remembered the girl trips she used to take to Las Vegas with her sister. With the sunroof open, they would sing "Viva Las Vegas!" every time they passed a sign that told them how many miles were left.

6. **Incubate:** Not needed.

7. **Go Deeper:** She brought a traffic light up and got a green signal to GO. For the first time in many months, Kim was excited about something and felt great.

8. **Implementation:** Kim's daughter was delighted, and didn't even want to bring a friend along. The new Las Vegas has plenty of activities for kids. They made their hotel plans and left the work behind. With a nice long drive, they would have plenty of time to talk, sing, and laugh.

203

POWERHUNCH TOOL

Managing Time

A few months ago, Joan had to let her assistant go—it was too much work to train her. Now, Joan is overloaded. Should she learn to manage her time better, or find help? Joan asks her intuitive mind, "How can I manage my time better?" The image that comes is a red mustang. From the various associations in the amplification process, the image of two in the front seat stands out. What a PowerHunch! Hiring someone to assist her is imperative.

Do you need help managing your home, finances, work, or the children? Borrow the car metaphor and ask if you need to hire someone else to help you manage your time. After you get centered and receptive, actively elicit a car image. Are you riding alone or with someone else? Are you sitting in the driver's seat, as a passenger, or in back of the car?

Create Priorities

Does the phrase "I don't have time" inhabit your vocabulary? If so, turn it around and say, "I have all the time I need to get everything done." How can you make that switch? For starters, establish priorities so you can set realistic schedules. As you prioritize your activities, complete the most important ones first. If you have been putting something off, find a fun way to get it done rather than worry about it all day. Schedule your most difficult chores at a time when you will not be distracted or interrupted.

This all sounds so logical. Where does the intuitive mind come in? Your intuition will show you how to KISS your prioritizing activities. This means *Keep It Simple Sweetie!* Just like a child with a single focus, take life one thing at a time. Whenever I have to dig into the piles of paper sitting on my desk, I choose not to be overwhelmed by the confusion or clutter. Instead, I look at that pile and let my eye intuitively go to any one item, then I make that the starting point.

Commit your "to do" lists to paper so you can empty your head of all the mental "to do" lists you carry around. I actually feel exhilarated when I cross an item off my list.

Let your intuitive mind dramatize the starting point in a funny manner. You can let one item jump off the list right into your arms, or see a red border surrounding your starting item. Or, hear a whistle blow when you come to that place on the list. Tap into your PowerHunch source to connect with the list. You can see, hear, or feel that starting point in your body.

Are you stretched to the limit because of involvement in too many pursuits? Does a time battle rage between your many pursuits—work, partner, children, social, spiritual, and recreational? Managing time is often painful for people who get involved in their work to the exclusion of family and other pursuits.

Bob is a motivational speaker, and his job requires a lot of travel. He wanted to know how to balance his social, family, and work life. So he asked his intuitive mind to come to his rescue and show him how to manage his time. One night, at yet another strange hotel, he pondered this question and focused his attention on the geometric patterns on the hotel curtains. As soon as he became receptive (he used a breathing and relaxation exercise he made up), he used another of his favorite intuitive tricks: He conjured up the image of a box and looked inside. He saw a salamander, and the word "poison" spontaneously came into his mind. The words he associated to poison were "toxic," "venom," "death," "antidote," and "tonic." He was still confused, so he took time out to walk around the hotel courtyard. Suddenly, in a flash, he remembered reading that salamanders are very sensitive to subtle changes in the environment—especially increases of temperature. He realized that he must maintain a proper environment and a balance in his life or else he would become extinct. Bob wanted his family and social life to act as a tonic and balance his work life, or else the demands would poison him. The answer he received from his intuitive mind reaffirmed his devotion to his friends and family. He was now determined to spend more time with them and look for a tennis partner.

205

POWERHUNCH TOOL

Create Your Priorities

Do you have difficulty trying to get all the things you want to do completed? How many things are you trying to manage simultaneously? What are your priorities? It's time to find out!

First, list five tasks you want to complete.

Take three deep breaths. Inhale to a count of seven, hold for three counts, and then exhale to a count of seven. To feel more relaxed, do a "countdown" by imagining yourself standing at the top of a flight of ten steps. Count down from the tenth step until you reach the first one. (See the Breathing and Relaxation Exercises at the end of this book for complete instructions.)

Create a bar graph in your mind. Label each bar with one of the five activities that needs to be completed. Take another deep breath. See or sense the bars rising. The longest bar is the task that needs to be completed first. The next highest bar needs to be completed after that.

Manage Your Stress

The first step on the moon may have been one giant leap for humankind; a better understanding of stress and how to deal with it positively may well be another. Here are the two basic tenets for understanding stress:

- Stress is a fact of life.
- You can choose to have the stress motivate or debilitate.

Your life would be empty without stress. The problem is not what's *causing* stress, but how you *perceive* and *react* to it. We find ourselves in stressful situations nearly every day: stuck in commuter traffic, a boss who expects a sixty-hour work week, children crying out for attention, an impending trip to the dentist, a hurtful argument with your partner. . . . These situations create stress, which in turn produce emotional reactions like anxiety, uncertainty, frustration, or anger. Stress also creates physical responses, such as rapid heartbeat, pounding headache, stomachaches, and soaring blood pressure. The impact on your health can be debilitating.

Stress tends to arise when we feel a lack of control. Here's a musical analogy: An orchestra has different instrumental sections: brass, woodwinds, strings, percussion. You have four different sections playing in your orchestra: physical, mental, emotional, spiritual. You can use your intuition to help you manage and alleviate stress in any of these areas of your being.

Your Physical Self: Breathe!

Your body is constantly sending you intuitive messages about what you need to do to alleviate stress. Do you pay attention when your back begins to ache, or do you keep working at your computer? Did you have to catch a cold in order to stop and get some rest? Do you have to get surgery before you discover that you are holding anger and frustration in your heart? Your body will always tell you when you are stressed. The challenge is listening and becoming more aware of these bodily messages. There is always something you can do to work with your body as a partner to alleviate stress.

207

You can find plenty of good advice on nutrition and exercise, and I have listed some books on these topics under Suggested Reading. Basically, my advice is probably a lot like your mother's: Get plenty of rest, get enough exercise, and eat a balanced diet. Here's where my advice may differ a bit: I want you to remember to breathe deeply and completely—the breath of life is just that.

Many people habitually hold their breath, which can lead to all sorts of problems, from a hunched posture to panic attacks. Deep breathing can help restore your sense of balance and well-being. Engaging freely and fully in the breath of life will help you release tensions and feel regenerated. Breathing goes beyond the simple act of drawing air in and out of the lungs. Breath is the linking point between mind, body, and spirit. Every change of mental state is reflected first in the breath and then in the body.

Take a moment now and then to notice how tightly you hold your toothbrush, pen, or car steering wheel. When you are aware of holding on tightly, remind yourself to lighten up by taking in a deep breath of fresh air. Begin to notice how every tense situation causes a change in your breathing. The more stressed you feel, the more shallow your breathing becomes. Other changes of feeling are registered in our breathing. While anger produces shallow inhalation and often strong, panting exhalation, fear creates rapid and shallow breathing. Spasmodic or broken breathing is associated with the sobs of sorrow. In contrast, regular breathing as the chest cavity relaxes occurs when positive emotions like love and joy flood the body.

Becoming aware of your breath will help you revive as well as nourish any aching part of the body. My energy gets blocked when I am writing intensely. I have to force myself to pause, and take a deep breath that I direct right down to my solar plexus, the area just above the navel. You can focus attention on any part of the body in need of life energy for revitalization. When my left eye in particular feels tired, I stop and direct a deep breath into both eyes.

My throat is another area that holds stress and makes it difficult for me to swallow when I am tense. When that happens, I take a deep breath and direct the energy to my throat. You have been practicing breathing and relaxation exercises since you read about receptivity in chapter 3. All these exercises are excellent physical stress reducers—and the less stress you have, the easier it will be to hear and see your intuitive messages. Use the directed breathing technique below to send the breath of life to any area that needs to be invigorated.

POWER**HUNCH TOOL**

Directed Breathing

On each inhalation, imagine you are bringing energy in. On the exhalation, let all the tension in your shoulders and neck go down your arms and out your fingertips. Repeat this twice. On the next inhalation, imagine you are bringing energy in. This time, exhale and let the tension go down the spine, down the legs, and out through the feet. Repeat this twice.

Now go to a specific part of your body that needs healing energy. Lay your hands over that area. As you inhale, see and feel the energy coming down through the top of your head to your hands, and as you exhale let that energy heal the afflicted area.

Imagine your pain and soreness going away with each complete breath. Continue until you feel a reduction in the actual physical pain. Now breathe the energy into that area, and let the tension flow down your legs to your feet and down into the earth. Record in your PowerHunch Journal the area you are working with, and note what happens as a result of the breathing.

Your Mental Self

Thoughts are incredibly potent. Anxious, guilty, self-deprecating, and angry thoughts can create unnecessary stress. Believe it or not, you *can* refuse to think certain thoughts. Think of it this way: If a salesperson is knocking at your front door and you don't answer, the salesperson might go around to the back door to see if you are home and even knock on the window. If you don't want to talk to the salesperson, you become resolute about not opening the door. Analogously, you can shut the door to negative thoughts by not letting these disturbing, intruding ideas come in. Of course, this is easier said than done! I still have to practice closing the door to these negative thoughts when I feel they are interfering with my productivity and sense of well-being. I *can* do this when I choose to.

Your intuition can help you realign your thoughts and mental processes to alleviate stress. Once again, the focus comes back to imagery—the pictures dancing inside your head—which will show you how to convert the agitating negative facets of the "outside world" into a more positive stance. As you have already learned to some degree, you can picture yourself learning a challenging new skill, making up with a family member, or overcoming a fear.

Using imagery can help you change a physical, mental, emotional, or spiritual state. Remember that any negative or disabling condition can be converted into a positive and life- affirming circumstance. Here are some of the ways you can use imagery to eradicate stress.

Use Your Intuition to Understand How Stress Manifests in Your Body. First, you can imagine what the stress or tension looks like inside your body, and then use imagery to picture its release. For example, if you feel tension from having "pins and needles" inside your body, create a way to have these pins taken away. You can imagine this by creating imagery that shows someone using tweezers to gently pull these pins out of your back.

POWERHUNCH TOOL

Picturing The Stress

Trying to imagine what stress looks like in your body can be fun and can even spark creativity. Jessie saw the pain in her back as a knife, and imagined someone coming along to pull the knife out. (She also explored the underlying pun—could a feeling that someone was "stabbing her in the back" be contributing to her discomfort?) Greta's shoulders ached with a feeling of heaviness. Using her intuition, she saw a circus act where the acrobats were standing on her shoulders, and then watched them jump off one at a time.

Use your intuitive Power Tools to picture your stress and then relieve it.

Use Your Intuition to Take a Mental Getaway. Using imagery, you can transport yourself to any enjoyable setting that will help you dissolve the stress. This may be a place you know and love, or a fantasy world that fulfills all your relaxation needs.

POWERHUNCH TOOL

Take a Fantasy Trip for Instant Relief

This can be the most fun you ever have without spending money! Even if you can't afford to fly to a tropical island or spend a week at a health resort, you can use your intuition to create the healing environment that is perfect for you. Maya loves a warm ocean and soothing tropical breezes. Nick's idea of a good time is a long soak in a hot tub under the desert stars. Fillippa wants the works: a total body massage, a mud bath, a facial, and a relaxing nap by the pool. What's your fantasy? Use the Power Tools at your disposal to create this space, and stay in it as long as you need to. It's free!

Use Your Intuition to Resolve a Frustrating Situation with an "Inside Out." Some times stress comes from a situation that is more frustrating than debilitating. When that happens, you might feel stuck and in need of some comic relief to cope with the frustration: facing an annoying project, involvement with an irritating person, or a plan that has come to a grinding halt. This is the time to turn these frustrations inside out. This inside out is just like the "turning it around" exercises you practiced in chapter 4.

Use Your Intuition to Change a Negative Perception into A Positive Impression. See yourself smiling and shaking hands with a person you viewed as menacing. Sometimes I see the negative person and do an "inside out" on the emotional situation, picturing the hate or wrath being turned into a loving situation. One day, a graduate student was hostile to me about the comments I made on her papers. As she talked, her face literally turned beet red. During group work assignments, she always chose to work alone. Even when she was raging at me, I looked past the words and saw a very frail girl inside—one who was crying out for love. Just as she was going to "fix" me by giving a negative evaluation of the class at the end of the semester, I smiled to myself knowing I was going to "fix" her, too—by sending her doses of love to reverse the rage fomenting inside her.

This was a tough case, but it worked. I learned from a colleague that this student had difficulty with every instructor she ever had in the graduate program. Weeks later, at a social gathering on the last day of class, she came over and thanked me for giving her understanding, which she felt no one had ever done. I looked into her eyes, smiled, and gave her a choice of receiving a hug, a handshake, or a surprise gift from me. She chose the handshake, which was one of the most touching incidents of my life. Symbolically, I felt that I had affected her in a gripping way.

Your Emotional Self: Let It Go

212

The emotional residues from resentment, criticism, guilt, and fear cause major stress blockages in your body. What can you do? Try weeding your garden. Imagine that you are like a garden that has many weeds—these are judgments from the unnecessary guilt, wounds, worries, and fears you carry around. Continue to let your intuition show you how to weed your mind of these hurt feelings and angry thoughts so you can clear the way for positive images to grow and flourish. By accentuating the positive, you are of course minimizing and possibly eliminating the debilitating stress.

Here's another analogy you can use in visualization. Imagine your body and mind as a pure reservoir. You don't want to pollute these waters by pouring in any toxic emotions. In order to keep pure and uncontaminated fluids flowing through your mind and body, you have to honestly monitor the thoughts and emotions that are filtering in.

Worry and guilt are the two most useless emotions for fostering optimal health. I would also include any emotion that knocks us off balance, such as fear, anger, anxiety, distrust, frustration, resentment, jealousy, irritability, and blame.

Gloria knows about combating fear. She was placed on temporary disability for a couple of months due to an automobile accident that happened in a company car. Since she had been off for months, she received a call asking her to come and see the company's doctor. She was overwhelmed by the fear this doctor would pressure her to get back to work, which she dreaded—she was still quite sore and couldn't sit at a computer all day. Gloria used the metaphor technique to halt her raging fear of the doctor. The image she got was a bowl of applesauce! She then realized that the company doctor might be someone who is soft and sweet. Gloria converted her fear to trust, which helped her before she met the doctor in person. Just as she had anticipated, she felt quite peaceful from this positive meeting.

Here's another way to turn the emotional debris into something more productive. Jacob was assaulted with worries about how to generate income for his consulting business. He turned to his intuitive mind for an image to combat this fruitless anxiety. The image of a New Year's celebration came into his mind. Although it was the middle of the year, intuitively he knew this was his personal *new year*. Immediately, intuitive insights sparked his productivity for a new action plan.

213

POWERHUNCH TOOL

Making A Conversion

Emotional stress is often the final straw for many who are already barely coping. Every once in a while, I get down in the dumps and realize that my pilot light has gone out. I know then that I have to bring some joy into my life to light my inner fire again. Hard as it may seem at the time, I can usually find some new goal, happy memory, or something in my environment—like hearing the purr of my cat—to help me put the light back into my life.

Use the intuitive PowerHunch Tools you know to convert negative emotions into a positive by showing how you will actually carry this out in real life. For example, I can convert my anger at a friend into a loving gesture by suggesting we have lunch so we can defuse the negativity together.

Many negative emotions are rooted in childhood conditioning. As you practice the "Correct Your Conditioning" exercise in chapter 4, you will continue to weed your garden. In the following example, David uses the PowerShift to reach into his childhood and retrieve an insight into his periodic bouts of uncontrollable anger.

1. **Issue:** David asked, "How do I deal with my anger?"
2. **Centering:** He focused on the rug and listened to the water running in his fountain.
3. **Receptivity:** The breathing helped him relax his body and clear his mind. David used the stretch and breathing technique to relax and get into a quiet space.
4. **Imagery:** He saw himself as a child being told, "I can't believe you feel that way." "I know you could not possibly believe what you are feeling," "We don't express our feelings." Then David saw a large bag being stuffed with great handfuls of cotton. The cotton was being forced into the bag. The bag was full, yet more and more was being stuffed into it. The bag was becoming tighter and tighter, and at the same time the tension in David's chest was growing tighter and tighter. The bag began to rip along its seams, and he realized his heart was being broken.
5. **Deciphering the Image:** David realized that the cotton represented his stuffed feeling because he was not allowed to express his anger. He saw a balloon burst, and knew that it represented his anger exploding into rage. He then saw the face of a clown with a tear running down his cheek, and realized it was his sadness in knowing that he had been

angry deep inside all his life, and now was begging to be understood.

6. **Incubate:** He put the situation on hold for a few days.

7. **Go Deeper:** David became silent and imagined himself being treated as an angry little child being disciplined. The child was in his room, crying in anger. He heard yelling and doors slamming, followed by angry words. It was a very traumatic situation. He realized the little child was him acting out: yelling, slamming doors, and being out of control with anger. He knew if he continued to behave like that angry little child, he would be treated like a child.

8. **Implementation:** He accepted the fact that in his past he was expected to stuff his feelings and not show any anger. But now he knew he must move on.

When was the last time you were annoyed or upset with someone? Did you have a major emotional clash with someone at work, or with a family member? What do you suppose happened to all the emotional debris that was churned up?

Here's a PowerHunch Tool to help you clear your emotions. You may feel angry when you start this exercise, but you will probably get such a charge out of putting the source of your annoyance into a Ziploc bag that you might even start laughing. Just the act of chuckling is of course releasing your anger.

POWERHUNCH TOOL

Releasing Emotions

Releasing emotions can be fun. The purpose of this exercise is to release any anger by putting it in an imaginary container like a Ziploc bag. First, write a brief letter to someone who makes you feel angry explaining why you are so annoyed. Express yourself strongly by saying anything you want. Put the letter in a Ziploc bag (or a paper bag that can be recycled!) and throw it away. As you do this, imagine that your anger is fading and your relationship is being transformed with this particular individual.

Now, get centered and relaxed and imagine your last encounter with this person. Face him or her and hold hands. Add a loving touch as you strongly feel the love coming from your heart to this other person's heart. Your imagery ends as you are radiating love mightily and forming a bond with this person. How do you feel after completing this exercise?

Your Spiritual Self: Finding Your Place in the World

Have you ever had that "dispirited" sense that you have nothing to live for? Have you ever lapsed into a "Why bother?" attitude because you feel you will only fail? These depressions may be spiritual stress confronting you at the core of your being. Try to remember that these moments are but a brief ripple upon the sea of life. As you strengthen your spiritual beliefs, you will realize that it takes both rain *and* sunshine to make a rainbow. You, like the moon, are cyclical and will wax and wane.

As a therapist, I have many opportunities to give my clients analogies about the cyclical nature of life. I ask people to look outside at the lush scenery. Then I remind them how tumultuous rains create the beautiful flowers and trees. You can liken any pain or disappointment in your life to heavy rain, which is vitally needed to help you flower and blossom. We all go through these up and down cycles of life. Just as some people are more anxious than others when they feel the bumps from airplane turbulence, some people will feel the ripples of life more than others. The point to remember is that when you are down, you *will* come up.

Violet was feeling bleak after a breakup with her boyfriend. One day, in meditation, she heard a voice say, "You are going up the down staircase." What a vivid perspective! Now her intuitive mind was giving her a "thumbs up" sign. When she asks for a symbol to show her what is going on, she sees a derailed railroad train being put back on the track. She is now back on track and moving forward again.

POWERHUNCH TOOL

Converting a Downer into an Upper

You can spiritually acknowledge your potential to reach the heights in anything you do. Watch a young downy swan waddling to the lake. Can you see past its stumbling, awkward appearance to the graceful swimming creature it will one day be? When you are beginning your spiritual walk, you may appear awkward to others, and may even stumble about. But when you are in tune with your spiritual nature, you will become as graceful and spectacular as that swan and be able to express love, success, and most important, feel peace.

The swan is expressing the cycles of life. How do you characteristically respond to the cyclical ups and downs of life?

Understanding your place in the world is crucial for eradicating spiritual stress. In Ralph Waldo Emerson's fable "The Mountain and the Squirrel," the squirrel says to the mountain, "Talents differ.... If I cannot carry forests on my back, neither can you crack a nut." Just as the mountain and squirrel each have their own unique function to perform, the energy and talent you provide is vitally needed in the quilt of life.

Many people miss this spiritual connection. At twenty-six, Joe couldn't see anything spiritual about his job. He spent his days in front of a computer for an Internet company that deals with pharmaceuticals. His main job was to help physicians access information on appropriate medications for specific diagnoses. He missed the point: His spiritual connection was giving order to a chaos of information, and giving it to someone who needed it. He was contributing to the healing of human beings. This is the greater work that he couldn't see.

Everyone has important work to do on this planet. As Deepak Chopra says, "There are no extra pieces in the universe. Everyone has a place to fill and every piece must fit itself into the whole as if it were a big jigsaw puzzle. And for any single thing to happen in this universe, you and everyone else must take part in it." Seeing the importance of our individual role was dramatically illustrated for me when I gave a stress management seminar for a health care provider. When I tried to identify the problems at the agency, everyone was vocal and agitated. I then had them form small groups and answer the following questions: What is your organization here to do? What is your role in the process? What are you bringing to someone else? In other words, I was having them fine-tune their vision and see the role they played in the greater whole.

218   After a few minutes, the agitation in the air began to fade. As I walked around to each group, inspiring ideas were surfacing. For example, one group felt the agency was here to assist needy people on the road to recovery. Another group collectively felt that the agency was providing services to empower people to get back on their feet and be productive after an incapacitating illness. Gradually, every person in the room realized the transformative role they played in guiding people back from the ravages of disease and discouragement to radiant health. All moved past the daily annoyances to realize they were real life success stories.

The lesson? Always remember the part you play in the greater whole, and who you are here to serve by doing your work. I always try to distinguish between our *job*, which we tend to perform between 9 A.M. and 5 P.M., and the spiritual underpinnings of the *work* we are here to do. You also have ongoing work to do in your home, with your family, and neighborhood community. In your office and work site, you, too, can discover the spiritual bottom line of what you can and should be doing.

POWERHUNCH TOOL

Finding Your Place in the World

In this exercise, you will be searching for your true purpose with your job as well as discovering who will benefit from your work ultimately and in the short term. Use your intuition to answer the questions if you get stuck in your logical mind.

1. Describe your activities at work.
2. Who will benefit from this work in the short term? How?
3. Who will benefit from this work ultimately? How?

How has this exercise changed your awareness of the importance of the work you are here to do?

Do this exercise again. In place of work, put the words "family," "relationship," "community," and so on.

219

Healing

When stress escalates, dis-ease sets in and healing is needed. The mind-body connection is always at work. For example, one of the deteriorating effects of anger comes from holding onto the annoyance, which acts like corrosive acid on the body to create an environment in which ulcers, high blood pressure, hardening of the arteries, and other problems can take hold. (For further illustrations of the workings of the mind-body connection, see my book *The Intuitive Healer*.)

Be aware of how you use language to describe your mind-body disharmony. The power of words is quite amazing. Alan said, "I was experiencing chronic pain in my foot for several months, and could barely walk on it. X-rays and other exams found nothing wrong. I was in a very conflicted situation with some family members at the time and found myself exclaiming to several friends, 'I'm having such a difficult time putting my foot down.' Finally someone pointed out the connection. I began saying, 'I can easily set limits with my family.' The pain went away within two days!"

POWER**HUNCH** TOOL

Watch Your Words

An interior designer told me about her serious nerve disorder. She started searching inwardly and realized that for years, when faced with difficult people, she'd tell her husband, "That person really gets on my nerves." And so they literally did. She's getting better now through her work on herself.

Do these phrases sound familiar? "I've bitten off more than I can chew," "That's hard to swallow," "That's hard to digest," "What a pain in the neck," "He'd cut my throat," "I can't stand that," or, "I can't see that clearly." Become vigilant in noticing these mind–body connections and record them in your PowerHunch Journal.

What health malady assaults all of us now and then? You guessed it—the common cold. The onslaught is rarely random and doesn't happen because you sat next to someone with a cold. Delving into the mind-body wisdom of why the cold was created will actually help with its relief. Here's Wanda's process. She had a cold for a couple weeks. Congestion lingered in her throat and sinus area.

1. **Issue:** Wanda asked, "How do I release this congestion and be healthy?"
2. **Centering:** She used the focusing word "relax."
3. **Receptivity:** Wanda became still in her chair and took three "Total Breaths." She took a deep inhale, extended her stomach, and on the exhale let go and released the breath. She then relaxed from her toes to the top of her head.

4. **Imagery:** The image representing the congestion was a huge baseball glove that was reddish brown and inflexible.

5. **Deciphering the Image:** At first, Wanda interpreted the image as a form of protection. Then she felt angry because the glove was blocking her way, and frustrated that it lingered. She engaged the glove in a dialogue and heard it say it wanted to protect her from all the "stuff" hurled her way. Then the glove was darting rapidly catching fly balls and flinging them away. The glove wanted Wanda to slow down and not work so hard. The glove also said it wanted oil massaged gently into the leather to soften it and make it flexible. Wanda felt this was telling her to take oil or bubble baths with nothing to do but luxuriate in the soft gentle water. And then have someone apply lotion on her body with a gentle nurturing touch to soften the skin and make it supple and flexible. She asked the glove, "What concerns are still present?" The glove was concerned that everything wouldn't get done in the set time frame. She then asked how she could take a step toward meeting the image's needs. The glove replied that she could take time out and do absolutely nothing. She could start this week with fifteen minutes and build on it.

6. **Incubate:** Wanda slept on this information.

7. **Going Deeper:** Wanda realized that baseball was called hardball when she was a kid. The associations flew from hardball to hard game to hard work, which reflected her current activities. She was engaged in a lot of hard work and the glove did in fact protect her when all her responsibilities with work, school, and family were hurled at her.

8. **Implementation:** For the next day, Wanda had several intervals where she stopped for fifteen minutes and did nothing. Later that evening, she poured a glass of wine, sat down on big pillows, and engaged in tender conversation with her husband. She relaxed on the couch as her husband played beautiful music on his electric piano. The congestion was gone the next day.

Remarkable cures can come from the dreaming mind. Henry Reed, author of *The Intuitive Heart*, dreamed that an East Indian doctor was telling him he should put a certain medicine in his ear. Perhaps the presence of a doctor in a dream should have told him that he was getting a message important to his health. But Henry was not inclined to "stick it in his ear," and later regretted ignoring that dream. Years later, Henry came across that dream in his dream journals. This time, the suggestion of an ear remedy caught his attention. Since the initial dream visited him, he had developed tinnitus—a ringing in the ear—brought about by the constant vasoconstriction in the tiny capillaries of the inner ear caused by habitual cigarette smoking. Although he quit smoking, the ringing remained. Investigating his unusual dream prescription, he found out that that very medicine he dreamt about causes blood to come to the surface of the skin where it is applied. Had Henry "stuck it in his ear," he might have prevented the tinnitus.

In a daydream or a night dream, you can imagine you are going to the office or to the dwelling place of the greatest healer in the world. Trust and believe and know it will be accomplished. Cay Randall May went to a Native American talking circle and met a shaman, shook his hand, and had a brief conversation. That night, she had a dream that she went to the shaman's office and he did an operation on her. He removed an ovarian cyst and she paid him $80. She had been having some cramping and other symptoms and it never came back again after that dream. Is this possible? With all you have read and practiced throughout this book, you know that with intuition as your guide, anything is possible.

Living an Intuitive Life

The key to success in anything you do with your career, family, and relationships is using your intuition daily. Then you can incorporate intuition as an equal partner with logic in anything you do: to make a decision, to understand a difficult person, to forge a new trail through life.

Dr. Jonas Salk, inventor of the polio vaccine, rightly said that the intuitive mind will tell the thinking mind where to look next. He said, "It is always with excitement that I wake up in the morning wondering what my intuition will toss up to me, like gifts from the sea. I work with it and rely upon it. It's my partner."³ It is just that partnership between the intuitive mind and the creative mind that puts the power in your PowerHunches!

Remember, it is the intuitive person who retrieves that gift from the sea, the creative or intuitive idea that the thinking person then implements. In our daily problem solving, we use these two different minds to retrieve the bright idea (intuition) and then find a practical application (logic). I delight in watching my students as they begin to incorporate this ability into their lives. Ken, a co-owner of a company that sells computers, never would have used the "I word" to describe his decision-making activities. Now, he realizes that he is constantly called on to give an immediate opinion. In retrospect, he realizes how often he arrives at a conclusion intuitively and then thinks about reasons to justify why he has taken that particular position.

223

In the final section of your PowerHunch Journal, or in a separate notebook, devote some pages to recording the "gifts from the sea" that you pick up on your intuitive journey. These gifts may be quotes, cartoons, or inspiring stories. Here's my offering for your journal, the words of Paramahansa Yogananda:

Anything that ripples the consciousness,
sensual or emotional,
distorts whatever is perceived,
but calmness is clarity of perception, intuition itself.

Finally, I want to borrow the magnificent words of a brilliant and intuitive man, Dr. Albert Einstein, who had reverence for all creation. He said, "The intuitive mind is a sacred gift and the rational mind is a faithful servant. We have created a society that honors the servant and has forgotten the gift."

Through this book, I extend my invitation to you to remember your gift.

POWERHUNCH WORKSHOP

A Partnership Affair

Take what you have learned out into the world as you invite friends, family, and co-workers to collaborate with you in your intuitive endeavors. Here's what Judy did:

Judy's frequent sinus infections were driving her crazy. They took so much time out of her life, and she was ready to heal them. Surgery was not an option, and she thought she had tried everything else. Finally, she invited four friends to join her in a group PowerShift exercise. The images they came up with were star, tears, exercise, sailboat on the ocean, and carrot. The first clue came from the orange carrot—they all agreed that the orange color represented balance because it is situated between red (emotions) and yellow (intellect) on the color spectrum. Then they associated to the rest of the images, and the water theme predominated in the associations. Since the water element is strongly linked to emotion, they concluded that Judy needed more emotional balance in giving and receiving, especially in relation to her grown children. She is the one who gives gifts, initiates phone calls, and visits them. Now it is time for these actions to be reciprocated. Judy realized this was not her children's fault—she had never really told them she expected different behavior on their part. As she thought about beginning this new phase of their relationship, she could feel the pressure in her face lightening up.

Now it is time to invite others into intuitive collaboration. Here are some suggestions:

* Invite like-minded friends to join you in an ongoing PowerShift group to resolve puzzling dilemmas.

- Invite family members and friends to form a dream group where you can unravel puzzling dreams.
- Form a creative think tank with your co-workers to improve life at work for everyone.
- Share the wonderful synchronicities of life with your partner, and see how it changes your relationship.
- Invite friends and family to explore their PowerHunch sources and discover their dominant intuitive modalities so they can hear the whispers as well as the shouts from their intuitive mind.

Appendix
Breathing and Relaxation Exercises[4]

Breathing

You can practice these breathing exercises whenever you like. The best posture, unless directed otherwise, is sitting upright with your feet flat on the floor and your hands uncrossed and resting in your lap.

The Total Breath

The Total Breath helps increase breathing stamina and enhances mental alertness. Morning and evening are particularly good times to practice this technique.

1. Inhale slowly, and feel as if a balloon is inflating inside your stomach.
2. When the balloon is full, raise your arms so that your elbows are even with your shoulders and inhale more air into your lungs.
3. Hold your breath for a slow count of three, and then exhale as you lower your arms and let the balloon deflate.
4. Repeat twice.

The Reenergizing Breath

The Reenergizing Breath acts as a power boost for mind and body. Try it when you are feeling sluggish.

1. Exhale all the air from your lungs.
2. Take six short inhales in quick succession through your nose.
3. Hold the sixth inhale for a moment, and inhale again.
4. Hold the inhale for a moment, then exhale completely.
5. Repeat twice.

The Ha! Breath

The Ha! Breath works to relieve stress. You can do this breath sitting or standing. When you first practice this breath, place your hands on your stomach just above the waist, with your fingertips meeting near your navel, and push your stomach in with your fingertips as you exhale.) Many people begin to laugh when they first do the Ha! Breath—in fact, laughter is a form of the Ha! Breath exhaled in rapid succession.

1. Inhale slowly, and feel as if a balloon is inflating inside your stomach.
2. When the balloon is full, exhale with an explosion of air as you say out loud, "Ha!"
3. Repeat five times.

The Hang-Sah Breath

The Hang-Sah Breath, especially when used with soft music, is effective for centering and receptivity. You can also use this breath if you are having difficulty falling asleep. If you are using it for relaxation and centering, be sure to sit upright and remind yourself not to fall asleep!

1. As you inhale, whisper "Hang." This lifts the diphthong in the back of your throat, just like when you are yawning.
2. As you exhale, whisper "Sah." This is like sighing, which will quickly put you into a relaxed state.
3. Repeat ten times.

Directed Breathing

Use this breath to direct healing energy to specific parts of the body.

1. Inhale, and imagine you are bringing energy into your body.

2. Exhale, releasing all the tension in your shoulders and neck, down your arms, and out your fingertips.
3. Repeat steps 1 and 2 two more times.
4. Inhale, and imagine you are bringing energy into your body.
5. Exhale, and release the tension down your spine, down your legs, and out through your feet.
6. Repeat steps 4 and 5 two more times.
7. Now lay your hands on the specific part of your body that needs healing energy. Inhale, and imagine the energy coming through the top of your head and down through your hands. Exhale the energy into the afflicted area. Feel as if the pain and soreness are going away with each breath.
8. Continue until you feel a reduction in actual physical pain.

Relaxation

The Abbreviated Autogenic Technique

You can either sit or recline when you do this exercise. Begin with your toes and work your way up through your body. As you send the message to each part of your body, picture steam or hot air rising out of that part until it becomes relaxed.

1. Send these messages from your mind to each part of your body:
   • I am relaxing my toes. My toes are relaxing.
   • I am relaxing my feet. My feet are relaxing.
   • I am relaxing my ankles. My ankles are relaxing.
   • Continue through your knees, thighs, pelvis, buttocks, back, abdomen, stomach, chest, shoulders, arms, hands, neck, back of the head, forehead, eyes, nose, mouth, jaw, and head.
2. When you are finished, tell yourself: "I am allowing myself to be completely relaxed." If any tension is left, return to that area and gently tell that part of your body to relax. It will!

Autogenic Relaxation

This technique focuses on specific areas. Combine Autogenic Relaxation with the Hang-Sah Breath and an affirmation to help you eliminate tension in your body.

1. Begin by doing the Hang-Sah breath ten times.
2. Say, "My feet feel warm and relaxed. My feet feel warm and relaxed. My feet are warm and relaxed." Repeat this message for your legs, midsection, chest and back, arms, shoulders, neck, and face and head.
3. Silently affirm, "Every cell in my body feels relaxed and comfortable. Every cell in my body feels relaxed and comfortable. Every cell in my body is relaxed and comfortable. I am now totally relaxed."

Stretching and Breathing

This is a good exercise to do first thing in the morning, when you come home from work, or when you return from any stressful activity.

1. Shrug your shoulders, inhale through your nose, and raise your shoulders toward your ears. Hold a moment.
2. Let your shoulders drop as you exhale through your mouth with a sigh of relief.
3. Repeat this three more times.
4. As you exhale, let your neck bend forward until your chin rests on your chest.
5. Inhale as you bring your head upright.
6. As you exhale the last time, let your neck bend gently back, letting your jaw relax as you open your mouth and say "Aaah!"
7. Inhale as you bring your head up, stretching your neck.
8. Repeat steps 4 through 7 three more times.
9. As you exhale, bend your neck to the left, letting your left ear attempt to rest on your shoulder.

10. Inhale as you bring your head up.
11. As you exhale, bend your neck to the right, letting your right ear attempt to rest on your shoulder.
12. Inhale as you bring your head up.
13. Repeat steps 9 through 12 three times.
14. Roll your head around on your neck three times to the right and three times to the left.

Tense and Release

Sit or lie in a comfortable position. Breathe in deeply through your nose and be aware of your chest rising and falling. Follow the air as it comes in through your nose. Be aware of the areas in your body touched by this breath of life. Hold the air and note how you feel. Finally, let the air come together from the various body parts to unite in a large current of air that will be expelled from your nose or mouth.

231

1. Inhale deeply through your nose. Hold the breath and curl your toes as tightly as you can.
2. Exhale and release the tension from your toes and feet.
3. Repeat once.
4. Inhale, extending your legs straight out, and hold the breath while you tighten your leg muscles.
5. Exhale and release the tension from your legs.
6. Repeat once.
7. Inhale, holding the breath as you tighten your stomach and buttock muscles.
8. Exhale and let these muscles relax.
9. Repeat once.
10. Inhale, holding the breath as you make a fist with both hands, and tighten the muscles in your arms.
11. Exhale and let your arms relax.
12. Repeat once.

13. Inhale, holding the breath as you tighten your shoulder and neck muscles.
14. Exhale and let your neck and shoulders relax.
15. Repeat once.
16. Inhale, holding the breath as you tighten all the muscles in your face, clenching your teeth.
17. Exhale and let these muscles relax.
18. Repeat once.
19. Take a deep breath as you inhale, hold for a moment, and exhale.

If any spot is stubbornly hanging on to the tension, tell it to "relax and be still." It will listen to you. As you practice, your body will respond more quickly.

Progressive Relaxation

Use Directed Breathing in this Progressive Relaxation technique. Close your eyes and imagine energy coming into your body each time you inhale. It helps to visualize the energy as colored light, like rays of sunshine.

1. As you exhale, imagine the tension flowing out through the soles of your feet, like the ocean tide as it goes out. Inhale the energy in and exhale the tension out.
2. Inhale, and direct the rays of energy to your legs. Exhale, and imagine the tension flowing down your legs and out through the soles of your feet. Inhale the energy in and exhale the tension out.
3. Inhale, and direct the energy to your midsection. Exhale and let the tension ease out of your waist and hips.
4. Inhale, bringing the golden rays of energy into your chest and upper back. Exhale, and let the tension flow down your spine, through your legs, and out through the soles of your feet. Repeat.

5. Inhale and direct the rays of energy into your arms and hands. Exhale, and imagine the tension flowing down your arms and out through your fingertips. Repeat.
6. Inhale and direct the golden rays of energy into your shoulders. Exhale, and imagine the tension flowing down both arms and out through your fingertips. Repeat.
7. Inhale and direct the energy into your head and neck. Exhale, and let the tension flow down your spine, down your legs, and out through the soles of your feet. Repeat.
8. Take a deep inhale and hold for a moment. Exhale.
9. Open your eyes.

Countdown

Use this exercise in conjunction with any one of the other relaxation techniques, or to enter an even deeper relaxed state. The stronger and more clear your imagery, the more quickly you will become relaxed.

233

As you do this exercise, picture yourself standing at the top step. Walk downstairs until you arrive at the bottom step. With each step, feel yourself becoming increasingly relaxed. Use imagery to count off each step by seeing the step light up with a number. Begin, and say to yourself:

10 ... 9 ... 8 ...   I am beginning to feel relaxed
7 ... 6 ... 5 ...   I am feeling more and more relaxed
4 ... 3 ...   I am feeling very relaxed
2 ... 1 ...   I am feeling completely relaxed

Notes

1. If you have read my other books, you are already familiar with the Intuitive Problem Solving Formula and the Mindshift Method. The PowerShift is another variation of this proven technique. See *Dr. Marcia Emery's Intuition Workbook: An Expert's Guide to Unlocking the Wisdom of Your Subconscious Mind* (New Jersey: Prentice Hall, 1994) and *The Intuitive Healer: Accessing Your Inner Physician* (New York: St. Martin's Press, 1999).

2. The current formulation is an outgrowth of the intuitive dream interpretation process presented in my other books, *Dr. Marcia Emery's Intuition Workbook: An Expert's Guide to Unlocking The Wisdom of Your Subconscious Mind* (New Jersey: Prentice Hall, 1994) and *The Intuitive Healer: Accessing Your Inner Physician* (New York: St. Martin's Press, 1999).

3. Salk, J. *Anatomy of Reality*. New York: Columbia University Press, 1983.

4. The exercises in the appendix are adapted from *Dr. Marcia Emery's Intuition Workbook: An Expert's Guide to Unlocking the Wisdom of Your Subconscious Mind* (New Jersey: Prentice Hall, 1994).

—

Dr. Marcia Emery's Resources

Intuition Development Training

Books

Dr. Marcia Emery's Intuition Workbook: An Expert's Guide to Unlocking the Wisdom of Your Subconscious Mind. New Jersey: Prentice Hall, 1994. A book to develop your intuition.

Inreaching: Cultivating Intuitive Potential. Berkeley, CA: Self-published, 1998. A collection of experiential exercises from top intuition authors.

Audiotapes

Intuition: How to Use Your Gut Instinct for Greater Personal Power. Six audiotapes. Nightingale Conant, 1995. 1-800-323-5552.

Intuition: How to Use Your Gut Instinct for Greater Personal Power. Two-audiotape cassette series. New York: Simon & Schuster, 1999.

Integrated Problem Solving. Four-audiotape cassette series by James Emery, M.M. Experiential exercises to complement Dr. Marcia Emery's Intuition Workbook.

Intuitive Problem Solving: An Everyday Guide to Successful Living. One audio tape. Experiential exercises to enhance your intuitive living skills.

A Breathtaking Experience. One audio cassette tape. Consists of five breathing techniques and a guided visualization.

Intuition and Healing

Book

The Intuitive Healer: Accessing Your Inner Physician. New York: St. Martins Press, 1999. Communicate with your body to find out what's really wrong, and then begin your wellness journey.

Audiotapes

The Intuitive Healer: Accessing Your Inner Physician. Two-audio-tape cassette series. New York: Simon & Schuster, 1999. Based on the book.

Intuition and Dreams

Infinity Series on Dreams: Exploring Your Dreams and Precognitive Dreams. Two-audiotape cassette series. Berkeley, CA: IMCC. Experiential exercises to program your dreams for problem solving.

Meditation

Ocean View Mountain Trail: Earth, air, fire, water. One-audiotape cassette by James Emery, M.M. A guided visualization/mediation.

All audiotapes are available from: Marcia Emery, Ph.D., 1502 Tenth Street, Berkeley, CA. 94710. Phone: (510) 526-5510. Fax: 510/526-9555. Email: PowerHunch@aol.com

Intuitive Conversations

Videotapes

The Intuitive Factor: Genius or Chance? Featuring Jeffrey Mishlove, Ph.D., Marcia Emery, Ph.D., Professor Bill Taggart, and Gary Zukav. Victoria Weston, producer. (1997). Phone: 404/816.0602 *vweston@zoiefilms.com*

Audiotapes

Intuition: One on One: Conversations with America's Leading Experts on Intuition and Spirituality! featuring Marcia Emery, Ph.D., Jeffrey Mishlove, Ph.D., and Gary Zukav. Victoria Weston, Producer. (1997). Phone: 404/816.0602. Email: *vweston@zoiefilms.com*

Workshops and Consultations

Dr. Marcia Emery is available to give workshops, seminars, talks, and keynotes in the United States and abroad. Her topics include: PowerHunch: Developing Your Intuition, The Intuitive Healer, Intuition and Dreams, Intuition: The Sacred Art of Living, Intuitive Leadership, Managing Stress, and Intuition and Love. For people who want intuitive guidance, she does personal coaching, medical consultations, and consulting.

E -mail: *PowerHunch@aol.com*
Website: *www.PowerHunch.com*
Telephone: 510-526-5510
Fax: 510-526-9555

Suggested Reading

Adrienne, Carol. *The Purpose of Your Life*. New York: William Morrow, 1998.

Agor, Weston. *Intuitive Management*. Englewood Cliffs, New Jersey: Prentice-Hall, 1984.

Aron, Elaine. *The Highly Sensitive Person*. Secaucus, New Jersey: Birch Lane Press, 1996.

Arrien, Angeles. *The Four-Fold Way: Walking The Paths of the Warrior, Teacher, Healer, and Visionary*. New York: HarperCollins, 1993.

Beasley, Victor. *Intuition by Design*. Blue Hill, Maine: Medicine Bear Publishing, 1995.

Choquette, Sonia. *Your Heart's Desire*. New York: Three Rivers Press, 1997.

Contino, Richard. *Trust Your Gut!* New York: American Management Association, 1996.

Csikszentmihalyi, Mihaly. *Flow*. New York: Harper Perennial, 1990.

Day, Laura. *Practical Intuition*. New York: Villard, 1996.

Dean, Douglas, et.al. *Executive ESP*. Englewood Cliffs, New Jersey: Prentice Hall, 1974.

De Becker, Gavin. *The Gift of Fear*. New York: Dell, 1998.

Einstein, Patricia. *Intuition: The Path to Inner Wisdom*. Rockport, MA: Element, 1997.

Feinstein, David, & Stanley Krippner. *The Mythic Path*. New York: Tarcher/Putnam, 1997.

Ferguson, Gail. *Cracking the Intuition Code*. Chicago: Contemporary Books, 1999.

Fishel, Ruth. *Time For Joy*. Centerville, MA: Spirithaven, 1988.

Ford, Arielle. *Hot Chocolate for the Mystical Lover*. New York: Plume, 1999.

Frantz, Roger, & Alex N Pattakos. *Intuition at Work*. San Francisco, CA: New Leaders, 1996.

Franquemont, Sharon. *Do It Yourself Intuition*. Oakland, CA: Self-Published, 1997.

Franquemont, Sharon. *You Already Know What to Do*. New York: Tarcher/Putnam, 1999.

Fuller, R. Buckminster. *Intuition*. San Luis Obispo, CA: Impact, 1983.

Garfield, Patricia. *The Healing Power of Dreams*. New York: Fireside, 1992.

Goldberg, Philip. *The Intuitive Edge*. Los Angeles, CA: Tarcher, 1983.

Goleman, Daniel. *Emotional Intelligence*. New York: Bantam Books, 1995.

Jaffe, Azriela. *Create Your Luck*. New York: Adams Media, 2000.

Levy, Joel and Michelle. *Living in Balance*. Berkeley, CA: Conari Press, 1998.

May, Cay Randall. *Pray Together Now*. New York: HarperCollins, 1999.

Miller, Marlane. *Brainstyles: Change Your Life Without Changing Who You Are*. New York: Simon & Schuster, 1997.

Millman, Dan. *Everyday Enlightenment: The Twelve Gateways to Personal Growth*. New York: Warner, 1998.

Mishlove, Jeffrey. *Roots of Consciousness*. New York: Marlow, 1997.

Myss, Caroline. *Anatomy of Spirit*. New York: Harmony Books, 1996.

Myss, Caroline. *Why People Don't Heal and How They Can*. New York: Harmony Books, 1997.

Nadell, L. with J. Haims & R. Stempson. *Sixth Sense*. New York: Prentice Hall, 1990.

Naparstek, Belleruth. *Your Sixth Sense: Activating Your Psychic Potential*. New York: HarperCollins, 1997.

Orloff, Judith, M.D. *Second Sight*. New York: Warner Books, 1996.

Orloff, Judith, M.D. *Dr. Judith Orloff's Guide to Intuitive Healing*. New York: Times Books, 2000.

Page, Christine, M.D. *Mind, Body, Spirit Workbook*. Essex, England: Saffron Walden, The C.W. Daniel Co. Ltd., 1999.

Peirce, Penney. *The Intuitive Way: A Guide to Living from Inner Wisdom*. Hillsboro, OR: Beyond Words Publishing, 1988.

Peirce, Penney. *The Present Moment*. Chicago: Contemporary Books, 2000.

Pert, Candace B. *Molecules of Emotion: Why You Feel the Way You Feel*. New York: Scribner, 1997.

Potter, Beverly. *High Performance Goal Setting*. Berkeley, CA: Ronin Press, 2000.

Ray, Michael and Rochelle Myers. *Creativity in Business*. New York: Doubleday, 1986.

Reed, Henry. *Exercise Your Intuitive Heart: Discover All Your Heart Knows*. Mouth of Wilson, VA. Hermes Home Press, 1997.

Reed, Henry and Brenda English. *The Intuitive Heart*. Virginia Beach, VA: ARE Press, 2000.

Reeves, Paula. *Women's Intuition*. Berkeley, CA: Conari Press, 1999.

Ritberger, Carol. *Your Personality, Your Health*. Carlsbad, CA: Hay House, 1998.

Ritberger, Carol. *What Color Is Your Personality?* Carlsbad, CA: Hay House, 2000.

Robinson, Lynn. *The Complete Idiot's Guide to Being Psychic*. New York: Macmillan, 1999.

Robinson, Lynn. *Divine Intuition*. New York: Dorling Kindersley, 2001.

Rosanoff, Nancy. *Intuition Workout*. Boulder Creek, CA. Aslan Publishing, 1988.

Rosanoff, Nancy. *The Complete Idiot's Guide to Making Money Through Intuition*. New York: Macmillan, 1999.

Salk, Jonas. *Anatomy of Reality: Merging of Intuition and Reason*. New York: Columbia Press, 1983.

Schulz, Mona Lisa. *Awakening Intuition*. New York: Harmony, 1998.

Segaller, S. and Berger, M. *The Wisdom of the Dream: The World of C. G. Jung*. Boston: Shambhala, 1989.

Shealy, Norman, M.D. & Caroline Myss. *The Creation of Health*. Walpole, NH: Stillpoint, 1988.

Smith, Jonathan. *Creative Stress Management*. New Jersey: Prentice Hall, 1993.

Taggart, Bill. *Accessing Intuition: A Research Bibliography*. 1994. Available at www.The-Intuitive-Self.com.

Travis, J. and R. Ryan. *Wellness Workbook*. Second Edition, Berkeley, CA: Ten Speed Press, 1988.

Vaughan, Alan. *The Power of Positive Prophecy*. New York: Aquarian Press, 1991.

Vaughan, Alan. *Doorways to Higher Consciousness*. Williamsburg, VA: Celest Press, 1998.

Vaughan, Frances E. *Awakening Intuition*. Garden City, New York: Anchor Books, 1979.

Weston, Victoria. *Into the Future*. Atlanta, GA: Oscar Dey, 1991.

Zukav, Gary. *The Seat of the Soul*. New York: Simon & Schuster, 1989.

About the Author

For Marcia Emery, Ph.D., psychologist, consultant, author, international lecturer, media personality, and college professor, intuition is a trusted old friend that's becoming a breakthrough management tool.

Her extensive clinical, academic, and business experience have yielded rare insights into intuition's extraordinary manifestations and its strength as a tool for facilitating personal and professional transformation.

In 1983, Marcia Emery launched her "Power Hunch" seminars. Now highly acclaimed, they've been presented to thousands of individuals through such organizations as Lucent Technologies, Amway Corporation, Blue Care Network, Donnelly Corporation, Herman Miller Co., Hewlett Packard, and many more.

In 1984, Dr. Emery pioneered the first college course in whole-brain thinking at Aquinas College, Grand Rapids, Michigan. Entitled *Integrating Intuition and Logic for Managers*, her students—Master of Management candidates from international corporations, government, and small business—became the first wave of decision makers formally trained in the new technique. Today, Marcia Emery lives in Berkeley, California, with Jim, her husband and collaborator of nineteen years.

BEYOND WORDS PUBLISHING, INC.

OUR CORPORATE MISSION
Inspire to Integrity

OUR DECLARED VALUES
We give to all of life as life has given us.
We honor all relationships.
Trust and stewardship are integral to fulfilling dreams.
Collaboration is essential to create miracles.
Creativity and aesthetics nourish the soul.
Unlimited thinking is fundamental.
Living your passion is vital.
Joy and humor open our hearts to growth.
It is important to remind ourselves of love.

To order or to request a catalog, contact
Beyond Words Publishing, Inc.
20827 N.W. Cornell Road, Suite 500
Hillsboro, OR 97124-9808
503-531-8700 or 1-800-284-9673

You can also visit our Web site at *www.beyondword.com*
or e-mail us at *info@beyondword.com*.